Milestone Visual Documents in American History

The Images, Cartoons, and Other Visual Sources
That Shaped America

Milestone Visual Documents in American History

The Images, Cartoons, and Other Visual Sources
That Shaped America

Volume 3: 1941–2021

Craig Kaplowitz
Editor in Chief

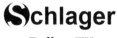

Dallas, TX

**MILESTONE VISUAL DOCUMENTS IN AMERICAN HISTORY:
THE IMAGES, CARTOONS, AND OTHER VISUAL SOURCES THAT SHAPED AMERICA**

Copyright © 2023 by Schlager Group Inc.

All rights reserved. No part of this book may be reproduced or utilized in any form or by any means, electronic or mechanical, including photocopying, recording, or by any information storage or retrieval systems, without permission in writing from the publisher. For information, contact:

Schlager Group Inc.
10228 E. Northwest HWY, STE 1151
Dallas, TX 75238
USA
(888) 416-5727
info@schlagergroup.com

You can find Schlager Group online at https://www.schlagergroup.com

For Schlager Group:
Vice President, Editorial: Sarah Robertson
Vice President, Operations and Strategy: Benjamin Painter
Founder and President: Neil Schlager

Printed in the United States of America 10 9 8 7 6 5 4 3 2 1
Print ISBN: 9781935306726
eBook: 9781935306733

Library of Congress Control Number: 2022943991

Contents

Reader's Guide...viii
Contributors..ix
Acknowledgments..x
Introduction..xi

Volume 1

Smallpox Epidemic among the Aztec Illustration..2
John White: Village of Secotan Illustration..8
Nova totius Map of the World..14
Nova Britannia Recruiting to the Colonies Flyer..20
Brockett's Map of New Haven...26
The Castello Plan: New Amsterdam Map...30
John Foster's Gravestone..36
Cherokee Delegation to England Portrait...42
"A View of Savannah" Map..48
Robert Feke: Portrait of Isaac Royall and Family...54
Dockside at Virginia Tobacco Warehouse Illustration...60
Benjamin Franklin: "Join, or Die" Cartoon..66
Slaves for Sale Advertisement..72
William Bradford: "Expiring: In Hopes of a Resurrection to Life Again" Newspaper Protest...................78
Thomas Jefferson: Advertisement for a Runaway Slave...84
Paul Revere: *The Bloody Massacre* Flyer..90
Philip Dawe: "Tarring & Feathering" Satirical Print...96
Philip Dawe: *Edenton Tea Party* Satirical Print..102
The Old Plantation Painting...108
"The Times, a Political Portrait" Cartoon..114
Colonial Cloth Makers Illustration...120
Painting of a Newly Cleared Small Farm Site..126
Elkanah Tisdale: "The Gerry-mander" Cartoon..132
The Plantation Painting..138
Carl Rakeman: "The Iron Horse Wins—1830" Painting..142
"Camp-Meeting" Lithograph...148
"King Andrew the First" Cartoon...154
William Henry Bartlett: Erie Canal, Lockport Illustration...160
Robert Cruikshank: "President's Levee" Illustration..166
Lowell Offering Masthead...172
Nathaniel Currier: "The Drunkard's Progress" Cartoon...178
Richard Doyle: "The Land of Liberty" Cartoon..184
Nathaniel Currier "The Way They Go to California" Cartoon..190
Currier & Ives: "Congressional Scales" Cartoon...196
McCormick's Patent Virginia Reaper Flyer..202
"Emerson School for Girls" Photograph..208
John H. Goater: "Irish Whiskey and Lager Bier" Cartoon..214
George Caleb Bingham: *The County Election* Painting..220
John L. Magee: "Forcing Slavery Down the Throat of a Freesoiler" Cartoon..226
"Picking Cotton, Georgia, 1858" Illustration..232

Volume 2

Cartoon Mocking Women's Rights Conventions..238
Louis Maurer: "Progressive Democracy—Prospect of a Smash Up" Cartoon..244
Photograph of Powder Monkey on USS *New Hampshire*..250

Andrew J. Russell: Ruins of Richmond Photograph..256
Photograph of the 107th U.S. Colored Infantry..262
James E. Taylor: "Selling a Freedman to Pay His Fine" Engraving..268
Alfred Rudolph Waud: "The First Vote" Illustration..274
"Reconstruction" Cartoon...280
Thomas Nast: "This Is a White Man's Government" Cartoon...286
Thomas Nast: "The American River Ganges: The Priests and the Children" Cartoon........................292
John Gast: *American Progress* Painting..298
Photograph of Nicodemus, Kansas..304
Joseph Keppler: "The Modern Colossus of (Rail) Roads" Cartoon..310
Haymarket Mass Meeting Flyer..316
Photograph of Carlisle Indian School Students...322
Jacob Riis: "Bayard Street Tenement" Photograph..328
Louis Dalrymple: "School Begins" Cartoon..334
Photograph of Freed Slaves at a County Almshouse...340
Buffalo Bill's Wild West Flyer...346
William McKinley Campaign Poster..352
"Dreamland at Night" Photograph of Coney Island..358
Edgar Thomson Steel Works Photograph...362
Louis Wickes Hines: Photograph of Boys Working in Arcade Bowling Alley......................................368
Photograph of Congested Chicago Intersection..374
Photograph of Garment Workers Strike...380
"Indian Land for Sale" Poster...386
Photograph of Health Inspection of New Immigrants, Ellis Island..392
Woman's Party Campaign Billboard..398
"Gee! I Wish I Were a Man": Navy Recruiting Poster...404
Photograph of Harlem Hellfighters Regiment...410
Photograph after Raid on IWW Headquarters..416
"The Only Way to Handle It" Cartoon...420
Assembly Line Photograph...426
Judge Magazine Cover: The Roaring Twenties..432
Edward Hopper: *Automat* Painting..438
Fazil Movie Poster..444
Photograph of Bread Line, New York City..448
John T. McCutcheon: "A Wise Economist Asks a Question" Cartoon..454
NAACP: "A Man Was Lynched Yesterday" Photograph..460
Photograph of Cab Calloway and Dancing Couples...466
Jacob Lawrence: *The Great Migration* Painting..472

Volume 3
Civilian Conservation Corps Poster...478
"We Can Do It!" Rosie the Riveter Poster..484
Photograph of B-17 Formation over Schweinfurt, Germany...490
Ansel Adams: "Manzanar Relocation Center" Photograph..496
Photograph of Navajo Code Talkers..502
"Kultur-terror" Pro-German, Anti-American Propaganda Poster..508
Alfred T. Palmer: "Detroit Arsenal Tank Plant (Chrysler)" Photograph...514
Rube Goldberg: "Peace Today" Cartoon..520
Photograph of Joseph McCarthy..526
Photograph of the 101st Airborne Division outside Little Rock Central High School......................532
Thomas J. O'Halloran: "Kitchen" Debate Photograph of Richard Nixon and Nikita Khrushchev...538
Photograph of Levittown, Pennsylvania...544
Photograph of Interstate 10 under Construction in California...550
Fred Blackwell: Woolworths Lunch Counter Sit-In Photograph..556

Hélène Roger-Viollet: Drive-in Restaurant Photograph	562
Herbert Block: "I Got One of 'em" Cartoon about Selma, Alabama	568
Photograph of Black Panther Party Demonstration	574
American Indians Occupy Alcatraz Photograph	580
United Farm Workers Strike Photograph	586
Photograph of Vietnam War Destruction	590
Herbert Block: "National Security Blanket" Cartoon	596
"Remember Wounded Knee" Patch	602
Marty Lederhandler: Photograph of Gasoline Rationing	608
Photograph of Anti-Busing Rally in Boston	614
Warren K. Leffler: Photograph of Phyllis Schlafly at White House Demonstration	620
Herbert Block: "Strange How Some Choose to Live Like That" Cartoon	626
Pat Oliphant: "There He Goes Again" Cartoon	632
"Silence = Death" Flyer	638
Photograph of Berlin Wall Teardown	644
Tom Olin: "Wheels of Justice" March Photograph	648
Greg Gibson: Photograph of Anita Hill Testifying before the Senate Judiciary Committee	654
Steve Greenberg: "Bill Clinton's Foreign Policy Vehicle" Cartoon	660
Steve Greenberg: "Contract with America" Cartoon	666
Oklahoma City Bombing Photograph	672
Bush v. Gore Election Photograph	678
Photograph of World Trade Center Towers after 9/11 Terrorist Attack	684
J. Scott Applewhite: "Mission Accomplished" Photograph	690
"We the People Are Greater Than Fear" Flyer	696
Mihoko Owada: Photograph of Rioters Breaching the U.S. Capitol	702
Steve Helber: Photograph of Robert E. Lee Statue Removal	708
List of Documents by Category	713
Index	717

Milestone Visual Documents in American History

The Images, Cartoons, and Other Visual Sources
That Shaped America

Civilian Conservation Corps Poster

Author/Creator Illinois WPA Art Project	**Image Type** Flyers
Date c. 1941	**Significance** Promoted the federally sponsored Civilian Conservation Corps as a source of paid employment for young men during the Great Depression

Overview

Two New Deal programs of the administration of President Franklin D. Roosevelt during the Great Depression of the 1930s are relevant to this poster. One is the Civilian Conservation Corps (CCC), whose benefits to young, unemployed men this poster is promoting. The other is the Federal Arts Project of the Works Progress Administration (WPA). The programs of the WPA were administered in the states, including Illinois, where this poster was created. The WPA was a work relief agency, created by executive order on May 6, 1935, with the goal of putting millions of unemployed persons to work; indeed, the WPA employed some 8.5 million people from 1935 to 1943. Those who worked under the WPA built public infrastructure, including parks, schools, and roads, including more than 620,000 miles of streets and more than 10,000 bridges.

One of the WPA's most famous projects was Federal Project Number One, which employed musicians, artists, writers, actors, and directors in arts, drama, media, and literacy projects. This poster was created by the Federal Art Project, one of several WPA undertakings; the others were the Federal Writers' Project, the Federal Theatre Project, the Federal Music Project, and the Historical Records Survey. The programs of Federal Project Number One contributed immensely to the preservation of the nation's historical and cultural heritage.

About the Artist

The poster was created by the Illinois WPA Art Project. The "Art Project" was the Federal Art Project (FAP), which was part of Federal Project Number One, which in turn was part of the Works Progress Administration. Federal Project Number One was funded under the Emergency Relief Appropriations Act of 1935 and operated from that year until June 1943 to provide employment to struggling artists, including musicians, actors, painters, and the like. Workers under the program created murals, easel paintings, sculptures, photographs, theater sets, and posters. The agencies operated through community art centers, where artists not only created artwork but also exhibited their work and educated others through exhibits and public presentations. In all, the project created some 200,000 pieces of art, much of it of historical significance. The Chicago FAP created numerous posters pertaining to art education and appreciation, reading and literacy, vaccinations, work, exhibitions held by

Document Image

A poster promoting the Civilian Conservation Corps
(Library of Congress)

various organizations, and other topics of interest to the people of Illinois.

Context

In October 1929, the Roaring Twenties—a period of optimism, a surging economy, rampant consumerism, and radical changes in culture and fashion—came to an abrupt end. That month, the U.S. stock market crashed. Billions of dollars in investments were lost, and by 1930, the Great Depression was underway. In the months and years that followed, people were mired in debt. Banks began to fail. In the first ten months of 1930 alone, more than 700 banks failed; in 1933, more than 4,000 banks failed, and during the 1930s a total of some 9,000 banks failed. People lost their jobs. At the height of the Depression, nearly 25 percent of the nation's workforce, some 12.8 million people, were unemployed. Those workers who were lucky enough to keep their jobs saw their wage income fall more than 42 percent from 1929 to 1933. Poverty was rampant. People were begging on the streets. Children wore rags and scavenged for food and stray pieces of coal to burn for heat. It was the worst economic crisis in the nation's history.

In 1932, Franklin Delano Roosevelt was elected president, carrying forty-two out of forty-eight states and garnering more than 57 percent of the popular vote. He won on a promise of a "New Deal" for Americans, one that would expand the scope of the federal government to confront the economic crisis; in contrast, his opponent, incumbent Herbert Hoover, was widely criticized as a "do-nothing" president. After he assumed office in 1933, Roosevelt and his administration went to work, launching programs designed to help Americans by putting them to work—and putting money in their pockets.

One of the most successful of these programs was the Civilian Conservation Corps, which the president created by executive order on April 5, 1933. The CCC was a work relief program formed to combat high unemployment. During its nine-year history, the CCC put some three million young men to work, about 5 percent of the U.S. male population. In his "Greetings to the CCC" in July 1933, President Roosevelt emphasized the personal benefits of the CCC to recruits: "You young men who are enrolled in this work are to be congratulated as well. It is my honest conviction that what you are doing in the way of constructive service will bring to you, personally and individually, returns the value of which it is difficult to estimate. Physically fit, as demonstrated by the examinations you took before entering the camps, the clean life and hard work in which you are engaged cannot fail to help your physical condition and you should emerge from this experience strong and rugged and ready for a reentrance into the ranks of industry, better equipped than before."

The CCC was regarded by many observers as one of the most successful New Deal programs of the Roosevelt administration. CCC workers were employed primarily in environmental conservation projects, leading to the CCC being called Roosevelt's "Tree Army." The workers planted 3.5 billion trees on land that had been made barren by erosion, fires, and poor agricultural practices. They built trails and shelters in more than 800 parks throughout the nation. A poster such as this one was designed to promote the CCC and entice young men into joining. Interestingly, some famous names were on the CCC roster. Actors Walter Matthau and Raymond Burr worked for the CCC in Montana and California, respectively. So too did baseball hall-of-famer Stan Musial and test pilot Chuck Yeager.

The CCC was a major undertaking. Most of the unemployed men who took jobs with the CCC lived in the nation's eastern cities. Most of the conservation work, however, was in the West. To solve the logistical problem, the U.S. Army went to work. It organized transportation for thousands of workers to CCC camps throughout the country. Those camps sprang up with remarkable rapidity: by July 1, 1933, 1,433 camps had been established, and more than 300,000 young men between the ages of eighteen and twenty-five had been put to work. (The age range was later widened to seventeen to twenty-eight, and veterans of World War I could enroll up to the age of twenty-nine. Women, incidentally, were not eligible to enroll.) The enrollment period was for a minimum of six months. Most of the corpsmen were unskilled and unemployed, although some were skilled foresters and craftsmen. About 88,000 Native Americans living on reservations were enrolled; African Americans who enrolled lived and worked in segregated camps. Most of the corpsmen's families were on some sort of government assistance. Under the guidance of the U.S. Forest Service, the National Park Service, and the Departments of the Interior and Agriculture, CCC enrollees planted trees, cleared roads, fought forest fires, and carried out soil-erosion control measures. They also built wildlife refuges, fisheries, water-storage facilities, and animal shelters. The president urged the CCC to build bridges and campgrounds as a way of encouraging Americans to get out and enjoy the nation's natural heritage. Enrollment peaked in August 1935, when 500,000 men were enrolled.

Each of the workers received $30 a month, plus room and board at a camp. They were required to send from $22 to $25 dollars of their monthly earnings to their families at home. Additionally, some of the corpsmen received basic and vocational education; it is estimated that as many as 57,000 corpsmen learned to read while serving in the CCC. Although the CCC had widespread support among the American public, it was criticized by organized labor. The basis of the criticism was that unskilled workers were being trained while many union members were out of work. The unions were also critical of Army involvement with the CCC, fearing that it could lead to the regimentation of labor.

Funding for the CCC was discontinued in 1942, when money was needed for World War II. In the aftermath, numerous monuments and statues commemorating the CCC were erected in parks across the country. The CCC became a model for future environmental reclamation projects. The National Civilian Community Corps, for example, part of AmeriCorps, employs young men and women for ten-month periods in nonprofit and governmental organizations, often those with an environmental purpose. The activities of the WPA were also suspended in early 1943, and the agency ceased to exist in June of that year.

Explanation and Analysis of the Document

The poster is dominated by a stylized image of a young man holding an axe. His facial features are indistinct. His face and neck are a uniform pale red, while his hat and uniform are light blue. At the top of the image is the start of a caption, "A Young Man's Opportunity." The words of the caption continue by arcing below the man to say "for work play study & health." At the bottom of the poster, the viewer is directed to submit his application to the Illinois Emergency Relief Commission. The purpose of the poster is not simply to recruit young men into the CCC but to highlight the advantages of the CCC to those who enlisted. The poster might have also provided a measure of reassurance to corpsmen's families, who would have bid good-bye to them for months at a time. As Harry Hopkins, administrator of the WPA, put it, "Give a man a dole, and you save his body and destroy his spirit. Give him a job and you save both body and spirit."

—Michael J. O'Neal

Questions for Further Study

1. What was the purpose of the CCC?

2. How effective might a poster such as this have been in recruiting young men into the CCC?

3. Why would labor unions have objected to the CCC?

Further Reading

Books

Bustard, Bruce I. *A New Deal for the Arts*. Seattle: University of Washington Press, 1997.

DeNoon, Christopher. *Posters of the WPA*. Los Angeles: Wheatley Press, 1987.

Maher, Neil M. *Nature's New Deal: The Civilian Conservation Corps and the Roots of the American Environmental Movement*. New York: Oxford University Press, 2009.

Mavigliano, George J., and Richard A. Lawson. *The Federal Art Project in Illinois: 1935–1943*. Carbondale: Southern Illinois University Press, 1990.

Pearson, P. O'Connell. *Fighting for the Forest: How FDR's Civilian Conservation Corps Helped Save America*. New York: Simon & Schuster Books for Young Readers, 2020.

Salmond, John A. *The Civilian Conservation Corps, 1933–1942: A New Deal Case Study*. Durham: Duke University Press, 1967.

Articles

Maher, Neil M. "A New Deal Body Politic: Landscape, Labor, and the Civilian Conservation Corps." *Environmental History* 7, no. 3 (July 2002): 435–61.

Websites

"Art of the Works Progress Administration WPA." UMMA Exchange, University of Michigan. https://exchange.umma.umich.edu/resources/23630.

"Posters: WPA Posters." Library of Congress. https://www.loc.gov/pictures/collection/wpapos/.

"Records of the Civilian Conservation Corps." National Archives. https://www.archives.gov/research/guide-fed-records/groups/035.html.

Documentaries

"Civilian Conservation Corps." *American Experience*, PBS, 2010.

"We Can Do It!" Rosie The Riveter Poster

Author/Creator	Significance
J. Howard Miller	Intended to bolster morale in the workplace and to encourage women to take jobs in war industries during World War II when large numbers of men were serving in the military
Date 1942	
Image Type Flyers	

Overview

This iconic poster, featuring a symbolic character who came to be known as "Rosie the Riveter," has become emblematic of the widespread participation of women in war industries during World War II. Although it is not absolutely certain who the model for the poster was, the most likely candidate is thought to be Naomi Parker Fraley (1921–2018), who worked on aircraft assembly at the Naval Air Station Alameda in California, but other candidates have been proposed. The poster was commissioned by the Westinghouse Electric Corporation and distributed by the War Production Coordinating Committee. The poster is often thought of as the "Rosie the Riveter" poster, but the name Rosie does not appear on J. Howard Miller's poster. In 1943, however, a popular song titled "Rosie the Riveter" was released, and that year Norman Rockwell produced an image for the cover of the *Saturday Evening Post* that included a somewhat similar figure of a working woman whose name, Rosie, was written on her lunchbox. In this way, Miller's poster became associated with "Rosie the Riveter."

"Rosie the Riveter" makes for a catchy slogan, but of course not all women in the war industries were riveters. Women—often combatting stereotypes and entrenched resistance to women in the workforce—worked in factories and in shipyards that produced war matériel of all types. They also took other jobs that had traditionally been filled by men, driving fire engines and trains, for example. Some served as code breakers for the military, and of course many women—some 350,000—joined the Women's Army Auxiliary Corps (later the Women's Army Corps or WAC), the Women Airforce Service Pilots (WASP), and the Women Accepted for Volunteer Military Services (WAVES). "Rosie the Riveter" and similar posters served as powerful symbols of the contributions that *all* Americans could make during the war.

About the Artist

The poster was created by J. Howard Miller, who painted forty-two posters during World War II in support of the war effort. Miller, however, remained largely unknown, and virtually nothing has been written about his life. Some sources cite the year of his birth as circa 1915, others as 1918. Some state that he died in 1990, others in 2004. It is known that he studied

Document Image

The iconic Rosie the Riveter poster
(National Museum of American History)

at the Art Institute of Pittsburgh, graduating in 1939. His work drew the attention of the Westinghouse Company and the Westinghouse War Production Co-ordinating Committee, which, through an advertising agency, hired him in 1942 to create posters. The Westinghouse committee was one of hundreds of labor-management committees organized and supervised by the national War Production Board. Miller's posters were put on display for the company's workers with the goal of boosting morale, reducing absenteeism, and lowering the risk of labor disputes and strikes. (The company had just signed a union agreement for the first time in 1941.) The company displayed each of Miller's posters for two weeks in the company's factories in East Pittsburgh and throughout the Midwest. Most of them featured men who were occupying traditional male roles. The "We Can Do It!" poster first went on display on February 15, 1943, at Westinghouse factories that were making helmet liners for the military—some 13 million over the course of the war.

Context

The number of men serving in the U.S. military in 1942, the year the poster was created, was more than 3.9 million. Their absence from the industrial workforce, largely because of service in overseas theaters of war, created huge personnel gaps at home in the industries that were producing the armaments and war matériel needed to prosecute the war—the ships, planes, munitions and bombs, tanks, parachutes, uniforms, helmets, boots, and everything else the military needed. Women in large numbers stepped up to fill those gaps. In 1939, about 5.1 million women (26 percent of women of working age) held paid employment. By 1943, the number had risen to more than 7.25 million, or 36 percent of women of working age, and by September of 1943, 46 percent of all women between the ages of fourteen and fifty-nine, and 90 percent of single women between the ages of eighteen and forty, were engaged in some form of work or national service. These numbers would be even higher if domestic servants had been included in the calculations.

Obviously, many women had always worked outside the home, but never in these numbers. According to the War Production Board, in some war plants women made up more than 50 percent of the workers; in others, 70 percent. In one plant, nearly every employee was a woman. The board cited one plant that before the war had a "No Women" hiring policy but after the outbreak of hostilities had a workforce consisting of 25 percent women, and the company was hiring more women as fast as they could be found. The board also cited the Norfolk, Virginia, navy yards, where 500 women were employed as welders, mechanics, and lathe and drill press operators and where they assembled engines and repaired radios, generators, and electric starters. The board, in calling on women to join the workforce, encouraged women in one recruitment pamphlet to ask themselves: "Can I be of greater service in my home or in a war plant?" The U.S. Employment Service stated: "It can hardly be said that ANY occupation is absolutely unsuitable for the employment of women. Women have shown that they can do or learn to do almost any kind of work."

Of course, women faced obstacles that were not physical but were social and psychological. Before the war, women who worked tended to be from the lower working classes. Many were minorities. Some members of the public believed that women from the middle and upper classes should not "demean" themselves by getting their hands dirty in a war factory. Others believed that women should hold only those jobs that men did not want; teaching and nursing were common examples. Still others believed that during the Great Depression of the 1930s, women should have given up their jobs for unemployed men. And of course it was widely believed that a woman's "place" was in the home, maintaining it for her husband and rearing children. These views were not held entirely by men with entrenched attitudes; many women at the time held similar views and looked down on women who worked.

These attitudes went by the wayside after the Japanese attack on Pearl Harbor on December 7, 1941, and U.S. entry into the war. A peacetime military draft had already been approved in September 1940, and by December 1941, 2.2 million citizen-soldiers were in the military. In January 1942, President Franklin D. Roosevelt ordered the establishment of the War Production Board, whose purpose was to aid in the conversion of peacetime industries—the producers of automobiles, appliances, and the like—into manufacturing plants for weapons of war. A second goal was to conserve materials such as metals, which were needed in the production of guns, ordnance, tanks, ships, aircraft, and other military equipment. One dramatic example of the transition to wartime industries is provided by the auto industry. In 1941, before U.S. entry into the war, about three million automobiles were manufactured in the United States. During the entire duration of the war from 1942 on, a mere 139 cars were produced. The Lionel toy train company produced items for warships, including compasses. Ford produced B-24 Liberator bombers. Alcoa, the aluminum company, made airplanes. The Mattatuck Manufacturing Company in Connecticut, which previously had made upholstery nails, made cartridge clips for Springfield rifles. By the end of the war, the United States was responsible for half of the world's wartime industrial production and was the arsenal of the Allied nations, including Britain and Russia.

After the war, most of the "Rosie Riveters" were let go and returned to the home. It was felt that their jobs belonged to the men who were returning from military service. But the wartime experience of women had positive and lasting effects. Women had proved that they could do any job, and over the next decades, women increasingly became a common sight in the workplace. Another positive effect was more immediate. Many of these women saved the money they earned; because of wartime rationing, there was not much to spend it on. This money became the down payment on new homes and contributed to the prosperity and burgeoning economy of the 1950s.

Explanation and Analysis of the Document

"We Can Do It!" presents an upbeat image of women in the workforce. The woman depicted has a determined look on her face and is flexing her arm muscles. She is attired for work, wearing on her head a red bandana with white polka dots and a blue work shirt. The badge on her collar identifies her as a floor employee at a Westinghouse Electric plant. The use of red, white, and blue clothing subtly appealed to the patriotism of the workers. The poster was originally intended for internal use at the Westinghouse plants—some 1,800 copies were made—with the intention of boosting employee morale and maintaining high production. The image, particularly after it became associated with Rosie the Riveter, became an iconic appeal to the patriotism of women in general in celebrating their willingness to take on demanding jobs while their husbands and sons, fathers, brothers, and boyfriends were in uniform.

—Michael J. O'Neal

Questions for Further Study

1. What was the underlying purpose of the "We Can Do It!" poster?

2. Why has this image been used in numerous contexts, such as book covers, notepads, T-shirts, lunch boxes, tote bags, and the like?

3. Why was it necessary for large numbers of women to enter the workforce during World War II?

Further Reading

Books

Colman, Penny. *Rosie the Riveter: Women Working on the Home Front in World War II*. New York: Crown Publishers, 1995.

Dumenil, Lynn. *American Working Women in World War II: A Brief History with Documents*. Boston: Bedford/St. Martin's, 2019.

Endres, Kathleen L. *Rosie the Rubber Worker: Women Workers in Akron's Rubber Factories during World War II*. Kent, Ohio: Kent State University Press, 2000.

Frank, Miriam, Marilyn Ziebarth, and Connie Field. *The Life and Times of Rosie the Riveter: The Story of Three Million Working Women during World War II*. Emeryville, CA: Clarity Educational Productions, 1982.

Gluck, Sherna Berger. *Rosie the Riveter Revisited: Women, the War and Social Change*. Boston: Twayne, 1987.

Knaff, Donna B. *Beyond Rosie the Riveter: Women of World War II in American Popular Graphic Art*. Lawrence: University Press of Kansas, 2012.

U.S. War Manpower Commission, Information Service. *America at War Needs Women at Work*. Washington, D.C: U.S. Government Printing Office, 1943.

Weatherford, Doris. *American Women and World War II*. Edison, NJ: Castle Books, 2009.

Articles

Goldin, Claudia D. "The Role of World War II in the Rise of Women's Employment." *American Economic Review* 81, no. 4 (September 1991): 741–56.

Kossoudji, Sherrie A., and Laura J. Dresser. "Working Class Rosies: Women Industrial Workers during World War II." *Journal of Economic History* 52, no. 2 (June 1992): 431–46.

Websites

"Powers of Persuasion." Online Exhibits, National Archives. Accessed August 16, 2022. https://www.archives.gov/exhibits/powers-of-persuasion.

"Women in the Work Force during World War II." Educator Resources, National Archives. Accessed August 16, 2022. https://www.archives.gov/education/lessons/wwii-women.html.

"If Hitler Came to Mobile." War Manpower Commission. Accessed August 16, 2022. https://www.archives.gov/files/education/lessons//images/wwii-flyer.pdf.

Documentaries

"The Life and Times of Rosie the Riveter." *American Experience*, PBS, 1988.

Evans, Redd, and John Jacob Loeb. "Rosie the Riveter" (song first released by the Vagabonds, 1943). https://www.youtube.com/watch?v=55NCElsbjeQ.

Photograph Of B-17 Formation Over Schweinfurt, Germany

Author/Creator U.S. Army Air Force **Date** 1943 **Image Type** Photographs	**Significance** Illustrates the emergence of strategic bombardment, one of the most terrifying evolutions of modern warfare, in which aircraft such as the B-17 Flying Fortress, with its thirteen .50-caliber machine guns and durable construction, allowed American airmen to deliver thousands of bombs while repelling enemy attacks

Overview

This photograph depicts a devastating air raid by the Allied Powers in Germany on August 17, 1943. During the January 14–24, 1943, multinational Casablanca Conference, the Allied Powers publicly committed to the unconditional surrender of the Axis Powers. Secretly, this conference would determine the future strategy of the war effort. During the meeting, American and British leaders decided to combine aerial bomber forces, with the Americans bombing during the day and the British bombing at night. Allied leaders directed these air forces to focus on "the progressive destruction and dislocation of the German military, industrial, and economic system, and the undermining of the morale of the German people to a point where their capacity for armed resistance is fatally weakened." Primary targets were German aircraft and submarine manufacturing facilities, transportation hubs, oil production facilities, and other war-supporting industries.

The dreaded Messerschmitt Me 109 fighter aircraft was primarily built in Regensburg, and significant war industries were concentrated in Schweinfurt. Combined Bomber Command put together an ambitious plan for American forces to strike both facilities while the British simultaneously attacked a rocket research compound. This was the first Allied attempt at a "shuttle mission" in which bombers would hit one target, land and rearm, then strike a second target before returning home. The 376 B-17s destroyed the Messerschmitt factories, caused a massive loss of production of war materiel, and killed more than 200 civilians. Despite these significant impacts, the German war industry quickly recovered, and production shortages were rapidly replaced through stockpiles. The Regensburg-Schweinfurt raid resulted in fifty-five B-17 bombers lost, over ninety B-17s badly damaged, and nearly 600 American airmen killed, wounded, or captured. With such heavy losses, the Combined Bomber Command could not follow up this attack for another two months. The August 17, 1943, Regensburg-Schweinfurt raid was a critical turning point in the war. Its failure convinced leaders that, despite the heavy armament of the B-17, long-range fighter escorts were necessary for the continued growth of strategic bombing to be effective.

Document Image

The B-17 formation flying over Germany on August 17, 1943
(Library of Congress)

About the Artist

The witness who took this photograph is unknown; however, it was likely one of the American Army Air Force crewmembers flying above the formation pictured as they delivered their ordnance to factories of war industries in Schweinfurt, Germany.

Context

Aerial bombing is a military strategy that uses fear and the destruction of transportation and industrial centers to reduce enemy morale and compel an enemy nation to surrender. Though other militaries made isolated use of bombs dropped by kites, balloons, or aircraft much earlier, the first large-scale use of aircraft to drop bombs on cities occurred during World War I. While these bombing raids were relatively ineffective at destroying enemy cities or industrial centers, they effectively inspired fear. Military thinkers like Giulio Douhet, Hugh Trenchard, and Billy Mitchell argued that aerial bombardment could rapidly win wars without armies or navies.

The concept of fear is as essential to the strategy as destruction. Ideally, enemy populations will become demoralized and, seeing peace as the best option, convince or force their government to surrender. Aerial bombing strategies are generally either tactical (in support of ground or naval forces) or strategic (an effort to eliminate the enemy's ability to continue to wage war). Mass production techniques, easy access to resources, a highly educated population, and industrial capacity were necessary to produce large bomber aircraft in numbers significant enough to make the desired strategic effects possible. In World War II, the Axis and Soviet militaries preferred tactical strategies. Much of the aircraft built and operated during this period by these nations were a hybrid of fighter and bomber aircraft. This reduced the number of bombs an aircraft could carry but theoretically increased the different missions these aircraft could conduct. American and British forces employed many hybrid aircraft and developed a sizeable strategic bombing capacity in purpose-built long-range, large-capacity bomber aircraft like the B-17.

While the Allied Combined Bomber Offensive was theoretically a unified effort of the British and American forces, the two nations effectively operated as supporting efforts. The strategic bombing campaign was designed to cause the Germans to divert forces from the front lines to defend Germany's industrial, economic, and transportation centers while increasing fear in its population. The British, who had been fighting for over twenty-seven months before the Americans officially entered the war, were more averse to subjecting their bombers to the dangers of daylight bombardment. Because of this, the British developed techniques and equipment focused on nighttime area bombardment. The Americans developed precision optical bombing sights and other equipment specifically to increase the precision of their bombing efforts. The Americans bombed during the day because American bombardiers had to see their targets to hit them with any accuracy. Daytime bombing was far more dangerous as Axis ground and air defenders could easily see the large American bombers. American leaders argued that the defenses, speed, and altitude capabilities would allow their bombers to defend themselves or avoid the dangers of ground-based anti-aircraft guns.

The Regensburg-Schweinfurt raid was a fully invested test in the effectiveness of strategic bombing and the application of precision-bombing practices. While the mission would not be a sweeping success, it would be a turning point in the war as American and British forces would develop long-range escort aircraft to defend their bombers. This development was critically important to the defeat of the Nazi state. Even though the Nazis were capable of continuing to produce aircraft, they did not have people to train as pilots in large enough numbers to replace the number the Allied air offensive was destroying.

Explanation and Analysis of the Document

The B-17 was a product of the United States Army Air Force's thinking during the interwar period. Initially conceived of as airborne artillery, the B-17 was outfitted with four powerful engines to fly faster than most bombers and at high altitudes. However, its 2,000-mile range and mission meant that the aircraft would not be able to have a dedicated fighter escort, so designers traded bomb payloads for thirteen .50-caliber M2 Browning machine guns. When flown in formations like the one above Schweinfurt, B-17s could easily provide mutual defense for one another. At the same time, the flight crew operated the secret Norden bombsight—one of the first transportable analog computers used by American forces.

Not long after the American entry into World War II, the B-17 Flying Fortress production shifted from building one aircraft every twelve to thirteen days to building fourteen to sixteen aircraft every day. While the B-17 was one of the first American aircraft to see combat in the Pacific, the aircraft would become most famous for its role in the European theater. The American Eighth Air Force would become the largest offensive bombing force, equipped entirely with B-17 aircraft. The aircraft's durability made it the preferred choice of many aircraft crewmembers and leaders, despite its limited capacity compared to other heavy bombers like the B-24 Liberator, the B-29 Superfortress, the British Avro Lancaster, or the Handley Page Halifax.

Although the costly raid did not produce the strategic effects the Combined Bomber Command had promised, it did cause a change in military thinking. After modified P-51 Mustang fighter aircraft joined the Eighth Air Force in the fall of 1943, losses of B-17 aircraft dropped so drastically that shipment of replacement aircraft was halted.

By the conclusion of World War II, more than 12,700 B-17s had been built. These aircraft operated in every combat theater flying with American, British, Soviet, Free French, Australian, and Canadian air forces. German and Japanese forces captured approximately forty-three B-17s that were put into service for the Axis for secret reconnaissance missions and to develop effective tactics against the B-17. The B-17 was one of the most iconic aircraft of the war, dropping nearly half of the almost 1.5 tons of American bombs targeted against Nazi Germany. Seventeen American B-17 crewmembers would be awarded the Congressional Medal of Honor, the highest recognition of military bravery awarded by the U.S. government.

Within weeks of the end of World War II, President Truman ordered a panel of experts to review the effectiveness of the bombing campaign in Europe and Asia. The 208-volume *United States Bombing Survey* report declared that strategic bombing played a decisive role in defeating the Axis powers. However, the report did offer that it was impossible to separate the effects of bombing from all other elements of governmental and economic collapse. The report also stated that although accuracy improved over the war, approximately 300,000 tons, representing about 20 percent of all American "precision delivery" of bombs, hit their assigned targets over the entire war.

—Bryant Macfarlane

Questions for Further Study

1. The useful creation of fear in everyday people by attacking their homes and places of employment is a central argument made by people who advocate for the use of strategic bombardment. How do you think military and governmental leaders in the United States convinced the American people that this strategy was not morally or ethically wrong?

2. How could a photo like this be used in Allied nations to raise morale? How could it be used as a tool of intimidation in Axis nations?

3. Today, only the United States and a handful of other nations continue developing and flying heavy bombers. Given that only about 20 percent of all "precision" bombing raids hit their targets, why do you think the United States decided to continue developing, producing, and employing these weapons after World War II?

Further Reading

Books

Biddle, Tami Davis. *Rhetoric and Reality in Air Warfare: The Evolution of British and American Ideas about Strategic Bombing, 1914–1945.* Princeton: Princeton University Press, 2002.

Clodfelter, Mark. *Beneficial Bombing: The Progressive Foundations of American Air Power, 1917–1945.* Lincoln: University of Nebraska Press, 2010.

Crane, Conrad C. *American Airpower Strategy in World War II: Bombs, Cities, Civilians, and Oil.* Lawrence: University Press of Kansas, 2014.

Johnson, David E. *Fast Tanks and Heavy Bombers: Innovation in the US Army, 1917–1945.* Ithaca: Cornell University Press, 1998.

Sherry, Michael S. *The Rise of American Air Power: The Creation of Armageddon.* New Haven: Yale University Press, 1987.

Vlaun, Brian D. *Selling Schweinfurt: Targeting, Assessment, and Marketing in the Air Campaign against German Industry.* Annapolis: U.S. Naval Institute Press, 2020.

Websites

Correll, John T. "The Cost of Schweinfurt." *Air Force Magazine*, February 1, 2010. https://www.airforcemag.com/article/0210schweinfurt/.

Crawford, Bruce. "Death on the High Road: The Schweinfurt Raid." Historynet.com. https://www.historynet.com/world-war-ii-eighth-air-force-raid-on-schweinfurt/.

Mighty Eighth Air Force Museum website. https://www.mightyeighth.org.

"Schweinfurt—The Battle within the Battle for the U.S. 8th Air Force." Air University website. https://www.airuniversity.af.edu/Portals/10/ASPJ/journals/Chronicles/reichert.pdf.

Documentaries

The Air Force Story: Chapter 14—Schweinfurt and Regensburg August 17th 1943. U.S. Air Force, director. U.S. Department of Defense, n.d.

All The Fine Young Men. Karen Rutledge, director. National Broadcasting Company News, 1984.

Bombers without Escorts. Jonathan Martin, director. A&E Television Networks, 1998.

The Bombing of Germany. Zvi Dor-Ner, producer and director. PBS American Experience, 2010.

The Case of the Tremendous Trifle. U.S. Signal Corps, director. U.S. War Department, 1944.

Victory through Air Power. James Algar, Clyde Geronimi, Jack Kinney, and H.C. Potter, directors. Walt Disney Productions, 1943.

Ansel Adams: "Manzanar Relocation Center" Photograph

Author/Creator
Ansel Adams

Date
1943

Image Type
Photographs

Significance
Portrays one of the ten detention centers where more than 120,000 Japanese Americans were forced to relocate after the passage of Executive Order 9066, just a few months after the bombing of Pearl Harbor on December 11, 1941

Overview

This photograph is of a typical Japanese American detention center created by the U.S. government in February 1942. The order allowed the creation of an exclusion zone that effectively excluded Japanese Americans from living or working in the western half of California, Oregon, Washington, and the southern half of Arizona. This order extended to anyone with one-sixteenth Japanese ancestry. When President Franklin Roosevelt signed the order, the government had no facilities ready to house the roughly 120,000 Japanese Americans living in the exclusion zone. Interestingly, the approximately 150,000 Japanese Americans living in Hawaii or Alaska were not forcibly relocated. With limited results, the government urged Japanese Americans to voluntarily evacuate from the exclusion area. Many had no relations or friends living outside the ethnic Japanese enclaves along the Pacific Coast to support their relocation. The Western Defense Command ordered the military to enforce a mandatory evacuation in March 1942.

As the photograph shows, these centers were generally located in remote inland areas. Roughly 110,000 individuals and families—approximately 70,000 of whom were American citizens—were classified as a potential threat to the American government. These people were provided only a few days to sell or otherwise safeguard their belongings before being loaded onto trucks, buses, or trains with only a suitcase to hold all their possessions. They were initially housed in one of fifty-nine hastily converted racetracks, fairgrounds, jails or prisons, or other similar locations called assembly centers. Many non-Japanese who were married or closely related to the Japanese Americans voluntarily left with their loved ones for the relocation centers. The first to leave these facilities were volunteers transported to Manzanar. They began erecting tents and building flimsy tar-paper wooden buildings that can be seen along the left side of the photograph. Manzanar, whose inmate population was mainly from Los Angeles, Central California, and Bembridge Island, Washington—was the first of the ten facilities estab-

Document Image

The Manzanar Relocation Center
(Library of Congress)

lished to detain Japanese Americans. Just over 11,000 Japanese Americans would be incarcerated, and about 150 would die, in Manzanar before the camp was closed in November 1945.

About the Artist

Ansel Adams was born in San Francisco in 1902. Witnessing the Great Quake of 1906, he fell in an intense aftershock and broke his nose—a disfigurement he would bear for the rest of his life. Very shy and self-conscious about his nose, Adams spent much time alone, often taking in views of the beaches of San Francisco or the Yosemite Valley. After spending several long summers in the wilderness hiking, exploring, and photographing his world, he grew more self-assured. Adams joined the Sierra Club in 1919 and became one of the early American conservation movement's most ardent advocates. His early photography work was a product of the fashion in photography in the 1920s of pictorialism—an effort to make photographs appear more like paintings. In 1927 Adams's work caught the eye of Albert Bender, a wealthy San Francisco art supporter. With Bender's patronage, Adams's work developed sharply focused and carefully framed images rich in tonality, a trademark that in Adams's photography would become famous.

By chance, Adams's friend and fellow Sierra Club member Ralph Merritt had been appointed the director of Manzanar in November 1942. After a turbulent and violent start to his directorship, Merritt invited Adams to Manzanar to record daily life. Adams wanted to present the loyalty and Americanness of the Japanese Americans detained in the camp. He also wanted to show the resiliency of the Japanese Americans to persevere despite the ugliness of their situation through their creation of a vibrant society inside the compound. Adams published his nearly 200 Manzanar photos in *Born Free and Equal: The Story of Loyal Japanese-Americans* (1944) and in an intensely controversial Museum of Modern Art exposition in New York. With World War II still being fought, many felt that Adams's work was an act of disloyalty. However, Adams also performed significant, yet quiet, work for the American war effort by secretly photographing Japanese military installations in the Alaskan Aleutian Islands.

Adams would go on to form the photography department at the California School of Fine Arts, cofound *Aperture*, the first serious American journal of photography, and become the first photographer to make an official presidential portrait for President Jimmy Carter. Adams died in 1984.

Context

The bombing of the naval base at Pearl Harbor, Hawaii, was a galvanizing moment in twentieth-century America. Panic, fear, and greed shook the dust off the cracks in American society, which allowed wartime hysteria and racism to deny civil liberties. Shortly after the attack, President Franklin Roosevelt ordered an investigation into what happened. While the report made some vague references to potential information gathering by Japanese agents before the attack, popular opinion—inflamed by media reports and political rhetoric—saw Japanese Americans as a potential fifth column threat. This led to the creation of the War Relocation Authority (WRA), which forcibly relocated and detained over 110,000 Japanese Americans without charges, hearings, or trials.

Many Americans saw an opportunity and supported the forced removal of their Japanese American neighbors so they could purchase their farms, land, homes, and businesses for a small fraction of their value or wait for the properties to become vacant and simply take them. The Japanese Americans were the largest and most publicly recognized group to be detained, but the U.S. Department of Justice also operated smaller, less-visible camps for German and Italian American sympathizers.

The WRA wanted its inmates to become more American but did allow for a degree of personal freedom. Inmates could choose to practice traditional Japanese customs but were strongly encouraged to assimilate to American ways. The camps' school system was taught in English and stressed American history. Inmates were allowed to work in camp facilities like the newspaper, recreation centers, medical facilities, or stores. At the same time, Nisei (second-generation Japanese Americans who had American citizenship under the Fourteenth Amendment) were encouraged to work in local war industries or agriculture to support the war effort. The WRA required religious facilities and services and encouraged attendance of either Christian or Buddhist services as individuals saw fit. The WRA's democratic forum of "self-governance" set up in the camps was intended to reflect the American town hall and give the inmates a sense of participation in the operation of their community. This severely limited Issei (first-generation Japanese Americans who could not by law attain citizenship) participation and required that the inmates maintain the fences, guard towers, and other facilities.

As early as April 1942, the WRA recognized it would not have the capacity to effectively control such a large mass of people without the hope of reintegration into American society for the inmates. To foster this hope, work release, college exemptions, voluntary relocation of American citizens (with a sponsor and at the inmate's expense), and volunteer service in the U.S. military were all methods provided for inmates. To help identify inmates for potential reintegration, the WRA administered a loyalty questionnaire to all Japanese Americans aged seventeen or older. The questionnaire ended with two questions that caused much confusion and resentment within the camps. Question twenty-seven asked if Nisei were willing to serve in the military or vital war industries. Question twenty-eight asked all inmates if they would swear allegiance to the United States and renounce any loyalty to the emperor of Japan. Because at least one-third of inmates were Issei, if they answered yes to Question twenty-eight, these people would be losing the only citizenship they had. Despite threats of fines or long prison sentences, approximately 20,000 refused to answer or answered no to both questions in protest, with some requesting repatriation to Japan. Called "no-no's," these Japanese Americans were designated "disloyal" and sent to Tule Lake's maximum-security segregation facility.

Explanation and Analysis of the Document

The photo presents the Manzanar Relocation Camp as a rural mountain town, not unlike other rural mountain towns across the American West. Taken from a guard tower elevation, Ansel Adams specifically framed this photo to present a positive view of Manzanar. Photographically, this image is a departure from his famed tonality-focused landscapes, but the composition communicates feelings of optimism for the future. The road draws the eye from the foreground to the horizon, from what is to what will be. Adams created much of this visual story, as he did with many of his works, through his darkroom development of the film negatives by selectively increasing or decreasing portions of the photo.

Note what is missing from this photo that you might find in an average image of a prison compound. There are no clearly represented fences, guard towers, or other signs that this is a restricted or secured area—though if you look closely enough at the end of the main street, a blurry guard tower can be seen. People can be seen walking or chatting to others along the sleepy main road with a few vehicles that may suggest a semi-prosperous and contented life. Adams was invited to photograph Manzanar the spring after Ralph Merritt, the director of the internment camp, had put down an inmate uprising. Despite many popular news outlets portraying the riot as a pro-Japanese celebration of the Pearl Harbor attack, the riot demonstrated that the WRA was struggling to contain the friction between groups of inmates and, in several cases, had poorly selected camp administrators. The WRA never was capable of understanding or developing methods to counteract the generational or cultural conflicts that were preexisting and grew only worse among the inmates.

The area has a main road and has electrical power. A baseball game is being played on the right of the photo, and many "residents" are lining the third-base line into the outfield. A family's laundry is drying on a line in front of the barracks block in the left foreground. What is not seen in the image are traditionally Japanese activities or symbols. Many of the inmates specifically wanted to demonstrate their Americanness by embracing American cultural activities—baseball instead of aikido or judo, poker or dice instead of shogi, chess instead of go, and so on. This attitude was reflected by inmates who served in segregated, all–Japanese American army units of the 442nd Regimental Combat Team, who adopted the motto "Go for Broke." This gambling phrase was an encouragement to risk it all to win big, a thought that reflected the motivation of these Japanese Americans to give everything to demonstrate their loyalty to the United States.

President Harry Truman rescinded the exclusion order at the end of the war. Though the WRA had transported the Japanese Americans to the internment camps, inmates were given twenty-five dollars and had to find their own way home. Manzanar's inmates had a tough time finding housing in their former communities, and many were unwilling to leave, requiring the WRA administrators to force arrangements onto inmates. This refusal caused the camp to remain open until November 21, 1945. Little remained of the camp by the early 1950s.

In the late 1940s and 1950s, Japanese Americans and others began advocating for a formal apology and monetary compensation from the American government for violating their Constitutional rights and causing their loss of property. Although the U.S. government paid a fraction of the initial nearly $132 million in claims from Japanese Americans, the passage of the 1952 McCarran-Walter Act allowed Issei to become naturalized citizens. Through the 1960s and 1970s, Japanese Americans and others continued to agitate in public and in the courts for an apology and compensation for all inmates as a formal recognition of the American government to uphold civil rights in the face of war hysteria, flagrant racism, and fundamental failures by elected political officials and institutions. These efforts resulted in the Civil Liberties Act of 1988, which formally recognized these failures of the American government. In November 1989, the federal government issued individual compensation of $20,000 and a letter of apology to the roughly 82,000 surviving Japanese Americans who had been inmates of the WRA. In March 1992, Manzanar was recognized in Public Law 102-248 as the National Historic Site for interpretation of wartime removal and incarceration of Japanese Americans. After 9/11, Japanese American organizations and activists organized demonstrations denouncing the racism and hate that wartime hysteria could bring. In reminding the American people of their shameful past, these demonstrations sought to protect Arab, Muslim, and other American citizens or residents from actions or legislation based on racial profiling.

—Bryant Macfarlane

Questions for Further Study

1. Why do you think the Japanese Americans living in Hawaii and Alaska were not forcibly relocated along with the exclusion zone residents? What does this suggest about regional differences in America in the early 1940s?

2. What did Ralph Merritt hope to achieve by allowing Ansel Adams to photograph Manzanar and then exhibit the works at the New York Museum of Modern Art?

3. Imagine you were a Nisei inmate at Manzanar and were asked to volunteer for military service. How do you react to the request? Why? Would your reaction change if you were drafted? Why?

4. The American government apologized and paid surviving former Japanese American inmates a $20,000 lump sum for their suffering, property loss, wrongful imprisonment, and denial of their Constitutional rights. Was this suitable and effective compensation for the survivors? Why or why not?

Further Reading

Books

Adams, Ansel. *Born Free and Equal: The Story of Loyal Japanese-Americans.* New York: U.S. Camera, 1944.

Bosworth, Allan R. *America's Concentration Camps.* New York: W.W. Norton & Co., 1967.

Drinnon, Richard. *Keeper of Concentration Camps: Dillon S. Myer and American Racism.* Berkeley: University of California Press, 1987.

Duus, Masayo Umezawa; Peter Duus, trans. *Unlikely Liberators: The Men of the 100th and 442nd.* Honolulu: University of Hawaii Press, 1987.

Hosokawa, Bill. *Nisei: The Quiet Americans.* Niwot, CO: University Press of Colorado, 1992.

Houston, Jeanne Wakatsuki. *Beyond Manzanar: View of Asian American Womanhood.* Santa Barbara, CA: Capra Press, 1985.

Ichioka, Yuji. *The Issei: The World of the First Generation Japanese Immigrants, 1885–1924.* New York: The Free Press, 1988.

Myer, Dillon S. *Uprooted Americans: The Japanese Americans and the War Relocation Authority during World War II.* Tucson: University of Arizona Press, 1971.

Websites

"Go for Broke National Education Center." Go for Broke, 2022. https://goforbroke.org.

"JACL Curriculum Guides and Resources" Japanese American Citizens League. https://jacl.org/resources.

"The Japanese American Legacy Project." Densho, 2022. http://www.densho.org/.

"Manzanar National Historic Site." National Park Service, 2022. https://www.nps.gov/manz.

"A More Perfect Union: Japanese Americans & the U.S. Constitution." Smithsonian National Museum of American History, n.d. https://amhistory.si.edu/perfectunion/non-flash/index.html.

"Virtual Museum Exhibit: Manzanar." National Park Service, n.d. https://www.nps.gov/museum/exhibits/manz/index.html.

Documentaries

From a Different Shore: An American Identity. Jeremy Cooper, director. The Open University, 1999.

Manzanar Fishing Club. Cory Shiozaki, director. From Barbed Wire to Barbed Hooks LLC, 2012.

Rabbit in the Moon. Emiko Omori, director. JALL, 1999.

Stand Up for Justice: The Ralph Lazlo Story. John Esaki, director. Visual Communications, 2004.

Photograph Of Navajo Code Talkers

Author/Creator U.S. Marine Corps	**Image Type** Photographs
Date 1943	**Significance** Two of the Navajo who used their language as an unbreakable code that kept the Japanese military in the Pacific mystified during World War II

Overview

During World War II, it was crucial for Allied troops to maintain secrecy in their radio and telephone transmissions. To that end, messages were encoded, but the ongoing concern was that Japanese (and German) code breakers could break the codes and thereby know the disposition, movement, and intentions of Allied troops. In 1942, the United States hit on a solution for more effectively conducting the war in the Pacific by keeping codes secret: it recruited Navajo as "code talkers." These soldiers, including the two shown in this photograph (Henry Bake and George Kirk), were members of the U.S. Marine Corps. They used their language to encode messages in battlefield transmissions. Navaho was chosen because of the complexity of the language, because it was largely unwritten, and because even other Native Americans could not understand it. The Japanese were never able to break the code.

About the Artist

It is unknown who specifically took this photograph. The photo, however, is part of a series of photographs of Navajo code talkers taken by the U.S. Marine Corps, which were collected at the National Archives in 1947 and arranged in an exhibit by the Defense Audiovisual Agency (DAVA) in the early 1980s. The photos, along with photos from other branches of the military, were made available for events such as Black History Month and other memorials acknowledging the contributions of women and minority groups to the war effort. DAVA was created as a Department of Defense agency in 1979 to "provide centrally managed acquisition, distribution, and depository support and services for selected audiovisual products to all Department of Defense components." DAVA was decommissioned in 1985, and its responsibilities were turned over to the various military departments.

Context

On March 6, 1942, General Clayton B. Vogel, the commanding general of the Amphibious Corps, Pacific Fleet, wrote a letter to the Marine Corps commandant. In the letter he recommended the recruitment of 200 Navajo to the Amphibious Corps. He made the recommendation after Philip Johnston, the Anglo son of a missionary who grew up on a Navajo reservation and spoke the language, demonstrated to him that the Marines could use Native Navajo speakers as "code

Document Image

Najvajo code talkers Henry Bake and George Kirk
(National Archives)

talkers," thwarting Japanese efforts to break U.S. radio codes.

Vogel wrote: "Mr. Johnston stated that the Navajo is the only tribe in the United States that has not been infested with German students during the past twenty years. These Germans, studying the various tribal dialects under the guise of art students, anthropologists, etc., have undoubtedly attained a good working knowledge of all tribal dialects except Navajo. For this reason the Navajo is the only tribe available offering complete security for the type of work under consideration.... It should also be noted that the Navajo tribal dialect is completely unintelligible to all other tribes and all other people, with the possible exception of as many as 28 Americans who have made a study of the dialect. This dialect is thus the equivalent of a secret code to the enemy and admirably suited for rapid, secure communication."

In this way, the Navajo code talker project was born. (Note that "dialect" is somewhat of a misnomer; Navajo is a language, like French or Chinese; a dialect is a variant of a language.)

On the island battlefields of World War II, it was essential for the military to maintain secrecy. In particular, messages had to be encoded so that the enemy could not decipher them. The process of encoding and decoding messages, however, often required hours of work. The Marines in the Pacific, under rapidly changing battlefield conditions, needed a quicker way to send and receive messages in a code that the Japanese could not break.

In 1970, Philip Johnston wrote a paper entitled "Indian Jargon Won Our Battles." The paper described the genesis of the Navajo code-talker program. He stated that he came upon the idea of Navajo code talkers after reading a newspaper article about the U.S. Army's use of Native Americans during training maneuvers in Louisiana. The Army had tried them out as signalmen because during World War I, the Canadian army had success using them to send secure messages the German military could not decipher. In 1942, he pitched the idea to naval authorities. The Naval Office in Los Angeles sent Johnston to the headquarters of the Eleventh Naval District in San Diego, which in turn directed him to Camp Eliot in San Diego, where a demonstration was scheduled for February 28, 1942.

Prior to the demonstration, Johnston sent a report to General Vogel explaining why he believed the plan would work. In that report, he included population statistics about the Navajo and a specific explanation of the potential of the Navajo language as a code. He noted the complexity of the language; its largely unwritten status because it had no alphabet of purely Native origin (with the exception of the work of a few anthropologists); the tribe's relative seclusion, which made it linguistically and culturally autonomous compared to other tribes; and the fact that the language was unintelligible to other Native tribes. He emphasized that a person could achieve fluency in reading Navajo only by making an extensive study of it—and that very few people had done so. He indicated that the languages of the Sioux, Chippewa, and Pima-Papago could work, but Navajo was the best choice because the Navajo had the largest population to draw on for recruitment. Additionally, many Navajo had attended schools that taught English, trades, and occupations and had been prepared for jobs in the non-Native community.

Vogel was impressed by the results of the demonstration. The four Navajo whom Johnston recruited accurately sent and translated six messages. For example, the message "Enemy expected to make tank and dive bomber attack at dawn" was deciphered as "Enemy tank dive bomber expected to attack this morning." The only problem was that the Navajo language did not contain words for military terminology. Accordingly, over the next year, a lexicon was developed that would be consistent and universally applicable. Initially, 211 words were included, but over the course of the war, the list expanded to 411. Thus, for example, a fighter plane was called "da-ha-tih-hi," meaning "hummingbird." A dive bomber was a "gini," meaning "chicken hawk." A commander was a "war chief," an observation plane was an "owl," and the British Isles were "Between Waters," to cite a few more examples. The code talkers also created a system to refer to the twenty-six letters of the English alphabet so that any words not included in the list of terms could be spelled out. Thus, for example, the letter *A* was represented by "wol-la-chee," meaning "ant" in Navajo; the letter *E* was represented by "dzeh," meaning "elk." Concern grew that the code could be broken because of too many repetitions. Accordingly, the vocabulary was expanded to include alternatives for the most frequently used letters: *E, T, A, O, I, N, S, H, R, D, L,* and *U*. Thus, "be-la-sana," meaning "apple," and "tse-nihl," meaning "axe," were alternatives to "ant" for the letter *A*.

The Marine Corps approved the program, with the stipulation that the recruits had to meet all the usual requirements for enlistment and undergo basic training. In May 1942 the first twenty-nine recruits arrived in San Diego for basic training. They were then assigned to the Fleet Marine Training Center at Camp Elliott, where they were trained in radio operations and the transmission of messages. The Navajo quickly became adept at memorizing the code and transmitting messages under adverse conditions. The success of the first batch of recruits led to the recruitment of an additional 200. In October 1942, Johnston, a World War I veteran, himself enlisted in the Marine Corps and worked as the trainer for additional Navajo recruits in an intensive eight-week course. The problem the Marine Corps faced for the duration of the war was the lack of qualified recruits. Despite intense efforts on the part of the Corps, the goal of recruiting a thousand code talkers remained elusive, and many military units in the Pacific did not have a code talker, making use of the code pointless. Another problem that arose was lack of consistency. Different contingents of code talkers had trained at different times and different places, leading to differences in the "dialect" of the code, impeding communication. To combat this problem, officers often reassigned Navajo from one unit to another and advised quarterly training sessions to review the code, radio procedures, and radio headings.

The Battle of Iwo Jima in 1945 provided perhaps the best example of the success of the code-talker program. During the monthlong battle, the code was used to transmit some 800 messages. A Marine captain, in his report on the battle, called the Navajo code "the simplest, fastest, and most reliable means" of transmitting secret orders by radio and telephone circuits.

It is estimated that between 375 and 420 Navajo served as code talkers. They never returned home to parades because program remained classified until 1968. Then in 2000, Congress passed the "Honoring Code Talkers Act" recognizing the Navajo code talkers, and in 2001 the first twenty-nine soldiers were awarded the Congressional Gold Medal at a ceremony at the U.S. Capitol. Many Americans became familiar with the code-talker program from a 2002 major motion picture titled *Windtalkers*, starring Nicholas Cage.

The Navajo code-talker program was fraught with one irony. As Native Americans were confined to reservations in the nineteenth century and Native children were taught in government boarding schools, the children were forbidden to speak their native languages or to follow their traditional customs and practices. The needs of total war cast an entirely different light on the value of preserving American Indian tongues.

Explanation and Analysis of the Document

The four inch by five inch, black-and-white photograph is simple. It shows two Navajo code talkers at work on Bougainville Island in Papua New Guinea. The two men have carved out a hiding place from the jungle bush. The man on the left, Corporal Henry Bake Jr., has a writing implement and a pad on which he is presumably writing out a coded message. The man on the right, Private First Class George H. Kirk, is the radio operator. He is wearing headphones, and the radio appears to be slung from his shoulder. He is talking into a handheld microphone, presumably transmitting the message. No specific date is given, but the Japanese had occupied the island in March–April 1942, Allied troops had launched their initial assault on the island in Operation Cartwheel in November 1943, and the Japanese launched a counterattack in March 1944, so it is possible, but not certain, that this photo was taken sometime during that battle. The photo demonstrates the harsh, adverse conditions under which the code talkers, and the Marines in general, had to operate as they dislodged the Japanese from the islands they had occupied in the early years of the war.

—Michael J. O'Neal

Questions for Further Study

1. Why were the Navajo selected for the code-talker program?

2. Why did some Navajo choose to take part in the program (and to enlist in other branches of the military during World War II)?

3. In what way did the code-talker program help to combat stereotypes of Native Americans?

Further Reading

Books

Durrett, Deanne. *Unsung Heroes of World War II: The Story of the Navajo Code Talkers*. Lincoln: University of Nebraska Press, 2009.

Kawano, Kenji. *Warriors: Navajo Code Talkers*. Flagstaff: Northland Publishing, 1990.

McClain, Sally. *Navajo Weapon: The Navajo Code Talkers*. Tucson: Rio Nuevo Publishers, 2002.

Nez, Chester. *Code Talker: The First and Only Memoir by One of the Original Navajo Code Talkers of WWII*. New York: Dutton, 2012.

Paul, Doris A. *The Navajo Code Talkers*. Pittsburgh: Dorrance Publishing, 1973.

Turner, Jim. *Navajo Code Talker Manual*. Tucson: Rio Nuevo Publishers, 2019.

Articles

Meadows, William C., "Honoring Native American Code Talkers: The Road to the Code Talkers Recognition Act of 2008 (Public Law 110-420)," *American Indian Culture and Research Journal* 35, no. 3 (2011): 3–36.

Websites

Johnston, Philip. "Indian Jargon Won Our Battles." Colorado Plateau Archives, Northern Arizona University, 1970. Accessed August 15, 2022. http://archive.library.nau.edu/digital/collection/cpa/id/39511/.

"Memorandum Regarding the Enlistment of Navajo Indians." National Archives, March 6, 1942. Accessed August 15, 2022. https://www.archives.gov/education/lessons/code-talkers.

"Navajo Code Talkers and the Unbreakable Code." CIA, November 6, 2008. https://www.cia.gov/stories/story/navajo-code-talkers-and-the-unbreakable-code/.

"Navajo Code Talkers' Dictionary." Naval History and Heritage Command. Accessed August 15, 2022. https://www.history.navy.mil/research/library/online-reading-room/title-list-alphabetically/n/navajo-code-talker-dictionary.html.

Documentaries

True Whispers: The Story of the Navajo Code Talkers. PBS, 2002. https://itvs.org/films/true-whispers#:~:text=Native%20American%20men%20devised%20a,during%20the%20World%20War%20II.

"KULTUR-TERROR"
PRO-GERMAN, ANTI-AMERICAN
PROPAGANDA POSTER

AUTHOR/CREATOR
Harald Damsleth

DATE
c. 1943

IMAGE TYPE
FLYERS

SIGNIFICANCE
An example of pro-German, anti-American propaganda in the German-occupied Norway, Denmark, and Netherlands alleging that an American invasion freeing these areas from German control would bring about disastrous results

Overview

This poster was part of the work done by the Norwegian artist Harald Damsleth and his advertising agency, Heralden, undertaken for the extreme right-wing administration of Vidkun Quisling (1887–1945) in Norway during World War II. From the time Nazi troops seized control of most of Norway in April 1945, Quisling's regime had aligned itself with Germany—and ultimately the Axis Powers of Germany, Italy, and Japan—against the Allies, France and Britain. After France was overrun and capitulated to the Germans on June 25, 1940, and England had fended off Hitler's Reich for over a year, the Soviet Union was attacked by German forces in Operation Barbarossa on June 22, 1941. Then on December 7, 1941, the Japanese assault on Pearl Harbor brought the United States into the war on the Allied side. By 1943, and most assuredly by 1944, the tide of war had turned against the Axis Powers, with the United States taking the role of the most powerful of the Allies. The Axis forces had been driven out of North Africa; Italy had surrendered to the Allies on September 8, 1943; the Russians had weathered the German onslaught and were counterattacking; and British and American bombers were operating against targets throughout Axis-occupied Europe. Underground resistance movements became more active as prospects for liberation by Allied forces became a more realistic possibility. This gained momentum after the successful D-Day landings at Normandy Beach launched on June 6, 1944. To counter the image of Americans and other Allies as liberators, the Nazi propaganda machine commissioned Damsleth to design posters such as "Kultur-terror" to cast Americans as barbaric, uncultured, and brutal.

About the Artist

The poster itself is unsigned, but the artist has been identified as the Norwegian cartoonist/illustrator Harald Damsleth (1906–1971). Born in Bremen, Germany, Damsleth moved to Norway, where he first worked for advertising agencies and the Norwegian Tourist Board. His political views were far-right, nationalist' racialist, and in 1933 he joined Vidkun Quisling's fascist-oriented Nasjonal Samling Party. In 1933 and 1934 he lived in the United States and worked for the Foster & Klieber Advertising Agency. From 1939 to 1945 he partly owned and operated the Heralden Agency in Oslo. In April 1940, the invading Nazis installed Quis-

Document Image

The "Kultur-terror" poster
(Hoover Institution Library & Archives)

ling as head of a puppet Norwegian government; and Damsleth was commissioned to design Norwegian postage stamps and, as codirector of Heralden, churned out propaganda posters, such as "Kultur-terror." His output, some 200 or so, was quite prolific, and the posters were widely disseminated in the German-occupied countries of Norway, Denmark, and the Netherlands. The Waffen SS employed Damsleth for a while as a war correspondent, and he also produced many of their recruiting posters. Following the German surrender and liberation of Norway, Quisling was placed under arrest (May 9, 1945), tried and convicted of treason and executed by firing squad on October 24, 1945. Damsleth was arrested as a collaborator on May 15, 1945 and similarly tried for treason. After protracted proceedings he was found guilty in 1950 and sentenced to five years' imprisonment at hard labor. After two years he was released on pardon. Heralden had been liquidated and Damsleth resumed his artistic career as a freelancer, mainly designing Christmas cards, postcards and book jackets, and illustrating children's books. He died on March 1, 1971.

Context

Throughout World War I, Norway, Denmark, and the Netherlands had maintained neutrality; the Netherlands even served as a place of refuge for the deposed Kaiser Wilhelm II of Germany in November 1918. When World War II began on September 1, 1939, the Norwegian, Danish, and Dutch governments hoped that their neutrality would again be respected. However, Adolf Hitler and his generals saw the control of western Scandinavia and the Dutch coast and ports as essential to their plans for a massive attack on the main Western Allies, France and Britain, during the spring of 1940, and they feared that the British navy might preempt them and seize control of the ports themselves. For this reason, these countries, plus neutral Belgium and Luxembourg, were targeted for attack and occupation under the German military operation Case Yellow. Accordingly, Denmark and Norway were attacked on April 9, 1940, and the Netherlands, Belgium, and Luxembourg were struck on May 10, 1940.

Denmark was particularly vulnerable, and what defenses it had crumbled very quickly. In fact, its fall came to be dubbed the Six Hour War. But almost immediately, resistance groups sprang up, at first employing nonviolent tactics but, as time went on, adding more forcible methods. Denmark successfully evacuated most of its Jewish population by the end of 1943. In Norway, the fighting was far more intense and raged on through May 5, 1940. However, German forces, aided by Quisling and his fifth column, steadily gained ground, and British intervention proved ineffective. King Haakon VII (1872–1957) and the Norwegian royal family escaped and formed a government in exile in London, and resistance groups against the Nazis and Quisling's government were speedily established. Overtures were even made to the United States, with Crown Princess Martha (1901–1954) taking up residence there, after fleeing via Sweden, in August 1940. There she served as a very effective promoter of the Norwegian and Allied cause, even maintaining a close friendship with President Franklin D. Roosevelt (1882–1945). The Netherlands was subjected to a German blitzkrieg that employed massive paratroop drops and a saturation bombing of civilian areas of the city of Rotterdam. Dutch troops surrendered after five days, and the Dutch royal family, headed by Queen Wilhelmina (1880–1962), fled and set up a government in exile in London.

As the Axis forces were being pushed back in 1943 and 1944, the Nazi occupiers and their Norwegian, Dutch, and Danish surrogates became increasingly desperate, repressive, and eager to use any tactic whatsoever—including the invention of false information besmirching America and the Allies—to keep control over their conquered territories.

Explanation and Analysis of the Document

In the poster, Damsleth patched together a conglomerate American "Frankenstein's monster"—in Damsleth's words, a "terror." In his attempt to drive home his message, Damsleth drew on a variety of common stereotypes regarding American society. The large heading at the top proclaims "Kultur-terror," and the caption held at the bottom sarcastically states, "USA vil redde Europas kultur fra undergang. Med hvilken rett?"—"The USA will save European culture from ruin. By what right?" The caption is held by a little elfish creature with huge ears—a staple in many of Damsleth's works, which could be derived from Norwegian folklore. Damsleth tries to convince his audience that, to the contrary, America will bring death, destruction, and the obliteration of European culture in its wake. The monster's left foot, a blood-soaked bomb, is about to smash some fine Medieval structures and a fountain, while dead bodies litter the town square. While the viewer cannot see the right foot, it has already stomped on a Renaissance-era church, which is in the process of disintegrating into black smoke and fire. The two bomber wings attached to the shoulder of the figure serve to emphasize the USA as an engine of wanton destruction from the skies. At the left, off in the distance and in opposition to the European town, appears the Statue of Liberty with the New York skyline. Details in the figure emphasize the Nazi depiction of the United States as a racially mongrelized, morally depraved nation with a degenerate culture. Two of the monster's four arms are those of a muscular black man. One of these arms is holding a sound disk, representational of American jazz, which Nazi ideology classified as primitive and barbaric. The other arm is wearing a boxing glove, emblematic of the supposed American obsession with sports and a reference to the African American heavyweight champion Joe Louis (1914–1981), whose epic matches against German boxer Max Schmeling had been touted by Nazi propaganda as clashes between the Nordic Aryan "Superman" against the member of a perceived "inferior" race. The gloved hand holds a moneybag, which in turn is being clutched by a caricature of a Jewish man, referring to alleged American materialism, controlled by Jewish financiers. The anti-Semitic motif is further emphasized by the monster's loincloth, on which is printed the Star of David. Of the two lower arms, the one on the monster's right bears a prison-striped sleeve, a pair of handcuffs dangling from the wrist, and a submachine gun—all emblematic of lawlessness and organized crime. The left arm holds a hand grenade.

The presumed American focus on sexual promiscuity is also portrayed, first in the monster's right leg, which is that of a woman (the ribbon tied around its thigh reads "World's most beautiful leg"), and second in the two small, scantily clad women. The one on the monster's left wing (to the viewer's right) holds an American flag and bears a sash stating "Miss Victory," and the one sitting on the back of the monster's neck wears a Native American headdress and is labeled "Miss America." The headdress of "Miss America" emphasizes America's interracial mixing, and the trumpet she is playing represents, again, the "degenerate" art form of jazz. Continuing in this cultural vein, the monster's chest is a cage in which are placed two African American men apparently dancing the jitterbug. A martial drum makes up the rest of the monster's body.

Perhaps the most bizarre aspects of the image are the hangman's noose wrapped around and dangling from one of the monster's black arms, signifying lynching, and the Ku Klux Klan hood covering the monster's head. It seems a bit contradictory on Damsleth's part to include the hood since the Nazis and the extreme right-wing party would have agreed with the KKK's ideas about white supremacy, often expressed by lynching African Americans throughout the early twentieth century and beyond. The Ku Klux Klan was indeed an influential force in U.S. political life, but it was one the Nazis would have embraced, not mocked.

The Nazi propaganda message that Damsleth seemed to want to convey to the population of occupied Norway, the Netherlands, and Denmark was that liberation by the Allies, and especially the Americans, would not be beneficial at all and instead would result in the destruction of thousands of years of European culture.

—Raymond Pierre Hylton

Questions for Further Study

1. What methods does the artist use to make an argument for his point of view? What fears and half-truths might he draw upon?

2. What does the image reveal concerning issues confronting the United States in the early twentieth century?

3. How would you frame a counter-argument to the allegations in "Kultur-terror"?

Further Reading

Books

Dahl, Hans-Fredrik; Anne Marie Stanton-Ife, trans. *Quisling: A Study in Treachery*. Cambridge, UK: Cambridge University Press, 1999.

Darman, Peter. *Posters of World War II: 1939–1945*. New York: Book Sales, 2011.

Vigness, Paul Gerhrdt. *The German Occupation of Norway*. New York: Vantage, 1970.

Warmbrunn, Werner. *The Dutch under German Occupation: 1940–1945*. Stanford: Stanford University Press, 1963.

Welch, David. *World War II Propaganda: Analyzing the Art of Persuasion during Wartime*. Santa Barbara: ABC-CLIO, 2017.

Alfred T. Palmer: "Detroit Arsenal Tank Plant (Chrysler)" Photograph

Author/Creator	**Significance**
Alfred T. Palmer	Illustrates the rapid shift in manufacturing from consumer goods to war materiel for American and Allied forces during World War II, and the importance of the manufacturing capacity of American industry as the "arsenal of democracy" in the fight against the fascist forces of the Axis nations
Date	
1944	
Image Type	
Photographs	

Overview

Before American entry into World War II, American manufacturing had already shifted to producing a tremendous amount of equipment, vehicles, aircraft, ships, and ordnance to support the Allied forces. The Second World War was the first mechanized war, one where more soldiers were equipped with or supported by cars, trucks, and tanks than ever before. While American automobile manufacturers had shifted a portion of their production capacity to armored vehicles and trucks, the American production of tanks was at first nonexistent. The National Defense Act of 1920, which restricted tanks to infantry support use only, and a limited army budget led to the lack of American tank manufacture in the interwar years. However, this allowed the American military to develop and test new tank components while observing foreign tanks' manufacturing and battlefield performance.

This testing and observation paid dividends when Chrysler was tasked with building a new light tank—the M3 series of light tanks. Chrysler engineers developed an armored platform that the assembly line could construct to perform several roles in consultation with military officials. In late 1940, Chrysler broke ground on the first American purpose-built tank manufacturing plant—the Detroit Arsenal Tank Plant (DATP). The factory was explicitly designed to use mass-automobile production methods and was built using reinforced concrete. The 1.25-million-square-foot factory was giant. At five city blocks long and two city blocks wide, the sprawling facility covered 113 acres and was built to withstand bombing or shelling. More than 5,800 employees had to be hired and trained specifically for this new style of manufacture. DAPT would build just over eighteen tanks daily for use by British, American, and Soviet forces in every theater of the war. By the end of the war, DAPT alone had built nearly 22,500 tanks—over one-quarter of the American tanks built—and produced more tanks than German industry produced throughout the war.

About the Artist

Alfred T. Palmer was an avid photographer of life and specialized in subjects of Americana. Born in San Francisco in 1906, Palmer befriended and accompanied Ansel Adams on photographic explorations into the Yosemite Valley. Working for several shipping lines,

Document Image

The Detroit Arsenal Tank Plant
(Library of Congress)

Alfred T. Palmer: "Detroit Arsenal Tank Plant (Chrysler)" Photograph

Palmer traveled the world photographing all that caught his eye for the next thirteen years. In 1938 Palmer left the sea and made a living as a traveling freelance photographer for educational publishing firms.

In early 1940 President Franklin Roosevelt, predicting an American entry into World War II, began posturing American industry and defense for the challenge. Roosevelt ordered the creation of a National Defense Advisory Commission (NDAC). The NDAC started organizing a campaign to inform Americans about how the government was using their tax dollars and to rally popular support for the military buildup. The commission hired Palmer as its head photographer. The NDAC sent Palmer to restricted industrial and military facilities to capture images that would vividly capture Americans building the "arsenal of democracy." Media outlets and government agencies would publish Palmer's photos in newspapers and magazines across the nation. His work quickly became recognized for his unique compositions that captured gritty industrial geometry as symbolic forms of power. Palmer's work was known for conveying the intense devotion of the American workers. Palmer's work, like that of Ansel Adams, was known for its dramatic range of tone and sharp focus to create feeling even in the most industrial of subjects.

After the bombing of the naval base at Pearl Harbor, Hawaii, in December 1941, Palmer became a photographer for the Office of War Information. In his work there, Palmer captured all aspects of the American home front and its participation in the war effort. Here, Palmer's photographs were of particular significance in changing public opinion about the appropriate roles for women and African Americans in the workforce. Palmer's photos depicted women as feminine, capable, respectable, and patriotic members of the American workforce. Pictures of African American workers framed their labors with dignity, reverence, and honor. Palmer worked closely with the African American press to ensure that Americans saw people like themselves doing their part in the war effort.

After the war, Palmer worked as a photographer for the National Geographic Society before turning to filmmaking. As a filmmaker, Palmer produced films generally focused on marine subjects or sea life for government agencies, transportation companies, humanitarian organizations, and multinational corporations. Palmer continued to photograph and make films until he died in 1993.

Context

On May 26, 1940, President Franklin Roosevelt broadcast one of his famous "fireside chat" radio speeches discussing his concern about the lack of military capacity to defend the United States in the event of war. Europe had been at war for over half a year, Japanese forces had beaten down Asian territory for almost three years, and many feared it would not be long before events drew the United States into the war. The American government had already done much to provide equipment for the Allied war effort through the cash-and-carry provisions of the Neutrality Acts of 1937 and 1939 and the September 1940 Destroyers-for-Bases Deal. However, many American leaders felt the nation was still unprepared. Without question, America had the human resources to fight a war; but it lacked the equipment in large enough quantities to do so effectively.

Mass production and America's tremendous industrial manufacturing capacity were the answer to this rapid demand for equipment, vehicles, and munitions—but this also required a shift in production and the retooling of manufacturing plants, something President Roosevelt knew little about. In May 1940 President Roosevelt asked William Knudsen, a Danish immigrant and the president of General Motors, to accept an appointment as the chairman of the newly created Office of Production Management. As chair, Knudsen would also be a member of the NDAC. In this position, Knudsen would be responsible for setting material priorities to shift the manufacturing from consumer goods to war materials. Knudsen accepted, provided the federal government set his salary at one dollar annually.

On December 29, 1940, President Franklin Roosevelt broadcast another fireside chat about the significant territorial gains the Axis powers had made since the commencement of World War II. President Roosevelt's aim was not only to unseat American comfort with isolationism but also to rally American support in providing war materiel to Britain. President Roosevelt argued, "Europe does not ask us to do their fighting. They ask us for the implements of war ... which will enable them to fight for their liberty and for our security." The broadcast ended with President Roosevelt calling the American people to action: "We must be the great arsenal of democracy."

After accepting the appointment and conferring with military officials, Knudsen set out to produce light tanks that could move quickly to perform reconnaissance and support infantry and heavier tank units on the battlefield. Knudsen realized that no mass-production facility for tanks existed, so he contacted K. T. Keller, CEO of Chrysler, and tasked him with building and operating such a facility. Keller instructed Chrysler engineers to design a new tank and contacted industrial architect Albert Kahn to design the facility. Kahn had designed and overseen the construction of nearly 20 percent of the nation's factories, and his use of reinforced concrete offered many advantages. It was capable of withstanding bombardment, and the building was fireproof, inexpensive, and quick to build. In late 1940 the Detroit Arsenal Tank Plant (DAPT) was born, and Chrysler employees were producing M3 tanks in the winter of 1940–41 even before the walls or roof of the plant were finished. The first M3 rolled out of the factory in March 1941, and M3 tanks would see combat in North Africa and the Philippines in November and December 1941.

Explanation and Analysis of the Document

Alfred Palmer's photograph is intentionally composed to do many things with a single image. Palmer's use of sharp focus and tone create emotion in the gritty industrial geometry of the M3 tank production lines at DATP. However, by framing the tank hulls at an angle against the bright white lighted windows, Palmer suggests power, justness, and capability both in the M3 tank and in the cause to which American manufacturing capacity is being directed. The photograph relays how methodical and industrious the process of equipping Allied forces is. Nearly devoid of people, the photo suggests the tremendous need for workers to enter the war industry while highlighting the modern manufacturing processes involved in the mass production of tanks—including overhead cranes.

The M3 tank was the product of the American military development and testing of tank components, strategic military writers like J. F. C. Fuller and B. H. Liddell Hart, inspection of foreign tank manufacturing processes, and observation of the Spanish Civil War, Chinese Civil War, and the Second Sino-Japanese War during the interwar years. Testing and developing tank components by the American military led to easily maintained and resilient tank engine, suspension, track, and transmission components that provided a smoother ride, a better overland ability, and a more stable weapon platform. Military strategists developed a theory of mobile warfare that focused on using speed and maneuver to encircle an enemy, punch a hole in the defense with heavily focused firepower, and rapidly exploit the opportunity to defeat the enemy. This strategy fit well with the American value of tenacity while focusing on mass production and the use of machines to protect American lives.

As chairman of the Office of Production Management, William Knudsen's efforts to network with manufacturing executives, negotiate with labor unions, and prioritize resources allowed the American manufacturing industry to become the arsenal that President Roosevelt, and the free world, needed to win the war. However, this turnabout in production and efficiency had made many political enemies for Roosevelt, and political pressure was mounting to replace Knudsen with a political appointee. In January 1942, only weeks after the Japanese attack on Pearl Harbor made American entry into World War II inevitable, Knudsen was commissioned as a lieutenant general in the U.S. Army. This solution retained Knudsen's managerial and organizational capacity and relieved political pressure on Roosevelt when he needed political capital to fight the war. As of this writing, Knudsen remains the only civilian to have been commissioned into the regular army at such a rank. Lieutenant General Knudsen was assigned as the director of production, working directly for the Undersecretary of War. Here Knudsen became an organizer, troubleshooter, and problem solver who often traveled to engineering labs, factories, labor meetings, and battlefields to ensure that American manufacturing produced the quality and quantity of tools for the Allies to win the war.

Lieutenant General Knudsen's observation of tank success on battlefields suggested that light tanks needed to have better armor to survive tank-on-tank and anti-tank weapons; possess greater range and speed to take advantage of mobile warfare tactics; and be equipped with heavier weapons. As the photo records, the first M3 armor design used riveted plates. However, rivets were prone to shearing off in battle or rough travel. Within a few months of initial manufacture, Chrysler engineers shifted to casting and welding processes that increased production time and improved survivability. Early M3 tanks used aircraft radial engines, but by mid-1941, increased aircraft production led to Chrysler's adoption of the Cadillac 346 V8 and Hydramatic automatic transmission. The Cadillac components were easier to maintain, easier to operate, and much quieter than the earlier models. Despite this change, Soviet forces complained about the M3's narrow base, which often got stuck in Eastern European mud, and its need for high-octane fuel to produce maximum range and efficiency. These faults aside, the British revered the tank—naming the tank "Stuart" after Confederate cavalry general J. E. B. Stuart—and employed the tank with success in Asia and Northern Africa.

The M3 was well suited for use against Japanese forces. It was easily transported aboard navy landing craft, and its narrow base was effective in jungles and island terrain. The Japanese preferred the use of steel for ships, making Japanese tanks very lightly armored, and relatively few of these were ever manufactured. Despite its successes in the jungle, military commanders in Europe wanted more firepower and hoped that the M3 could use its speed and smaller size to be effective against German armor. Knudsen ordered the 37mm main gun be replaced by a 75mm main gun already equipped on the American M6 medium tank. Despite these changes, the M3 series was not well-suited for battle with the large number of medium and heavy tanks used by the German forces. Many American military commanders judged the M3 series obsolete by early 1944. Knudsen would resign his commission in 1945 and die of a stroke in 1947. However, the Detroit Arsenal Tank Plant would continue to produce tanks for the American military and other allies until its closure in 1996, when the U.S. Army shifted tank manufacturing to the Lima Army Tank Plant in Lima, Ohio. Though some military offices are still present, most of the former DATP has been divided for use by several different companies as manufacturing space.

—Bryant Macfarlane

Questions for Further Study

1. Why do you think William Knudsen agreed to leave General Motors and accept a government job with the provision that he be paid only one dollar per year?

2. Arguably, many American leaders believed that World War II would not come to their shores, so why in 1940 would the Detroit Arsenal Tank Plant be intentionally designed and built to withstand an enemy attack?

3. Imagine you were a graphic designer at the National Defense Advisory Commission, assigned to use Palmer's photograph of the DATP. What would the poster that you created say? How would you use this to help rally popular American support for the war effort?

Further Reading

Books

Automobile Manufacturers Association. *Freedom's Arsenal: The Story of the Automotive Council for War Production.* Detroit: Automobile Manufacturers Association, 1950.

Baine, A. J. *The Arsenal of Democracy: FDR, Detroit, and an Epic Quest to Arm an America at War.* Boston and New York: Houghton Mifflin Harcourt. 2014.

Herman, Arthur. *Freedom's Forge: How American Business Produced Victory in World War I I.* New York: Random House, Inc. 2012.

Hyde, Charles K. *Arsenal of Democracy: The American Automobile Industry in World War II.* Detroit: Wayne State University Press. 2013.

Stout, Wesley Winans. *Tanks Are Mighty Fine Things.* Detroit: Chrysler Corporation. 1946.

Wilson, Mark R. *Destructive Creation: American Business and the Winning of World War II.* Philadelphia: University of Pennsylvania Press. 2016.

Websites

Jackson, David D. "Chrysler Corporation in World War Two." *The American Automobile Industry in World War Two.* December 16, 2019. http://usautoindustryworldwartwo.com/chrysler.htm.

"Arsenal of Democracy" *Encyclopedia of Detroit.* Detroit Historical Society, 2022. https://detroithistorical.org/learn/encyclopedia-of-detroit/arsenal-democracy.

Documentaries

Assembly Lines of Defense. Chrysler Corporation, 1941.

Automakers and the Arsenal of Democracy. Brandt Rosenbusch, director. Stellantis North America, 2015.

Bill Knudsen. Jared Law, producer. Real History, 2013.

History of the Detroit Arsenal Tank Plant, 1940–1997. U.S. Department of the Army, 1999.

Our Block Goes to War. Chrysler Corporation, 1942.

Rube Godlberg: "Peace Today" Cartoon

AUTHOR/CREATOR Rube Goldberg	IMAGE TYPE CARTOONS
DATE 1947	SIGNIFICANCE Captured the American public's anxiety about atomic weaponry as Cold War tensions were unfolding in the late 1940s

Overview

This cartoon was published in the *New York Sun* newspaper on July 22, 1947, and was awarded the Pulitzer Prize for cartooning in 1948. The cartoon captures the precarious position of world peace in the late 1940s in light of the development of atomic weaponry and the increasingly hostile Cold War that was emerging between the United States and its allies and the Soviet Union and its satellite states. The United States had been the first nation to develop and use atomic weapons; the bombs dropped on Hiroshima and Nagasaki, Japan, in August 1945 finally brought an end to World War II. In the wake of the war, however, it was apparent to American intelligence agencies and war planners that the Soviet Union had its own atomic weapons development project underway. In this context, the cartoon suggests the anxiety Americans felt about the possibility that the Soviets could break the American monopoly on atomic weapons, and a nuclear exchange could take place.

About the Artist

Rube Goldberg was born as Reuben Lucius Goldberg on July 4, 1883, in San Francisco. Goldberg was an editorial cartoonist who frequently satirized what he saw as Americans' preoccupation with technology. The phrase "Rube Goldberg machine" continues to be used to refer to any chain-reaction contraption or sequence that makes an otherwise simple process outlandishly complicated. Examples include the Self-Operating Napkin, the Orange Squeezing Machine, and an Automatic Stamp Licker that sets in motion a small robot that overturns a can of ants on a page of postage stamps; the ants are then licked by a starving anteater.

Goldberg received a bachelor of science degree in engineering from the University of California in 1904. He then took a job designing sewer pipes for the city of San Francisco. The position did not satisfy him, so after a short period, he left to become a sportswriter and cartoonist for the *San Francisco Chronicle* (1904–1905) and for the *San Francisco Bulletin* (1905–1907). He then relocated across the country to take a position at the *New York Evening Mail* (1907–1921), where he created long-running comic strips that included *Boob McNutt, Foolish Questions, Mike and Ike (They Look Alike), I Never Thought of That*, and *The Inventions of Professor Lucifer Gorgonzola Butts*, which showcased Rube Gold-

Document Image

The "Peace Today" cartoon
(Sarin Images / Granger)

berg machines. These strips were syndicated throughout the country, and Goldberg became one of the nation's most popular cartoonists.

In 1938 Goldberg began to create editorial cartoons, working first for the *New York Sun*, then for the *New York Journal* and the *Journal-American*. He was the son of a Jewish immigrant from Germany, so he was a passionate opponent of the Nazi regime in Germany. During World War II, many of his cartoons dealt with the events of the war, often lampooning Adolf Hitler. After the war, he continued to focus on the international situation. He was a founding member and first president of the Cartoonists Society, and shortly after its founding in 1948, he became a teacher at the Famous Artists School, an art correspondence school with headquarters in Connecticut. He died in New York City on December 7, 1970.

Context

On July 16, 1945, the world changed forever. On that date, a massive fireball rose over the desert in New Mexico when scientists conducted the first test of an atomic bomb. On the evening of that day, President Harry Truman received a coded message telling him that the test, code-named "Trinity," had been a success. The message stated, "Operated on this morning. Diagnosis not yet complete but results seem satisfactory and already exceed expectations."

U.S. involvement in World War II had dragged on for nearly four brutal years, at the cost of many tens of thousands of American lives. As the war continued to rage in the Pacific, it was becoming increasing clear to American war planners that Japan would not surrender and that a bloody invasion of the Japanese mainland would be necessary. For Truman and many (but by no means all) of his advisers, the atomic bomb provided a way to put a quick end to the war. Further, by ending the war quickly, the bomb would prevent the Soviet Union from gaining a toehold in the Asian-Pacific region. Accordingly, on July 24, 1945, President Truman issued the order that would change the course of history. On July 25, the U.S. War Department issued an order stating: "The 509 Composite Group, 20th Air Force will deliver its first special bomb as soon as weather will permit visual bombing after about 3 August 1945." At 8:15 on the morning of August 6, the first "special bomb" detonated over the city of Nagasaki, resulting in the immediate deaths of 80,000 people, with 100,000 seriously injured. Three days later, a second bomb was dropped on Nagasaki at a cost of more than 40,000 lives. On August 14, Japan surrendered, bringing World War II to a close.

Americans were jubilant, but that jubilation would become muted and turn to unease: It was becoming apparent that a new "war" was underway, a "cold war" pitting the United States and its Western allies against the Soviet Union and the satellite states Joseph Stalin was gobbling up in Eastern Europe. Unease among the U.S. defense establishment deepened as details emerged about the efforts of the Soviets to develop their own atomic weapons. Although atomic research had begun in Russia as early as the 1920s and 1930s, it was not until the early 1940s that a Russian physicist, Georgy Flyorov, began to notice that American, German, and British scientists were no longer publishing papers on nuclear science. This led to the suspicion that they were developing some kind of "superbomb," or at least conducting secret nuclear research programs. In April 1942 Flyorov sent a pair of classified letters to Stalin urging the development of a uranium bomb "without delay." In response to these letters, Stalin authorized an atomic bomb project.

The matter became more urgent in August 1945 after Stalin learned of the atomic bombings of Japan. At that point, a special committee was appointed to oversee the development of atomic weapons. In April 1946 a "design bureau" was created to map out a bomb design based on the results of American research with weapons-grade plutonium. The first Soviet nuclear reactor, built near Moscow, became operational in October 1946.

As if all this was not unsettling enough, it was becoming increasingly apparent that the Soviet atomic development project was being accelerated by espionage. In the United States, some communist sympathizers were operating under the direction of Russian officials in North America. The number of these sympathizers had increased early in the war when it was feared that the German invasion of Russia in 1941 might be successful. These people were willing—in many cases, eager—to share classified information with the Soviets. The Russians also maintained an intelligence network in the United Kingdom that played a major role in helping to create spy rings in the United States.

One member of such a ring was Harry Gold, a Swiss-born chemist and active spy who conducted industrial espionage in the U.S. chemical industry. Gold served as a Soviet courier for classified information given to him by Klaus Fuchs, a German-born British theoretical physicist who worked on the Manhattan Project—the top-secret research program that developed the atomic bomb at a compound near Los Alamos, New Mexico, from 1943 to 1945. Also working for the Soviets was Theodore Hall, an American physicist who provided Russian scientists with detailed information about the implosion-type "Fat Man" bomb (the type of bomb used against Nagasaki). In 1944, Hall visited the offices of the U.S. Communist Party in New York City and established contacts that enabled him to pass along information about the Manhattan Project to the Soviets. Meanwhile, in 1943, the U.S. Army's Signal Intelligence Service launched the Venona project, a counterintelligence effort designed to decrypt messages sent back and forth between the Soviet Union and its American espionage assets. It was the efforts of the Venona project that exposed and eventually identified Karl Fuchs and numerous other Russian spies. With the help of these spies, the Soviets detonated their first atomic bomb in 1949 and their first thermonuclear (that is, hydrogen) bomb in 1953.

During and after World War II, the Soviets annexed a number of Central European states, turning them into satellite states collectively referred to as the Eastern Bloc. The Cold War between East and West can be said to have begun in February 1946, when George F. Kennan, a U.S. diplomat in Russia, wrote what was called the "Long Telegram," which became the basis of the Truman administration's policies with regard to the Soviet Union. On March 5, former British Prime Minister Winston Churchill delivered his famous "Iron Curtain" speech at Westminster College in Fulton, Missouri. In his speech, he called for an Anglo-American alliance against the Soviets. In July 1947 (the same month as Goldberg's cartoon), Kennan's telegram was published as "The Sources of Soviet Conduct" under the name X in *Foreign Affairs*. This document argued that the Soviet regime was expansionist and had to be "contained," and "containment" became the foundation of the Truman Doctrine. U.S. hostility toward the Soviets increased as Stalin and his foreign minister broke a number of postwar promises. Meanwhile, Stalin had responded to the Iron Curtain speech by comparing Churchill to Hitler and contending that the English-speaking nations were bent on world domination. He called the speech "a call for war on the USSR."

The Cold War tensions and the precarious nuclear peace captured in Goldberg's cartoon were underway. They would dominate international relations and policies for more than four decades.

In June 1947, an international group of researchers who had taken part in the Manhattan Project began including an image of the "Doomsday Clock" on the cover of the *Bulletin of Atomic Scientists*. Since then, the scientists have marked the movement of the minute hand toward midnight, when, presumably, a man-made catastrophe, including a nuclear catastrophe, would strike. In 1947, the setting was seven minutes to midnight. As of 2022, the clock was set at 100 minutes to midnight, where it had stood since 2019.

Explanation and Analysis of the Document

The cartoon depicts a large, black atomic bomb perched precariously on the edge of a cliff. Sitting on top of the bomb is a house and an American family seemingly enjoying the day under a patio umbrella. The scene is idyllic, with pets, a bird bath on the other side of the house, birds in flight, and a blue sky. The bomb, however, sits at an angle so that the family and its home (and the bomb itself) are in danger of sliding into an abyss labeled "World Destruction." The rock cliff on which the bomb is balanced is labeled "World Control." The implication is that the bomb poses two kinds of threats. One is that an atomic arsenal can give the nation that holds it control over the world. The other is that unleashing that arsenal can lead to world destruction. The balance between the two states of affairs, neither of which is desirable, is hazardous and unsteady, and disaster could strike at any moment. By calling the cartoon "Peace Today," Goldberg is implicitly saying that there can be little in the way of peace when the devastation of atomic warfare threatens.

—Michael J. O'Neal

Questions for Further Study

1. What might have motivated Goldberg to create this cartoon?

2. What effect might this cartoon have had on newspaper readers at the time?

3. What effect would this cartoon and others like it have had on American anxiety about the possibility of atomic warfare? Why?

Further Reading

Books

Boyer, Paul. *By the Bomb's Early Light: American Thought and Culture at the Dawn of the Atomic Age.* Chapel Hill: University of North Carolina Press, 1994.

Gaddis, John Lewis. *The Cold War: A New History.* New York: Penguin Books, 2006.

Kinnaird, Clark, ed. *Rube Goldberg vs. the Machine Age: A Retrospective Exhibition of His Work with Memoirs and Annotations.* New York: Hastings House Publishers, 1968.

Marzio, Peter C. *Rube Goldberg: His Life and Work.* New York: Harper & Row, 1973

McMahon, Robert J. *The Cold War: A Very Short Introduction*, 2nd ed. Oxford, UK: Oxford University Press, 2021.

Scheibach, Michael. *"In Case Atom Bombs Fall": An Anthology of Governmental Explanations, Instructions and Warnings from the 1940s to the 1960s.* Jefferson, NC: McFarland, 2009.

Westad, Odd Arne. *The Cold War: A World History.* New York: Basic Books, 2017.

Articles

Kennan, George F. "The Sources of Soviet Conduct." *Foreign Affairs* 25, no. 4 (July 1947): 566–82. (Originally published under the name X.)

Schlesinger, Arthur, Jr. "Origins of the Cold War." *Foreign Affairs* 46, no. 1 (October 1967): 22–52.

Websites

Wilson, Emily, "The Story behind Rube Goldberg's Complicated Contraptions," *Smithsonian*, May 1, 2018, https://www.smithsonianmag.com/history/story-behind-rube-goldbergs-complicated-contraptions-180968928/.

Documentaries

1945–1953: From World War to Cold War, directed by Emilie Lancon. Martange Production, 2018. Available from Prime Video. https://www.amazon.com/Episode-2/dp/B07W96J8N9/ref=sr_1_5?crid=25USP6FLP55HO&keywords=cold+war&qid=1657204563&sprefix=cold+war%2Caps%2C378&sr=8-5.

Photograph Of Joseph McCarthy

Author/Creator
Unknown

Date
1954

Image Type
Photographs

Significance
Shows Senator Joseph McCarthy toward the end of his influence, in a televised hearing that helped turn public support against him and illustrated the potential power of the emerging medium

Overview

This photo is quintessential Joseph McCarthy, a microphone in front of him and his hand raised in dramatic fashion holding folders of papers he claims contain indisputable evidence of treason and corruption by his adversaries. In this case, his opponents are those who accused him of pressuring the military to give special treatment to David Schine, an unpaid consultant to the Permanent Subcommittee on Investigations, which Joseph McCarthy chaired. In a significant transposition, McCarthy is the person being investigated in this photo.

Joseph McCarthy (1908–1957) was a power-hungry politician who for a time held power and influence over the executive and legislative branches of the U.S. government that rivaled the president. Playing off fears of communist subversion of the U.S. government stirred up by the House Un-American Activities investigations of accused spy Alger Hiss and others, McCarthy made a name for himself by making outlandish charges of treason and corruption against government officials and employees. While he claimed to know of hundreds or even thousands of traitorous conspirators in the U.S. government, he identified very few. Through demagoguery in Senate investigative hearings and abetted by journalists seeking to increase readership by printing sensationalist and salacious stories, McCarthy would force those he named to defend themselves against his generally absurdly ridiculous accusations. His skill as an orator and rapid-fire switching from allegation to allegation in a chaotic manner, however, often left them momentarily dumbfounded. By the time they recovered, McCarthy had moved on to other targets, depriving the defense of the same level of coverage as his accusations. Bureaucrats and his fellow members of Congress so feared the possibility of having to respond to a slew of McCarthy's allegations that by 1953 they largely acquiesced in his wishes.

McCarthy overplayed his hand, however, when he attempted to discredit the upper administration of the U.S. Army in live television hearings. The Army accused McCarthy and his chief counsel, Roy Cohn, of abuse of power, prompting the subcommittee to hold hearings on McCarthy and his staff. This photograph is one of many from those hearings.

Document Image

Joseph McCarthy
(Rue des Archives / GRANGER)

About the Artist

This photograph, or a virtually identical one shot at the same time from the same angle and distance, is in many sources and databases as a stock image of Joseph McCarthy, but none specifically identify the photographer. A prominent news photographer named Thomas J. O'Halloran is credited with some images of the Army-McCarthy hearings, but because there was widespread press coverage of the hearings, any one of a number of photographers could have taken this particular image, which is not definitively attributed to O'Halloran in the multiple photo repositories where it can be found. Some other photos of the hearing are credited to O'Halloran. If he were the photographer, it seems unusual that he would not be identified as such given the somewhat famous nature and widespread use of this photograph, especially when he is credited as the photographer of others.

Context

A climate of fear lingered in the United States after the shock of World War II. Americans genuinely believed that evil foreign forces were out to destroy or enslave them. These sinister hordes were seen as determined to succeed at whatever cost and even perceived as omnipotent. Americans thought some number of their fellow citizens were inexplicably aiding and abetting this diabolical effort. The facts that the Nazis were indeed inhumanely malevolent and that the Japanese had engaged, from the perspective of the average American, in a vicious and unprovoked attack against the United States provided a basis in reality for such conspiratorial beliefs.

Policymakers were not immune to these beliefs, leading to the Harry S. Truman administration's Federal Employee Loyalty Program (FELP) and congressional investigations such as those of the House Un-American Activities Committee (HUAC) and the Senate's Permanent Subcommittee on Investigations (PSI) to protect the country from these fiendish efforts. Some exploited this climate for their own partisan and political advantage. Truman's supporters used the Federal Employee Loyalty Program to remove followers of Henry Wallace, the man Truman replaced to become vice president and eventually president, from the federal bureaucracy. McCarthy used his chairmanship of the PSI and his aggressive, bullying tactics to build up the public support that allowed him to intimidate and extort the executive branch, giving him an extraordinary amount of power over it, especially for a junior senator.

McCarthy had already shifted his efforts to finding communist subversives in the military since, despite many headlines and much favorable publicity, his attacks on U.S. Department of State personnel failed to actually find any communist activity on the part of America's diplomats, and that line of inquiry had run its course. McCarthy's right-hand man and PSI's chief counsel, Roy Cohn, used the PSI's investigation into the military to intimidate it into shielding his good friend and unpaid "consultant," David Schine, from having to bear the burdens of military service when he was drafted. While Schine, a rich playboy with a reputation among his Harvard classmates for arrogance and behaving as a self-important spoiled brat, was inducted into the U.S. Army as a private in 1953, Cohn's pressure led the Army to ignore his absences in many basic training drills and grant him leave whenever he wanted once he completed basic training. Much of his time was spent consulting with Cohn from his Waldorf Astoria hotel room or in Washington.

The U.S. Army, however struck back, publicizing a report of the efforts of Cohn to secure preferential treatment for the wealthy Schine. McCarthy accused the military of harassing Schine, Public concern over these charges and countercharges, which were widely reported in the media, compelled the PSI to hold hearings to examine them. McCarthy was forced to temporarily step down as chairman since he was now the subject of the PSI's inquiry. Complete televised hearings began in April 1954 and lasted almost two months, drawing at peak times up to twenty million viewers. McCarthy's personality and temperament did not translate well on television. While his antics came across well when written up by sympathetic journalists, his arrogance and rudeness in the face of the calm demeanor of those he attacked in the hearings was off-putting to the public. By the end of the hearings, McCarthy's reputation and political career were in shambles. The Senate passed a censure resolution against him in late November 1954, and he died of alcohol-related liver disease in 1957 at forty-seven.

Explanation and Analysis of the Document

The photo depicts Joseph McCarthy and his chief counsel, Roy Cohn, at a table in the Army-McCarthy hearings. McCarthy is holding up a folder containing what he says is evidence of improper actions by Secretary of the Army Robert Stevens. While the single shot may not look particularly damning to McCarthy, when people saw him televised with his voice, tone, movements, and comportment in full view, he looked much less benign. Scholars see this as an early instance of television images defining public perception of a political issue, illustrating the potential power of the newly emerging medium.

McCarthy's demeanor and tactics toward witnesses did not change from his previous untelevised interrogations. What changed was that up to twenty million Americans saw his behavior for weeks on end. McCarthy was described as rude for his incessant interruption of the proceedings and witness testimony. He was belligerent, badgering witnesses, and to some observers appeared possibly drunk and rabidly aggressive at times. It was clear from the length of the hearings that this was not just McCarthy on a bad day; this was the nature of the man. Such emotions do not come out nearly so clearly in transcripts or newspaper coverage, especially if reporters do not stress them.

The composure of those McCarthy attacked heightened the depiction of McCarthy as an out-of-control lunatic. His primary targets in these hearings were Secretary of the Army Stevens and James Welch, an outside special counsel brought in to represent the U.S. Army in the hearings. Stevens, the highest-ranking man in the U.S. Army, remained calm throughout McCarthy's rants, although to some observers he came across as naïve. Welch proved to be the greater foil to McCarthy. He methodically exposed that some of the documents in the folder McCarthy held up in the photo were actually falsified. After getting both Cohn and David Schine to testify under oath that a photo McCarthy had introduced was not altered, Welch produced a wide-angle version of the picture showing that McCarthy's team had cropped the photo. While the photo itself was not significant to the case, the fact that McCarthy's closest aide and the man whose treatment in the Army was the basis for the hearings had both perjured themselves, and that their perjury was caught on a nationally televised broadcast, destroyed their credibility and seriously damaged that of their boss, who had been lauded in the hearings and in public as paragons of American virtues and values.

McCarthy himself was next. To support his charges that Stevens was enabling subversive activities in the Army, McCarthy introduced a letter from J. Edgar Hoover, director of the Federal Bureau of Investigation (FBI), that warned of communist activity at a military base. Welch quickly gathered information from Hoover, who stated that he did not write the letter and that while some parts of it were similar to an FBI memo, the letter, which McCarthy claimed was a carbon copy, did not exist in FBI files. Growing ever more desperate as Welch shredded his credibility, McCarthy attacked a junior attorney in Welch's law firm for having been a member of a left-wing legal organization. Welch famously replied, "Have you no sense of decency, sir?" Undeterred, McCarthy continued his increasingly agitated accusations while Welch calmly asked the chairman to call the next witness and continue the committee's hearings. The toll of the hearings on McCarthy's reputation was clear. In January 1954, Gallup surveys had McCarthy with a favorability rating of 50 percent favorable and 29 percent unfavorable. By June, as the hearings were winding down, McCarthy's ratings had fallen to 34 percent favorable and 45 percent unfavorable. Interestingly, the number of people with no opinion remained steady at 21 percent in both polls.

Even more than the introduction of photographs enhanced the ability of journalists to show more revealing elements of their stories, moving images with sound broadcast by television altered how the public perceived developments in the world around them. No longer dependent upon a reporter to set the tone, reproduce the words, and describe the action happening, people could see the event as it was occurring. McCarthy's style, methods, and tone were the same when he started his anticommunist crusade as it was in the Army-McCarthy hearings. With the hearings televised, however, the public no longer received information about his activity through the perspective of journalists, who were often sympathetic to him at least to the point of not wanting his credibility to be ruined and their easy source of future stories wiped out. The Army-McCarthy hearings exposed McCarthy for what he was: an out-of-control, lying bully with little to no respect for civil discourse or behavioral norms. While video broadcasts can certainly be structured to depict a particular perspective, live feeds, which these hearings largely were, are more difficult to manipulate, especially if multiple people are providing them. The Army-McCarthy hearings were one of America's first experiences with such live reports.

—G. David Price

Questions for Further Study

1. Who was Joseph McCarthy? How did he operate? What role did he play in American history?

2. What were the Army-McCarthy hearings? What were they investigating? How did they turn out for McCarthy?

3. What do the Army-McCarthy hearings suggest about the effects of changing technologies of covering news? Are these effects positive, negative, or just different? What do you base your conclusion on?

Further Reading

Books

Adams, John G. *Without Precedent: The Story of the Death of McCarthyism.* New York: Norton, 1983.

Bayley, Edwin R. *Joe McCarthy and the Press.* Madison: University of Wisconsin Press, 1981.

Griffith, Robert. *The Politics of Fear: Joseph R. McCarthy and the Senate.* Lexington: University Press of Kentucky, 1970.

Articles

Achter, Paul J. "TV, Technology, and McCarthyism: Crafting the Democratic Renaissance in an Age of Fear." *Quarterly Journal of Speech* 90, no. 3 (2004): 307–26.

Raines, Rebecca R. "The Cold War Comes to Fort Monmouth: Senator Joseph R. McCarthy and the Search for Spies in the Signal Corps." *Army History* 44 (Spring 1998): 8–16.

Websites

"McCarthy-Welch Exchange." American Rhetoric: Top 100 Speeches. Accessed August 10, 2022. https://www.americanrhetoric.com/speeches/welch-mccarthy.html.

Photograph Of The 101st Airborne Division Outside Little Rock Central High School

Author/Creator
Uncredited/Associated Press

Date
1957

Image Type
Photographs

Significance
Demonstrated the degree to which some states and school systems resisted racial integration, and the lengths to which the federal government went to enforce it

Overview

This photograph was published on September 26, 1957, in the midst of a tense local battle over school desegregation. Many Americans were shocked to see images like this one, showing a unit of the United States armed services deployed not against a foreign danger but in response to a domestic crisis on American soil. In response to court orders to racially integrate public schools, stemming from the Supreme Court decision in *Brown v. Board of Education of Topeka, Kansas* (1954), the school board in Little Rock, Arkansas, approved plans to implement integration, beginning at the high school level. Central High School was scheduled to accept nine African American students on September 4, 1957. These students were Elizabeth Eckford, Ernest Green, Minnijean Brown, Melba Patillo, Gloria Ray, Jefferson Thomas, Carlotta Walls, Terrence Roberts, and Thelma Mothershed, and they had been specially selected by the Arkansas State NAACP under the leadership of its president, Daisy Bates. On that day, however, a white mob had assembled to block their way, and Governor Orval Faubus of Arkansas made good on a prior threat to order the State National Guard to likewise prevent the students from entering. President Dwight D. Eisenhower, in an attempt to carry out the integration court orders without having the federal government involved, tried to persuade Faubus to admit the nine students. Faubus seemingly agreed and withdrew the State National Guard. But when, on September 23, the students entered through a side door and a riot broke out, the governor refused to act to restore order. Eisenhower assumed his powers as commander in chief, and on September 24, he called back the National Guard under his direction and ordered in 1,000 U.S. Army soldiers from to 101st Airborne Division, under the command General Edwin Walker. The students were successfully admitted to classes the next day. However, the situation remained tense, and there were many instances of the students, who would be dubbed the "Little Rock Nine," being harassed by white students. One, Minnijean Brown, was suspended for retaliating against this harassment.

About the Artist

An unnamed Associated Press photographer took this photo. The Associated Press is a news agency, founded by New York City newspapers in 1846, whose members

Document Image

The 101st Airborne Division shown outside Little Rock Central High School
(AP Images)

collaborate in providing each other with a pool of news stories and photographs.

Context

Following the Reconstruction era, the Democratic Party in southern states was run by white-supremacist conservatives. The party recaptured political control in all the states of the former Confederate States of America and established state governments that legalized the disfranchisement of African Americans and legislated segregation along racial lines. This would be later be characterized as the Jim Crow system and would prevail until legislation and court rulings began to dismantle it.

One of these rulings was the Supreme Court decision *Brown v. Board of Education* on May 17, 1954. The court ruled that having separate school systems based on race produced inequality and was therefore unconstitutional. The following year, in a ruling known as *Brown II*, the court specifically ordered desegregation to proceed "with all deliberate speed." Many states and school districts resisted and even pledged "massive resistance" to integration. White Citizens' Councils, a network of white supremacist organizations, were organized in the South to galvanize community efforts to prevent or at least minimize integration efforts, and the Ku Klux Klan saw an upsurge in membership. The gruesome murder of fourteen-year-old Emmett Till in Money, Mississippi, for allegedly whistling at a white woman on August 28, 1955, seemed to underscore a new white southern backlash of anger and resentment, and the extensive news coverage publicized the situation in the segregated South to the general public as never before.

In 1956, eighty-two congressional representatives and nineteen senators jointly signed what became known as the Southern Manifesto, denouncing the *Brown* ruling as a violation of states' rights and urging legal challenges. Some school systems accepted desegregation as inevitable but tried to put off action as long as they could while quietly planning to put into place limited and gradual integration, hoping to avoid publicity and trouble. One such plan was proposed by the Little Rock, Arkansas, school system, which decided to start with nine Black high school students and then, over time, slowly introduce Black students into the elementary and middle grades. When the white mob, backed up by Governor Faubus's National Guard units, prevented integration, President Eisenhower unsuccessfully conferred with Faubus and then invoked the Insurrection Act of 1807 to order the 101st Airborne to Little Rock. Eisenhower's decision was based on his conviction that there was a constitutional obligation to uphold Supreme Court rulings regardless of his personal beliefs—which were definitely anti-desegregation. This state of armed surveillance lasted for a year, though the 101st Airborne was withdrawn in November 1957 and the Task Force 153rd Infantry of the Arkansas National Guard took its place.

Anti-Black sentiment simmered and sometimes erupted into violence for months thereafter, and Faubus, who was a segregationist Southern Democrat, remained a strong political force for many years, maintaining the support of his hard-core following. The Little Rock Crisis would have a bearing on the passage of the Civil Rights Act of 1960 and on the sit-in movement that began in February 1960, which is credited with launching the nonviolent, direct-action phase of the civil rights movement.

Explanation and Analysis of the Document

The issue of school desegregation was an explosive one, and the crisis in Little Rock, Arkansas, encapsulated it and the larger issues of racism and race relations. Press coverage of the crisis was intense. Tensions in Little Rock undoubtedly conjured horrific memories among both whites and Blacks of the anti-Black riots earlier in the twentieth century in such diverse towns as Detroit, Michigan; Springfield and Chicago, Illinois; Tulsa, Oklahoma; Washington, D.C.; and Knoxville, Tennessee.

What strikes the viewer most vividly in this photograph is the stark simplicity of the scene depicted. The view of the two soldiers standing guard on either side, flanking more soldiers sitting in jeeps parked in front of Central High, gives the very large school the aspect of a fortress under siege. In many ways it was a community under siege. This image and other, similar ones depicting the intensive military presence bring forward the irony of the country's own armed forces compelling its citizens to abide by the laws that their own constitutional process had put in place. The impression is that the threat of violence is ever present and that the situation could turn deadly at any moment. This is also apparent in the iconic image of the crisis of the African American student Elizabeth Eckford walking to the school building surrounded by a sea of hostile whites, some of whom screamed at and spat on her. At the same time, the image depicting the 101st also plainly demonstrates the federal government's determination to uphold the rule of law.

The presence of the military did not completely shield the "Little Rock Nine" from suffering various instances of persecution and intimidation from some of the white students and being ignored by most of the others. Besides the events leading to Minnijean Brown's suspension, there were physical attacks reported on Gloria Ray (who was shoved down a flight of stairs) and Melba Patillo (who was burned when acid was flung in her face). Of the nine, only Ernest Green graduated from Central High, in May 1958. The others would later matriculate from other institutions.

In February 1958, the Little Rock School Board petitioned the courts that school desegregation be delayed for thirty months. On September 12, 1958, the Supreme Court ruled against the delay in the case of *Cooper v. Aaron*. In response, through a political maneuver by Governor Faubus, who signed a school closure bill on September 15, 1958, all four high schools in Little Rock were closed, and the city voters approved the measure by more than a two-thirds majority. It was not until nearly a year later, on August 12, 1959, that schools reopened under the mandate of a new school board. Though the classes resumed on a desegregated basis, Black students were still subject to being shunned and occasionally bullied for a long time to come. Central High now contains a civil rights museum and still functions as an educational institution.

Faubus would continue a long political career: he served six consecutive terms as governor, holding the office from 1955 to 1967. Though he would run again three times, the Democratic Party took on a more moderate philosophy, and Faubus's segregationist past hindered his attempts to secure his party's nomination. He became a relic of the past.

Despite a brief period of racial calm from 1958 to 1959, the Little Rock Crisis foreshadowed the more tumultuous civil rights campaigns of the early 1960s: the sit-ins, the freedom rides, the movements in Albany, Birmingham, and Selma, and the Mississippi Freedom Summer Project of 1964.

—Raymond Pierre Hylton

Questions for Further Study

1. What reaction might the photographer or editor have wanted to awaken in the consciousness of newspaper readers with this photograph?

2. Taking into account the times and attitudes of the 1950s and the events at Central High School, is the impression this image gives one of strength and stability or unrest and uncertainty? Please explain.

3. In your opinion, under what circumstances might the U.S. president be justified in calling out and stationing troops within the United States during peacetime? In what way might this have applied in Little Rock in 1957?

4. What lessons can be derived from the actions of President Eisenhower and Governor Faubus?

Further Reading

Books

Bates, Daisy. *The Long Shadow of Little Rock: A Memoir.* New York: David McKay, 1962.

Beales, Melba Pattillo. *Warriors Don't Cry: A Searing Memoir of the Battle to Integrate Little Rock's Central High.* New York: Simon & Schuster, 2007.

Burk, Robert F. *The Eisenhower Administration and Black Civil Rights.* Knoxville: University of Tennessee Press, 1984.

Jacoway, Elizabeth. *Turn Away Thy Son: Little Rock, the Crisis That Shocked the Nation.* New York: Free Press, 2007.

Lanier, Carlotta. *A Mighty Long Way: My Journey to Justice at Little Rock Central High School.* New York: Random House, 2009.

Films

Crisis at Central High. CBS, 1981.

The Ernest Green Story. Walt Disney Television, 1993.

Thomas J. O'Halloran: "Kitchen" Debate Photograph Of Richard Nixon And Nikita Khrushchev

Author/Creator Thomas J. O'Halloran **Date** 1959 **Image Type** Photographs	**Significance** Portrays a lively discussion between U.S. vice president Richard Nixon and Soviet leader Nikita Khrushchev on the benefits of their respective political and economic systems—concepts that formed the ideological underpinnings of the Cold War from 1946 to 1991

Overview

This photograph depicts Premier Nikita Khrushchev of the Soviet Union and Vice President Richard Nixon of the United States together in Moscow on July 24, 1959. They met as part of a world's fair–style exhibition of the United States' scientific, economic, and cultural achievements. The event, which was filmed and then broadcast soon after in both the United States and the Soviet Union, was the culmination of the U.S.-Soviet Cultural Agreement, which was signed the previous year. Each nation agreed to construct an exhibit in the other's country in hopes of educating the general population about what everyday life was like in that country. The hope was for the cultural exchange to open the door to mutual understanding and thereby ease Cold War tensions. A month earlier, the Soviet Union opened its exhibition in New York.

What has since become known as the "kitchen debate" was a series of impromptu exchanges between Nixon and Khrushchev on the relative virtues of capitalism and communism. For Nixon and many prosperous Americans, the debate encapsulated the pride that they felt in the ability for many to live so well under the capitalist system. While the *New York Times* referred to the event as a "lavish testimonial to abundance," for Nixon it was an opportunity to remind both Khrushchev and the world of the potential and might of both the American economy and the American way of life.

About the Artist

Thomas J. O'Halloran worked as a photographer for *US News & World Report* for 35 years. A native of Washington State, he served in Europe during World War II with the Army Air Force, where he installed photographic equipment in bombers. His career at *US News & World Report* began in 1951 as a staff photographer. He subsequently covered a variety of issues, including the civil rights movement, politics, and international affairs. During his tenure, *US News & World Report* saw its greatest success, and circulation passed two million in the 1970s. He retired as chief photographer in 1986.

Document Image

Richard Nixon (holding microphone) pointing at Nikita Khrushchev (in hat)
(Library of Congress)

Context

Under the direction of President Harry Truman (1884–1972), the United States pursued the elimination of trade barriers as a key to post–World War II peace, but it also marked a shift to a hardline stance vis-à-vis the Soviet Union and moved from a policy of unilateralism to multilateralism. According to historian Melvin P. Leffler in his book *For the Soul of Mankind*, "neither Truman nor Stalin wanted a cold war," but "conditions in the international system created risks that Truman and Stalin could not accept and opportunities they could not resist." The Cold War was not simply a rivalry over political control or military power but a struggle for worldwide influence. A number of major foreign policy initiatives were taken during the Truman administration that would have lasting effects, and American policy was greatly affected by such things as diplomat George Kennan's supremely influential Long Telegram (articulating a hard U.S. stance against the Soviet Union) and the National Security Act of 1947, which set the framework for containment policy.

Containment was the idea that if communism were not contained or isolated, that it would spread to neighboring countries, first in Europe and then around the world. Containment, along with a National Security Council policy report called the NSC-68 and the creation of the national security state, remain Truman's main legacy, as it created the template for U.S. foreign policy for the remainder of the Cold War. NSC-68 was not only a reaffirmation of the U.S. foreign policy of containment during the Truman administration but the template for U.S.-Soviet relations for much of the duration of the Cold War. This report stated that the Soviets were animated by a "new fanatic faith, antithetical to our own," and that they wanted "absolute authority over the rest of the world." Leffler sums it up thusly: "Germany and Japan had to be economically integrated into the Western world, militarily rearmed, and pulled politically and diplomatically into the U.S. orbit. Southeast Asian nations had to be insulated from the Communist virus, defended against Chinese ambitions, and convinced that their nationalist aspirations could be fulfilled in cooperation with their former imperial master and with the United States. Middle Eastern governments had to be protected from internal subversion and regional foes, dissuaded from pursuing neutralist options, and encouraged to offer their bases and oil to the freedom-loving democracies of the West in case of global conflict."

While Cold War animosity between the United States and Soviet Union remained high throughout the 1950s, there was some optimism that in a post-Stalin world, tensions could be relaxed. Although the paranoia of McCarthyism had begun to fade, still, according to historian Walter LaFeber, President Dwight D. Eisenhower (1890–1969) believed that "the overriding threat to world stability was communism, not starvation, inequality, or other wants that led the have-nots to rebel against the haves." Eisenhower felt that maintaining the preponderance of the world's resources was imperative to sustaining American world supremacy.

Eisenhower's New Look strategy featured the same foreign policy goals as Truman but used new ways to achieve them, notably with its emphasis on regional alliances and use of the CIA as a foreign policy tool. The so-called Eisenhower Doctrine made it policy to intervene in places either controlled by communism or perceived as threatened by it. This paved the way for interventions in places like Guatemala and Iran. While the United States flexed its power around the world, domestically it trumpeted the marvels of capitalism and consumer culture to a population hungry for such a message.

The Great Depression was not a distant memory for most of the nation. Fears that a new depression could be just around the corner made consumers cautious in the immediate post–World War II years. This is where advertisers came in. So-called Mad Men sold the public on all sorts of consumer goods, from toasters to cigarettes to washers to the latest food fad. Peace and prosperity were for sale, and the American consumer was ready to buy. Publications like *Good Housekeeping* featured images of futuristic kitchens, an idea featured heavily during the "kitchen debate."

The idea for a renewed push for cultural understanding initially came from Soviet Premier Nikita Khrushchev (1894–1971) in 1957. He called on the West to open opportunities for cultural exchange and trade. As part of a new Soviet effort that had begun shortly after the death of Soviet leader Joseph Stalin in 1953, Khrushchev wanted not only to reach strategic and political agreements with the United States but also to provide the Soviets access to information about U.S. developments in science and technology. Khrushchev knew that the United States maintained an edge over the Soviet Union in many technological areas. If the two sides could come together, he thought, the Soviets could better gauge the progress of their adversaries. Although initially reluctant, Eisenhower soon agreed, and the plan was codified in the U.S.-Soviet Cultural Agreement, signed on January 27, 1958.

The Soviet exhibit opened in New York City in June 1959. The Soviet exhibition focused on scientific advancement and included a model of Sputnik, which had successfully carried the first man into orbit two years prior. It also featured Soviet farm equipment and an art installation.

U.S. vice president Richard Nixon (1913–1994) arrived in Moscow on July 22. Before the exhibition, Khrushchev welcomed him at the Kremlin, where he proceeded to berate the vice president about the annual Captive Nations resolution, which had just passed in Congress, as it had every year since 1950. The resolution urged Americans to "study the plight of the Soviet-dominated nations and to recommit themselves to the support of the just aspirations of those nations." Thus tensions were high heading into the public exhibition two days later.

The American exhibit focused more on consumer goods and the conveniences they brought to the average American worker. While leaning away from propaganda, the exhibit did stress the higher standard of living in the United States as compared to the Soviet Union. Automobiles, color televisions, and modern kitchen appliances would themselves demonstrate the benefits of a free-market economy and a free society. The exhibit featured a complete reproduction of a house that exhibitors claimed was affordable for any American.

Wary of this message spreading, Soviet propagandists almost immediately attempted to draw attention away from the exhibit. Competing fairs and events were held, and reports were issued that claimed, with some truth, that such products were out of the financial reach of many Americans. Despite these efforts, over 2.5 million Soviets visited the exhibit during the forty-two days the fair was open, demonstrating a thirst among the Soviet population for information on their Cold War adversary. By introducing American culture and technology to the Soviet public, some have argued that the "kitchen debate," in the long run, helped contribute to the weakening of the Soviet Union.

While on the surface, the "kitchen debate" may not seem like much more than verbal sparring between two ideologically divergent characters, in reality, the debate fit very much into the U.S. containment policy of the Cold War. For the United States, the exhibit was an intellectual reflection of this policy. By demonstrating the superior standard of living of American citizens, technological innovation, and economic independence, the country hoped to use the debate as a way to curb the spread of communism.

Explanation and Analysis of the Document

The image comes from a staged press conference by Premier Nikita Khrushchev of the Soviet Union and Vice President Richard Nixon of the United States following their tour of the U.S. exhibit in Moscow on July 24, 1959. Aides and translators surround both men. The bright lights necessary for television allow the viewer to note easily the expressions on each man's face. Nixon, in a dark suit, holds the microphone stand with his left hand and points toward Khrushchev with his right. Khrushchev, wearing a light-colored suit and a large-brimmed hat, opens his left hand to Nixon. Here they are engaged in open debate, each thoroughly convinced of the superiority of their nation's respective economic and political systems.

Several exchanges are noteworthy. In one, Nixon, proud of the model home, enthusiastically guided Khrushchev toward the kitchen. Said Nixon, "I want to show you this kitchen. It's like those of houses in California. See that built-in washing machine?" "We have such things," Khrushchev replied. Nixon continued: "What we want to do is make more easy the life of our housewives." "We do not have the capitalist attitude toward women," was the Russian's dry retort.

Khrushchev was at times dismissive of U.S. accomplishments, such as when he claimed that American houses were built to last only twenty years so builders could sell new houses at the end of that period. "We build firmly. We build for our children and grandchildren," Khrushchev said. Nixon countered, arguing that American houses would last more than twenty years, but even so, after twenty years many Americans would want a new home or a new kitchen, their old one having become obsolete by then. The American system was designed to take advantage of new techniques.

Another interesting aspect of the debate is that both men were genuinely insistent on the free exchange of ideas. They insisted that both countries must have this free flow of ideas and information so that their citizens could learn from each other. To accomplish this, they agreed to broadcast the debate, translated (Khrushchev was adamant on this point) in their home country. In the broadcast, both smile as they shake on this agreement, each man bursting with confidence that his adopted system will win the day. All three major U.S. networks broadcast the debate on July 25, 1959, in color, surely to the annoyance of Khrushchev, as that technology was not yet available in the Soviet Union. The quick broadcast in the United States drew Soviet protests, as the agreement had been for the debate to be broadcast simultaneously. The Soviet broadcast finally occurred two days later.

—Matthew Jagel

Questions for Further Study

1. What kind of information might a Soviet citizen learn about the United States from such an exhibition? How valuable (or accurate) might that information be in helping a Soviet citizen come to a better understanding about their American counterparts?

2. Why do you think the American exhibition focused on the kitchen as opposed to another part of a house or another location? Do you think that choice helped make the American exhibition successful?

3. What do you think the impact of such an exhibition would have had in the Soviet Union? Think about both short-term and long-term implications.

Further Reading

Books

Kennan, George F. *American Diplomacy*. Chicago: University of Chicago Press, 1984.

LaFeber, Walter. *America, Russia, and the Cold War, 1945–2006*. New York: McGraw-Hill, 2008.

Leffler, Melvyn P. *For the Soul of Mankind: The United States, the Soviet Union, and the Cold War*. New York: Hill and Wang, 2007.

Websites

"Nixon-Khrushchev Kitchen Debate." C-SPAN.org. Accessed August 2, 2022. https://www.c-span.org/video/?110721-1/nixon-khrushchev-kitchen-debate.

A Visual Guide to the Cold War. Accessed August 2, 2022. https://coldwar.unc.edu/.

Photograph Of Levittown, Pennsylvania

Author/Creator
Unknown

Date
c. 1959

Image Type
Photographs

Significance
Shows the immense size of the Levittown housing development, indicative of the growing demand for housing during the baby boom in the wake of World War II

Overview

This photograph shows an aerial view of Levittown, Pennsylvania. The name "Levittown" became virtually synonymous with suburbia, particularly with the growth of sprawling American suburbs in the post–World War II era. The suburban homes of the era represented the fulfillment of the American dream, particularly for many men and women who had served in the military during the war, returned home, and were starting families. The suburbs, with their rows of houses, pools, community centers, playgrounds, and lawns, provided an alternative to crowded and oftentimes gritty and crime-ridden cities. The three Levittown communities—this one outside of Philadelphia, along with one on Long Island, New York, and one in New Jersey—are regarded as emblematic of the growth of the suburbs, and perhaps as emblematic of middle-class conformity. William Levitt, the president of the company at the time Levittown was built, is often regarded as a pioneer and the "father of the American suburb." Notably, Levitt refused to sell homes to African Americans, and covenants in the communities forbade residents from allowing non-whites to live in or use their Levittown homes. These emblems of suburban life, then, were founded in segregation.

About the Artist

It is unknown who took this photograph, one of many widely reproduced aerial photographs of the Levittown development.

Context

The Levittown planned development in Bucks County, Pennsylvania, was the second of three such communities developed and built by Levitt & Sons, Inc., a construction firm founded by Abraham Levitt in 1929. The land for the community—more than 5,700 acres, largely of spinach and broccoli farms—was purchased in 1951. Construction began in 1952 and was completed in 1958. When the first model home was opened for viewing in 1951, it was viewed by 30,000 people over the first weekend. Americans were hungry for affordable housing.

The first, and arguably more famous, Levittown was built on Long Island beginning in the late 1940s; a third

Document Image

Aerial view of Levittown, Pennsylvania
(Wikimedia Commons)

Levittown community was later built in New Jersey. The Pennsylvania community eventually comprised more than 17,000 homes, each on a lot that was roughly 7,000 square feet—an immensity to apartment dwellers from the cities. The basic planning unit for Levittown was the "master block." This was a roughly mile-square area that held three to five variously sized neighborhoods, also known as "sections." Each section contained an average of 300 to 500 homes. The goal was to create a neighborhood feel, even a small-town feel. The company offered six models of single-family homes: the Levittowner (the best-selling model), the Rancher, the Jubilee, the Pennsylvanian, the Colonial, and the Country Clubber. Homes from each model had minor exterior variations, and over time the owners made changes that added elements of distinction. The price of the homes was modest at $8,900, although a slightly larger home could be purchased for $9,900. Down payments were low, just $100, and military veterans did not need to make a down payment. Homes were initially not sold to African Americans.

The homes could be built inexpensively and rapidly because the president of the company at the time, William Levitt (the son of Abraham), developed a twenty-six-step building method that resembled an assembly line. He learned the construction method during the war, when the company won a government contract to build 2,200 defense housing units in Virginia and had to build them rapidly. Building materials, everything from siding to nails, were delivered in perfectly calculated amounts to each house site so that workers did not need to do any measuring or cutting. Construction workers moved from house to house, with each team of workers having a specific task, such as pouring slabs, framing, installing electrical fixtures, or installing washing machines. Levitt was the first major builder to construct houses on radiantly heated cement slabs. The company estimated that by not digging out a basement, it saved each buyer $1,000. (The practice caught on, and by 1952, a quarter of all new houses were constructed on slabs.) Standard building materials were used. To cite an example, the company ordered 1.75 million bamboo screens from Japanese companies, to be used in place of more expensive wooden interior doors. Landscaping, too, was standardized: each lot was allotted the same number of shade trees, fruit trees, evergreens, perennials, and flowering shrubs—a total of 400,000 plantings costing $8,000,000—and given that many new residents had been city dwellers, the company provided them with detailed instructions on how to care for the landscaping. The building process was highly regimented, and it is said that a finished Levitt home was completed every sixteen minutes. (A number of sources say "seconds," but this is a misstatement.) William Levitt himself stated: "We are not builders. We are manufacturers." When it was completed, Levittown, although not an incorporated municipality, was the tenth largest "city" in the state.

One of the reasons the Pennsylvania Levittown community became popular was that it provided housing for a growing population of industrial workers. In 1952, U.S. Steel opened the nearby Fairless Mill, which provided jobs for up to 10,000 workers. The mill was a popular destination for workers who wanted to leave Philadelphia and also for jobless coal miners from other parts of the state. This influx of people and their growing families—the 17,000 houses became home to 84,000 people—needed housing. Residents, however, were not always members of the working class. Medical professionals, lawyers, and other white-collar workers also called Levittown home.

Other suburban developments had sprung up in the years following World War II, but what made the Levittown developments, including the one in Pennsylvania, unique was that they were planned as complete communities. The streets were curved to slow down traffic and make them bike-friendly for children. No child had to walk more than a half mile to school or cross a major intersection. There were no four-way intersections in the community. The company donated property for an elementary school to be built in each of the development's neighborhoods. The company also set aside property for churches and other public buildings. Amenities included public pools, parks, greenbelts, baseball fields, playgrounds, a community center, and even a nearby, meticulously landscaped shopping center—which at the time was the largest shopping center east of the Mississippi River.

The context in which Levittown sprang up was the rapid growth of the United States during the postwar era. It was a time of prosperity, expansion, and optimism. The nation's population in 1950 was 151.3 million. By 1960, the year after the completion of Levittown, the population had risen to 180.7 million. In 1950, the median household income was just about $3,300 (about $36,500 in 2022 dollars). By 1960, that figure had risen to $5,600 (about $50,400 in inflation-adjusted dollars). Given growing incomes, many

American families were looking for newer, more modern housing with amenities in the suburbs, where they could find lower crime rates and less population density. Indeed, by 1950, for the first time in the nation's history, more Americans were living in the suburbs than in the cities, particularly because of the large number of servicemen and women returning from the war. They were starting families, and after the privations of the war years (and the Great Depression that preceded the war), they were eager to seize a share of the American dream of homeownership. The federal government encouraged this dream—at least for white Americans—by providing mortgage insurance and low-interest loans and by making mortgage interest payments tax deductible. Further, insurance rates on suburban homes and cars were lower than they were in the cities. By 1960, some 20 million people had been drawn to America's suburbs.

Other historic developments contributed to the rise of the suburbs. One was the construction of roads, particularly the interstate highway system, which was begun during the administration of President Dwight Eisenhower in the mid-1950s. By 1960, nearly 8,000 miles of the system had been built. These roads, along with commuter trains, made it easier for suburban residents to commute to work in the cities; in 1953, the Pennsylvania Railroad's Tullytown station was renamed Levittown-Tullytown in acknowledgment of the influence of Levittown. Another significant development was the skyscraper. Skyscrapers in the cities had the effect of making urban land much more expensive, placing it out of reach of the typical homebuyer. Land in outlying districts was much less expensive, resulting in lower-cost homes, along with access to shopping centers and temperature-controlled indoor malls with ample parking.

Many sociologists and social observers were critical of the suburbanization of the United States and of massive developments such as Levittown. They maintained that suburbs isolated people, in contrast to cities, where people congregated and could readily attend cultural, sporting, and other kinds of events that drew them together. The suburbs, according to some, created conformity, so that residents had to have the same green lawns, the same grills, the same furniture, the same cars, and initially, the same race, as African Americans were excluded from purchasing suburban homes. Suburbs contributed to congestion on the roads and to air pollution as more and more people had to drive into the cities to work. The suburbs had a detrimental effect on many downtown areas, whose businesses could not compete with businesses in the suburbs. Most importantly, social critics pointed to the psychological effects of the suburbs, arguing that suburbanites were stuck in a rootless, bland, standardized world that lacked the vitality of the city or the sense of belonging that could be found in small towns or in rural areas.

Explanation and Analysis of the Document

This image is an aerial photo of Levittown, Pennsylvania, taken in 1959, shortly after construction of homes in the development was completed. The photo gives the viewer a strong sense of the vast scope of the project, with hundreds of homes lined up along the streets of the community, far into the distance. The viewer can see that the community was divided into "neighborhoods" separated by parkways. For some viewers, the photo is a near-horrifying image of drab postwar middle-class suburban conformity. For other viewers, the photo documents the ability of American industry to rise up to meet the housing needs of a vast number of people with communities that were clean, well-maintained, and orderly.

—Michael J. O'Neal

Questions for Further Study

1. Would looking at such a photo induce a person looking for a home to buy a Levittown home? Why or why not?

2. What does the photo say about the suburbanization of the United States?

3. What did some social observers and others find objectionable about Levittown?

Further Reading

Books

Ferrer, Margaret Lundrigan, and Tova Navarra. *Levittown: The First 50 Years*. Charleston, SC: Arcadia Publishing, 1997.

Gans, Herbert J. *The Levittowners: Ways of Life and Politics in a New Suburban Community*. New York: Pantheon Books, 1967; reprinted, New York: Columbia University Press, 2017.

Harris, Dianne, ed. *Second Suburb: Levittown, Pennsylvania*. Pittsburgh: University of Pittsburgh Press, 2010.

Hayden, Delores. *Building Suburbia: Green Fields and Urban Growth, 1820–2000*. New York: Pantheon Books, 2003.

Jackson, Kenneth T. *Crabgrass Frontier: The Suburbanization of the United States*. New York: Oxford University Press, 1987.

Lane, Barbara Miller. *Houses for a New World: Builders and Buyers in American Suburbs, 1945–1965*. Princeton, NJ: Princeton University Press, 2015.

Wagner, Richard, and Amy Duckett Wagner. *Levittown*. Charleston, SC: Arcadia Publishing, 2010.

Websites

Blumgart, Jake. "What Will Become of Levittown, Pennsylvania?" *Bloomberg*, March 1, 2016. https://www.bloomberg.com/news/articles/2016-03-01/what-will-become-of-levittown-pennsylvania.

Dayanim, Suzanne Lashner. "Levittowns (Pennsylvania and New Jersey)." *Encyclopedia of Greater Philadelphia*, 2015. https://philadelphiaencyclopedia.org/essays/levittowns/#collections.

"Levittown: Building the Suburban Dream." State Museum of Pennsylvania. Accessed August 15, 2022. http://statemuseumpa.org/levittown/one/b.html.

Sheidlower, Noah. "The Controversial History of Levittown, America's First Suburb." *Untapped New York*, July 31, 2020. https://untappedcities.com/2020/07/31/the-controversial-history-of-levittown-americas-first-suburb/.

Documentaries

Levittown: A Living History. Shoshana B. Rubin, writer and producer. These5Guys Productions/SBR Productions, April 25, 2017. https://www.youtube.com/watch?v=WHrXIx4GrM0.

"1952: A City is Born: Levittown, Pennsylvania." *The March of Time*, 1952. https://www.youtube.com/watch?v=rnhzw3hu084.

Photograph Of Interstate 10 Under Construction In California

Author/Creator
State of California Department of Public Works/*Los Angeles Examiner*

Date
1961

Image Type
Photographs

Significance
Shows the extent of freeway construction in the United States following the passage of the National Interstate and Defense Highways Act (1956) during the Eisenhower administration

Overview

This photograph of Interstate 10 under construction at State Route 11 in California was published in the *Los Angeles Examiner*. It was taken by the State of California Department of Public Works, Division of Highways, on June 22, 1961, and it probably appeared in the *Examiner* at the end of July. The photo shows the construction of a freeway intersection between California's State Route 11 (now CA-110) and Interstate 10 (I-10), the freeway that connects Southern California with Florida, the southernmost route of the U.S. freeway system.

Both the interstate freeway and the state route have changed their names several times since the photo was taken more than sixty years ago. West of the intersection depicted in the photograph, I-10 is known as the Santa Monica Freeway. Further east, it is called the Rosa Parks Freeway and the Harbor Freeway. Other sections of the freeway are called the San Bernardino Freeway, the Veterans Memorial Highway, the Blue Star Memorial Highway, and the Sonny Bono Memorial Freeway.

Portions of California State Route 11 were laid out as early as 1924, when the Major Street Traffic Plan for Los Angeles widened Figueroa Street to improve traffic to the port of Los Angeles. In 1933, the California state legislature increased the state highway, labeling it Route 165. In 1934, Route 165 received new signage, labeling it State Route 11. Over the next eighteen years, other portions of the freeway were completed and added to the existing route, until the Harbor Freeway opened on July 30, 1952. State Route 11 was renumbered CA-110 in 1981.

The interchange between the two highways was planned as early as 1955. Construction began in 1957, and the interchange was open for traffic in 1962. It was renamed the Dosan Ahn Chang Ho Memorial Interchange in 2002. Ahn Chang Ho (1878–1938), also known by his pen name Dosan, was a Korean-born American who lived and studied in the United States intermittently from 1902 to about 1930. Dosan worked to improve the lives of Koreans in California while at the same time working to secure his native land's independence from Japan. He was arrested by the Japanese authorities in 1937 and died in Keijo Imperial University Hospital, in what is now Seoul, in 1938.

Document Image

Interstate 10 under construction in 1961
(*Los Angeles Examiner*)

Photograph of Interstate 10 under Construction in California

About the Artist

The photograph of Interstate 10 under construction is attributed to the California Department of Public Works, Division of Highways, known as Caltrans (California Department of Transportation) since 1973. The agency had its origins in 1895, when Governor James Budd created the Bureau of Highways with the mission of improving roads throughout the state highway system. Initially, the bureau proposed constructing a highway that would run across California from north to south, but the process foundered until the state legislature voted on funding in 1902, following passage of a constitutional amendment to allow the state to create a single highway system. It took another nine years for the California Highway Commission to divide the state into divisions, each of which had jurisdiction over a separate region of the state. It wasn't until 1934 that the state began assigning route numbers to state highways.

The main impetus behind the Highway Commission was to create roads and highways that would make it easier to move produce and other goods from one part of the state to another. Although railroads had been an important part of state transportation since the 1850s, parts of the state had never been connected to railheads at all. By 1915, trucking had become one of the most significant ways of moving produce and other farm goods to markets and to railheads, from where they could be shipped further east. In 1923, California enacted the first state gasoline tax, charging two cents per gallon to pay for the maintenance and improvements of highways. By 1937, California state records said that 40,000 freight-carrying trucks moved goods around the state. Two years later, California recorded that gasoline-powered trucks carried 70 percent of all goods within the state.

This photograph appeared in the newspaper *Los Angeles Examiner* in the summer of 1961. The *Examiner* had been founded in 1903 by the famous newspaperman William Randolph Hearst as a daily morning paper. The year after the photograph appeared, the *Examiner* merged with the *Los Angeles Herald-Express*, creating the *Los Angeles Herald Examiner*. The *Herald Examiner* ceased publication in November 1989.

Context

The Dosan Ahn Chang Ho Memorial Interchange, also known as the Harbor–Santa Monica Freeway Interchange, is one of the busiest intersections in the United States, used daily by hundreds of thousands of vehicles. It forms a crucial part of the infrastructure of the U.S. highway system, a series of high-speed roads that links together all the parts of the United States. But, although the interchange is a marvelous example of public engineering, it also represents parts of U.S. history that are not publicly celebrated.

One aspect of that history has to do with the construction of roads. Although infrastructure—also known as "internal improvements"—had been part of the national conversation since the days of George Washington, most nineteenth-century infrastructure was built using either state funds or private investment. Part of this had to do with constitutional questions. Did the U.S. constitution allow the government to spend money collected from all the states on improvements that benefited only one? In 1817, Congress passed a bill (known as the Bonus Bill) that allowed the government to pay for internal improvements in the aftermath of the War of 1812. that bill was vetoed by President James Madison on the grounds that it was unconstitutional. Madison's actions effectively killed direct government funding for infrastructure for almost a century and a half.

The lack of federal funding meant that states would have to fund improvements such as roads. As a result, the state of California footed the bill for the routes that crossed the state in the late nineteenth and early twentieth centuries, President Franklin D. Roosevelt called for the construction of a national system of superhighways as a way of employing people during the Great Depression. The Federal-Aid Highway Act of 1938 laid the groundwork for the later freeway system. During World War II, construction actually began on a few routes.

However, it was only in the 1950s, under President Dwight Eisenhower, that the U.S. government finally began to devote money and resources to a true transcontinental system of roads. Eisenhower had been impressed by the German autobahn that allowed the German army to move men and materials around the country rapidly. He pushed for a similar system of roads to be built across the United States, arguing that such a system would be less vulnerable to attack by hostile countries than railroads. In 1956, Congress passed the National Interstate and Defense Highways Act, and construction began in earnest.

But because the new freeways were meant to link into existing highways and other roads, they came with a concealed cost. The freeways made the automobile, with its reliance on petroleum-based fuel, the primary means of transportation in the country. Other forms of transportation, such as the railroads, were neglected and eventually superseded. Americans were now tied to the car, whether they liked it or not.

In rural areas of the country, the new superhighways followed routes that had belonged to the railroads. Interchanges in rural areas prompted the building of new commercial communities, where people lived and worked solely because of the freeway access. As a result, American civic planning changed permanently. In the cities, freeway planning often cut through neighborhoods where minorities lived—particularly predominantly Black and Hispanic neighborhoods. Freeway construction forced minority homeowners out of their homes, often paying only minimal prices for their properties. In some cases, whole neighborhoods disappeared under the new concrete superhighways. Once-thriving minority businesses were destroyed. The entire country may have paid for the construction of freeways, but some paid more than others.

Explanation and Analysis of the Document

The photograph of the Santa Monica Freeway interchange was taken by the state of California's Department of Public Works' highway division toward the end of June 1961. It appeared in the *Los Angeles Examiner*, a daily morning newspaper that had been started by the media magnate William Randolph Hearst in 1903. Only six months after the photo appeared in the *Examiner*, the newspaper merged with another Hearst property, the *Los Angeles Herald-Express*, to form a new paper: the *Los Angeles Herald Examiner*. The *Herald Examiner* lasted until 1989, when it was driven out of circulation by a combination of labor problems, loss of ad revenue, and competition from the city's largest newspaper, the *Los Angeles Times*.

Today, the *Examiner*'s archives and other papers are held in a special collection at the University of Southern California Libraries. A copy of the Department of Public Works' original photograph and a partial clipping form the copy published in the *Examiner* may be found there.

In the early 1960s, work on the freeway and its interchange had been ongoing for several years. The photo shows the outline of the new construction from Hoover Street (at the bottom of the print) looking eastward. In the center are the interchange with the Harbor Freeway and Washington Boulevard (running diagonally across the middle of the photo), one of the city's most important east–west thoroughfares. In the lower right-hand corner of the photo is 23rd Street, which runs through what is now the University Park neighborhood. In the background, on the far side of the incomplete interchange, is what is now the city's Fashion District.

The photograph is at least as interesting for what it does not show as for what it does. The need for an automobile-friendly route between the eastern suburbs of Los Angeles and the Pacific Ocean was recognized by city authorities back in the 1920s, but it took almost forty years for the project to break ground. In part, this was because local residents complained that the Santa Monica freeway would divide neighborhoods and destroy communities. As a result, the path the freeway should take—although not the question of whether it should exist—was hotly debated. Concerned citizens worried that the freeway might threaten schoolchildren's safety. Others saw the increase in pollution from car exhaust as a hazard. In the end, planners chose to run the freeway through poorer, and less influential, Hispanic and Black neighborhoods.

Even though the photograph appears to show the freeway nearing completion in 1961, a lot of work remained to be completed. Much of the construction to the west, the direction behind the camera's point of view, was not finished until 1964, and the entire length of the freeway was not opened to traffic until January of 1966. By that time, the disruption that the freeway had brought to the city had been forgotten or successfully ignored, and when the Santa Monica Freeway opened in its entirety on January 5, 1966, it was greeted with cheers by the local people and civic leaders alike.

—Kenneth R. Shepherd

Questions for Further Study

1. Are the buildings around the interchange primarily businesses, or do they appear to be residences?

2. What evidence can you see in the aerial photograph of the destruction of the neighborhoods surrounding the interchange?

3. The construction of the interchange in the photograph stretches for many city blocks. Why do you think it needs to cover so much area? Would it be related to an engineering issue, or might there be other reasons?

Further Reading

Books

Jackson, Kenneth T. *Crabgrass Frontier: The Suburbanization of the United States*. New York: Oxford University Press, 2012.

Johnson, Katherine M. *The American Road: Highways and American Political Development, 1891–1956*. Lawrence: University Press of Kansas, 2021.

Lewis, Tom. *Divided Highways Building the Interstate Highways, Transforming American Life*. Ithaca: Cornell University Press, 2013.

Seiler, Cotten. *Republic of Drivers: A Cultural History of Automobility in America*. Chicago: University of Chicago Press, 2009.

Websites

Masters, Nathan. "Creating the Santa Monica Freeway." KCET, September 9, 2012. https://www.kcet.org/shows/departures/creating-the-santa-monica-freeway. Accessed June 7, 2022.

Weingroff, Richard F. "The Greatest Decade 1956–1966: Celebrating the 50th Anniversary of the Eisenhower Interstate System." U.S. Department of Transportation Federal Highway System, Highway History. https://www.fhwa.dot.gov/infrastructure/50interstate.cfm. Accessed June 7, 2022.

Fred Blackwell: Woolworths Lunch Counter Sit-In Photograph

Author/Creator Fred Blackwell	**Image Type** Photographs
Date 1963	**Significance** Documentation of southern white people assaulting nonviolent civils rights demonstrators at a lunch counter sit-in

Overview

This photograph was initially published in the *Jackson Daily News* in May 1963. The photo documents part of a sit-in conducted at the Woolworths lunch counter in Jackson, Mississippi, on May 28, 1963, to protest the segregation of that lunch counter.

The lunch counter at Woolworths in Jackson, as was the case throughout the South during the Jim Crow era, denied service to Black customers. The sit-in was part of growing grassroots movement that advocated nonviolent protests to challenge the legalized segregation of the American South. Mississippi, like all the other southern states, was governed by Jim Crow laws—laws that allowed the segregation by race of both public and private facilities, businesses, modes of transportation, schools, and the rest of southern life. Inspired by earlier successful sit-ins in places like Greensboro, North Carolina, eight students and one faculty member from Tougaloo College in Jackson conducted a sit-in at the lunch counter at the Woolworths there. Students Anne Moody and Joan Trumpauer along with Professor John Salter are shown in the picture stoically enduring the assault.

Local police allowed white racists to verbally and physically assault the protestors, pouring condiments, sugar, drinks, and food on them, as well as burning them with cigarettes and cutting them with broken glass. After three hours the protest was broken up and the store closed.

The photograph was picked up by newspapers across the nation and served as a visible symbol of nonviolent protest and violent racism, inspiring further peaceful protests culminating in the March on Washington exactly three months later.

About the Artist

Fred Blackwell was a twenty-two-year-old photographer for the *Jackson Daily News* who stood on the lunch counter to take this photograph. A recent college graduate and native of Jackson, Mississippi, Blackwell was the only still photographer at the scene of the protest. He asked permission from the manager to stand on the lunch counter to get a proper angle for the photograph.

Document Image

The 1963 sit-in at Woolworths lunch counter in Jackson, Mississippi
(Fred Blackwell)

Context

In 1963, the civil rights movement accelerated its challenge to legalized segregation, systemic racism, and the continued discrimination against Black Americans. From the outset of the decade, a grassroots movement had spread across the United States, engaging in widespread nonviolent protests against Jim Crow segregation and other forms of discrimination. Groups like the Congress on Racial Equality (CORE), the National Association for the Advancement of Colored People (NAACP), the Southern Christian Leadership Conference (SCLC), and the Student Nonviolent Coordinating Committee (SNCC) conducted marches, rallies, freedom rides, and sit-ins to pressure President John F. Kennedy and the federal government to intervene in state and local affairs to end discriminatory laws and practices.

One of the primary examples of nonviolent protest was the sit-in. In February 1960, four students from North Carolina A&T, a college in Greensboro, North Carolina, instigated the use of sit-ins to fight segregation by conducting one at the segregated lunch counter in the Greensboro Woolworths. After several months of persistent protest, Greensboro city officials capitulated and allowed for Black customers to use the previously off-limits lunch counters in the city. The student-led protests resulted in the creation of SNCC and the adoption of the sit-in tactic by activists throughout the country. Initially, this sort of direct action was predominantly found in "progressive" southern cities like Greensboro and Nashville, Tennessee. As the decade progressed, the young activists increasingly sought to challenge Jim Crow in the Deep South.

The next major example of grassroots activism was CORE's Freedom Rides. CORE led a group of activists to challenge the federal government to enforce a recent Supreme Court decision that ordered the desegregation of train stations, bus terminals, and airports. The Freedom Riders boarded a bus in Washington, D.C., bound for New Orleans, Louisiana, with scheduled stops at stations along the way. The Riders saw their bus burned in Anniston, Alabama, and were viciously assaulted in both Birmingham and Montgomery. Undeterred, a new group of Riders finished the trip to New Orleans, while a second new group rode into Jackson, Mississippi. This group was immediately arrested, tried, and convicted of deliberately violating state laws, and they were sentenced to six months of hard labor in the state penitentiary.

Again, activists responded to this by increasing the pressure on state and federal officials, with activists successfully suing to gain entry in the University of Mississippi in 1962 and the University of Alabama in 1963. Dr. Martin Luther King Jr. began a large-scale protest movement in the city of Birmingham, Alabama, in the spring and summer of 1963. And SNCC promoted further sit-ins at still segregated lunch counters throughout the South, including the one pictured in Jackson, Mississippi.

The Kennedy administration, increasingly embarrassed by the pictures and videos of nonviolent protestors being attacked by white mobs or, as in Birmingham, by the police, reluctantly moved away from passive verbal support to a televised call for Congress to pass civil rights legislation. Kennedy was increasingly alarmed by the Soviets' exploitation of these images and videos as propaganda against the United States in Africa and Asia and felt he had no choice but to act.

Explanation and Analysis of the Document

The picture shows two female college students, one white and one Black, and a white professor sitting at the lunch counter in Jackson, Mississippi, being assaulted by a white mob. Most of the mob consists of young white males, egged on by an older white male in a hat. Joan Trumbauer, the white student in the picture, later stated that three white men in the background wearing sunglasses were FBI agents on the scene. The local police neither arrested the protestors nor prevented the mob from assaulting them, even as the assaults escalated from verbal harassment to pouring ketchup, mustard, and sugar on the protestors. Emboldened by the passive police response, members of the mob burned protestors with lit cigarettes and broke the sugar and condiment containers to cut a couple of the protestors with the broken glass.

The photograph captures the stoic defiance of the protestors even after the assaults turned physical. One of the key elements espoused by SNCC, CORE, and the SCLC in particular was a full commitment to nonviolence regardless of provocation. The civil rights activists believed that absolute nonviolence was necessary to win over northern white public opinion and to escalate the pressure on the federal government to intervene on behalf of the protestors. All of the activists were aware that any violent response, no matter what the provocation, would lead to negative press coverage and diminish the likelihood of eventual success in achieving the movement's goals of ending Jim Crow laws and bringing about racial equality in the United States.

Another key element espoused by the activists was persistent protest. One of the things learned by the Greensboro protestors in 1960 and passed along to SNCC as a whole was that protests had to be persistent in each action and over a period of days, weeks, or months. In Greensboro, city officials attempted to placate activists by opening negotiations; the initial price for those negotiations was a halting of the protests. After a couple weeks of talks, the students realized city officials were stalling, hoping that the semester would end and the problem would go away. The students immediately resumed the protests, sitting in at the lunch counters all day every day until city officials finally capitulated. The protestors in this picture maintained the sit-in for over three hours in the face of the mob's assault, stopping only when the store closed.

John Salter's participation in the protest demonstrated another key goal of the protest movement. Salter was a sociology professor at Tougaloo College who initially only intended, along with a number of other faculty, to observe the protest. Once it began, however, he decided to join in and became a full participant. Successfully recruiting active white support was a goal of the movement. Leaders like Martin Luther King recognized that without active white support at all levels, the likelihood of real change was small.

The photograph also highlights the importance of press coverage of the protestors and the white response to them. Photographer Fred Blackwell later said that he knew the pictures he was taking were vital in helping move the United States forward on the path to improved race relations. Hence, he stood on the lunch counter to shoot this image. Images like these forced Americans, especially northern whites, to confront the ongoing racism that African Americans were subjected to on a daily basis. Discussions of legal concepts did not move people the same way images of racism and violence on against peaceful protestors did. Segregation was no longer an abstract concept happening to others far away; it stared newspaper readers in the face on the front page.

Finally, it forced action by the Kennedy administration to undo the damage to America's global reputation as an example of freedom in a Cold War–dominated world. There was no disguising the violence of the mob and the contrast between the nonviolent protestors, who are only looking to be served a meal, and the naked force and hatred confronting them. This image, followed the next month by televised images of police attacking protestors in Birmingham, forced Kennedy to act, in this case by going on television and embracing the civil rights movement as a moral cause that the federal government had to support.

—Richard M. Filipink

Questions for Further Study

1. Why were protestors conducting a sit-in in Jackson, Mississippi, in May 1963? What were they protesting?

2. What message is the photographer trying to convey with this image? How has he framed the protestors and the mob?

3. Why would this picture help force the federal government to take action on the issue of civil rights?

Further Reading

Books

Chafe, William H. *Civilities and Civil Rights: Greensboro, North Carolina, and the Black Struggle for Freedom*. New York: Oxford University Press, 1980.

Lewis, George. *Massive Resistance: The White Response to the Civil Rights Movement*. London: Hodder Arnold, 2006.

Moody, Anne. *Coming of Age in Mississippi*. New York: Bantam Dell, 1970.

O'Brien, M. J. *We Shall Not Be Moved: The Jackson Woolworth's Sit-in and the Movement It Inspired*. Jackson: University Press of Mississippi, 2013.

Salter, John R., Jr. *Jackson, Mississippi: An American Chronicle of Struggle and Schism*. Lincoln, NE: Bison Books, 2011.

Articles

Vargas, Theresa. "'The Lunch Counter Now Has Two Empty Seats': She Is the Only One Left Who Can Describe What It Felt Like to Sit There That Hateful Day." *Washington Post*, January 16, 2019. https://www.washingtonpost.com/local/the-lunch-counter-now-has-two-empty-seats-she-is-the-only-one-left-who-can-describe-what-it-felt-like-to-sit-there-that-hateful-day/2019/01/16/f4aecc00-19bd-11e9-9ebf-c5fed1b7a081_story.html.

Hélène Roger-Viollet: Drive-in Restaurant Photograph

Author/Creator Hélène Roger-Viollet **Date** 1964 **Image Type** Photographs	**Significance** Reflects the intersection of suburbanization and the rise of roadside accommodations serving middle-class families, and illustrates the integration of automobile culture and the mass production of food for easy consumption

Overview

This photograph by Hélène Roger-Viollet presents a busy drive-in restaurant in Los Angeles, California. Roger-Viollet traveled the world capturing photos of people's daily lives. This image of a drive-in presents many features of daily life in 1960s United States.

The drive-in restaurant was a popular midcentury dining destination where patrons could enjoy a quick, affordable meal in an entertaining environment. Out front, cars in the parking lot represent the new diversity of models of automobiles. A place to see and be seen, drive-ins attracted customers by delivering hamburgers and ice cream to their car windows, allowing people to enjoy their meal in their bucket seats while admiring the fancy dashboard of their custom automobile.

Located in Los Angeles, this restaurant was photographed during a boom time in California. Many Americans were drawn to the promise of sunshine, good jobs, and homeownership, so they migrated to the suburbs of Californian cities. The population of California grew significantly after World War II ended in 1945. Drive-in restaurants were popular across the United States and could be found along major roads and highways that connected the country in the postwar era.

About the Artist

Hélène Roger-Viollet was a world-traveling photographer. The daughter of a French amateur photographer, she studied journalism in college. She married Jean Fischer. In 1938 she cofounded the Roger-Viollet photo agency in Paris with her husband. From the 1950s to the 1970s, Roger-Viollet made photographs of scenes in North America, Africa, and Asia using a Rolleiflex camera. She took interest in the ordinary aspects of daily life.

Little is known about her private life. Reportedly, her husband murdered her in 1985 when she was eighty-four years old. Fischer died the same year. The Roger-Viollet photograph collection is now housed in Paris, and the Roger-Viollet agency remains in operation in France.

Document Image

Hélène Roger-Viollet's photograph of a drive-in restaurant in Los Angeles, California
(Agence Roger Viollet / GRANGER)

Context

After World War II ended in 1945, manufacturers largely ceased production of weapons and military gear and began mass producing consumer goods. The U.S. economy boomed after the war, and wages increased. Many families welcomed an opportunity to purchase modern appliances, modular housing in the suburbs, and the flashy new automobiles that flooded the market in the 1950s. Oil was inexpensive at just 30 cents a gallon, and automakers devised clever marketing campaigns to link the ownership of a shiny new car to the sense of "individual free choice" that was central to the postwar conception of American national identity.

In general, Americans agreed that growing reliance on automobiles was positive, so they supported the largest federal works project to date: the National Interstate and Defense Highways Act of 1956. Federal funding helped to expand the interstate highway system to 41,000 miles of superhighway across the United States, sometimes destroying urban housing and communities of Black and brown Americans to make room for the roads. After this, American society revolved around the automobile. Unlike railroads or public transportation, the automobile offered privacy and autonomy to individual drivers, who could easily travel directly from home to their destination. By 1960, nearly sixty million cars were on the road, and housing, commerce, and public space transformed to accommodate them.

The rise of highways and automobiles was accompanied by rapidly developing suburban neighborhoods where families could own a small plot of land and a house for less money than renting an apartment in the city. The United States government subsidized the growth of the suburbs via the G.I. Bill, which granted veterans low-interest mortgages with which they could purchase a home. Racist lending and real estate policies kept Black and brown people from purchasing homes, so suburbs became segregated, white-only spaces. As home ownership became more accessible to more white people than ever before, it became the hallmark of the post–World War II version of the American Dream.

California's suburbs, such as those outside Los Angeles, drew residents from across the United States who were seeking a sunny version of the American suburban dream. Many suburbanites worked in the city and took the highway each day to get to work. Before drive-ins became popular, roadside stands offered travelers quick, convenient food. The first A&W Root Beer stand opened in Sacramento in 1923.

Across the United States, schools, shops, and restaurants that served suburban neighborhoods were segregated spaces as well. Some places had explicit whites-only policies, which civil rights activists in the early 1960s protested. The first protest of segregated restaurants was organized by Pauli Murray in Washington, D.C., in 1943 when students from Howard University employed the "stool sitting" technique. In what were later known as "sit-ins," protesters in the 1960s successfully challenged segregation by refusing to leave lunch counters until they were served. In 1964 the Civil Rights Act struck down segregation policies in places like restaurants. Then, in 1968, the Fair Housing Act made racist housing policies illegal. Nonetheless, several factors combined to maintain racial segregation of urban and suburban spaces for decades to come.

Explanation and Analysis of the Document

In this photograph, the eye is drawn to the variety of cars in the parking lot outside the restaurant. In the 1960s, car companies expanded the ways consumers could customize their vehicles. No longer producing limited options like the standard Ford Model T of previous generations, the 1960s car industry stratified its models at different price points, encouraging families to buy cars that fit their personalities and salaries. As a result, automakers offered gadgets and customizable features along a "ladder of consumption." Consumers could aspire to more expensive models or brands of car as their incomes improved. Also, old models went out of style. Automakers relied on the obsolescence of older models so consumers would want to purchase a newer, fancier car even if their old one still worked.

The 1964 Dodge Polara, for example, had multiple lines. Customers could choose from four styles of the body of the car and between a hardtop or convertible. The Polara 500 convertible had bucket seats, special trim, and attractive wheel covers. Customers could opt for upgraded engines, making their car not only cool-looking but fast.

The age of the automobile shaped the approach that small restaurant owners took to the layout of their buildings and parking lots. They needed to accommodate not only the customers but the vehicles that delivered them to their establishments. The parking lot featured in the picture was one way to do that. In the past, restaurants would draw customers in by placing their front door near the street or adjacent to a motel or gas station. In the 1930s, roadside stands offered coffee and meals to travelers. By 1964, 33,000 drive-in restaurants existed in the United States. Some included counters and booths for indoor dining as well.

Roadside stands evolved into drive-in restaurants, whose defining architectural feature was the canopy for shading the parked vehicles. Customers remained in their vehicle, and carhops delivered the food from the carhop station at the restaurant to the customer's car window. Car ownership was perceived to be masculine, and drive-in restaurants typically employed young women as carhops to entertain and titillate the customer for tips.

The parking lot was always in front of the building, showcasing the popularity of a restaurant by the cars filling the lot. The drive-in also became a place for young people to see and be seen without the direct supervision of adults. They hung out in groups near automobiles. Some teens enjoyed the privacy that a vehicle offered and often used the space for sexual activity. Others simply cruised from one drive-in to another to display themselves—and perhaps their fashionable cars—to one another as status symbols.

The large "Sandwich" sign visible from the road in the picture was a common feature. Drive-ins typically had large electric signs with easily recognizable words and symbols. Perhaps the most famous symbol is the golden arches of McDonald's, but even small, independently owned drive-ins attracted customers with flashing signs and light displays around their entrances. Menus at drive-in restaurants varied, though quick service and affordable prices distinguished them from other restaurants.

The high labor costs of the drive-in restaurant caused owners to innovate. Many restaurants abandoned the carhop service for walk-up windows. Some installed speaker boxes in the parking lot for customers to place orders themselves. Others installed drive-up windows. Wendy's was the first to include drive-through areas in their restaurants. Once paper plates and cups became more cheaply available, business models shifted to a carryout approach. This gave rise to places like Pizza Hut in the 1980s, which focused on selling food for families to buy on site and take home. By 1990, the carryout market exceeded the popularity of the drive-in.

—Mallory Szymanski

Questions for Further Study

1. How did suburbanization shape the ways people spent their money on transportation and dining out? To what extent is the drive-in restaurant still relevant in the age of ride-sharing and food delivery services?

2. What sorts of social interactions took place at the drive-in? How did the architecture of the drive-in impact the way people interacted with the space and one another?

3. Why do you think quick-service restaurants became so popular? What changes in society may have caused an increased demand for fast food? What are some pros and cons of this change?

Further Reading

Books

Chatelain, Marcia. *Franchise: The Golden Arches in Black America*. New York: Liveright Publishing, 2020.

Coontz, Stephanie. *The Way We Never Were: American Families and the Nostalgia Trap*. New York: Basic Books, 1992.

Jackle, John, and Keith A. Sculle. *Fast Food: Roadside Restaurants in the Automobile Age*. Baltimore: Johns Hopkins University Press, 1999.

Lears, T. J. Jackson. *Fables of Abundance: A Cultural History of Advertising in America*. New York: Basic Books, 1994.

Websites

Hot Rod 1960s Archive. https://ahrf.com/historical-library/photo-archives/1960s-archives/.

Roger-Viollet Photography. https://www.roger-viollet.fr/news/exhibition-helene-s-trips-a-life-time-spent-on-documenting-the-world-181.

Films/Videos

American Graffiti. Universal Pictures, 1979.

Marriage Today. McGraw-Hill Text Films, 1950. YouTube. https://www.youtube.com/watch?v=71iMD2DsPgA.

Herbert Block: "I Got One Of 'Em" Cartoon About Selma, Alabama

Author/Creator
Herbert Block (Herblock)

Date
1965

Image Type
Cartoons

Significance
Published two days after the incident in Selma, Alabama, on March 7, 1965, known as "Bloody Sunday," this cartoon expressed indignation over the violence the police inflicted on peaceful demonstrators

Overview

This cartoon by Herbert Block (known as "Herblock") was published on March 9, 1965, two days after the "Bloody Sunday" incident in Selma, Alabama. When the news broke that a nonviolent protest march of some 600 individuals had been set upon suddenly by law enforcement officers at the Edmund Pettus Bridge in Selma, and that sixty-seven people had been injured (including seventeen hospitalized for serious injuries), the overall reaction was one of shock and disbelief. Television cameras had been recording the event, and it was broadcast to the public within minutes by the American Broadcasting Company, which cut into its regular programming. The scenes of the actual attack were so disturbing and graphic that the incident was almost immediately dubbed "Bloody Sunday." The march had originally been planned to go from Selma to the Alabama State Capitol Building in Montgomery, a distance of a little over fifty miles. It was part of an ongoing civil rights campaign in support of voting rights legislation and had been organized by James Luther Bevel (1936–2008) and Dr. Martin Luther King Jr. (1929–1968) of the Southern Christian Leadership Conference (SCLC). King had a preaching engagement in Atlanta and would not be present, so the march was led by his SCLC colleague Hosea Williams (1926–2000), along with John Lewis (1940–2020) of the Student Nonviolent Coordinating Committee (SNCC).

Block, the famed cartoonist at the *Washington Post*, had long been a civil rights advocate and was among those who clearly demonstrated their disgust at the callous brutality of the officers involved and apparent indifference of Alabama state officials over what had occurred. The Selma movement and "Bloody Sunday" would accelerate the congressional passage and enactment of the Voting Rights Act of 1965.

About the Artist

Herbert Lawrence Block (1909–2001), who always signed his work as "Herblock," was one of the best-known and most prolific political cartoonists of the twentieth century. Born in Chicago, Illinois, on October 13, 1909, Block developed his artistic talents at an early age; in 1920 he began classes at the Art Institute of Chicago and started signing his work as "Herblock." From 1927 to 1929 he studied at Lake Forest College, but he withdrew to take up a position as a cartoonist

Document Image

"I got one of 'em just as she almost made it back to the church"
(Library of Congress)

for the *Chicago Daily News*. In 1943 he began service in the U.S. Army, where he drafted press releases and drew cartoons for the duration of the war. In 1946 he was discharged from service and resumed civilian employment as the leading cartoonist at the *Washington Post*.

Herblock became a strong supporter of President Franklin D. Roosevelt (1882–1945) and his New Deal initiatives, and his cartoons reflected an affinity with the Democratic Party. However, he could take an independent stand on occasion—notably assailing President Lyndon Baines Johnson (1908–1973) for his handling of the Vietnam War. He was among the most ardent critics of Senator Joseph McCarthy (1908–1957), a Republican, during the early 1950s and is credited with having originated the term "McCarthyism" to denote a political smear campaign based on character assassination and unfounded allegations. Herblock won the Pulitzer Prize in 1942, 1954, 1973, and 1979, and in 1994 he was awarded the Presidential Medal of Freedom by President Bill Clinton. He was still working at the *Washington Post* when he passed away, from pneumonia, on October 7, 2001, at the age of ninety-one.

Context

It had been a long, hard struggle, but on July 2, 1964, President Lyndon B. Johnson signed the Civil Rights Act of 1964, which comprehensively banned racial, religious, and gender discrimination in employment and public accommodation. This had been accomplished in the face of fierce resistance by Southern Democrats and conservative Republicans, which had included a seventy-five-hour filibuster in the U.S. Senate. The act struck a major blow against the so-called Jim Crow system of racially based segregation and discrimination that had largely prevailed throughout the southern, and certain other, states for some ninety years. However, there remained some areas that were not sufficiently addressed, among them voting rights and housing discrimination. From 1870 and well into the twentieth century white leaders had made concerted efforts to suppress or limit the African American vote through such tactics as poll taxes, literacy tests, so-called grandfather clauses, intimidation, and even lynching and other forms of lethal violence. These efforts had proven to be highly effective, and many feared that the political momentum that had brought about the Civil Rights Act of 1964 might have stalled, leaving the voting rights issue unresolved for a long time to come.

By January 1965, the city of Selma, Alabama, and Dallas County, inside which the city was located, had one of the most dismal records for voter suppression—only 2 percent of the eligible African American voting population had been allowed to register to vote. The vast majority had either been bullied or fobbed off by the manipulation of local election officials, who were entirely white. Then, on February 18, 1965, Jimmie Lee Jackson, a twenty-six-year-old African American who had taken part in a peaceful demonstration in nearby Marion, Alabama, was murdered by State Trooper James Bonard Fowler (1933–2015). This prompted Martin Luther King Jr. and James Luther Bevel, the SCLC's director of direct action and nonviolent education, to authorize the first Selma-to-Montgomery march, the ultimate purpose of which was to petition arch-segregationist Governor George C. Wallace (1919–1998) for voting rights reforms.

Protestors in Selma had already run afoul of the brutal segregationist Jim Clark (1922–2007), a Dallas County sheriff, and had been arrested. On March 7, 1965, the marchers paused, strategized, and prayed at Brown Chapel AME (African Methodist Episcopal) Church. Then, with Lewis and Hosea in the lead, they walked ten city blocks to the Edmund Pettus Bridge over the Alabama River. There, they were confronted by Alabama state troopers under Major John Cloud, who had been ordered there by Governor Wallace, and who was assisted by Clark and some white men he had deputized off the streets. Cloud told the marchers they had two minutes to disperse and leave but then, almost immediately, ordered his men to attack. The marchers were beaten with billy clubs and whips, tear-gassed, kicked, and even chased and beaten all the way back to Brown Chapel, where the wounded were sheltered and attended to. Lewis was among those most severely injured, having been viciously clubbed over the head, fracturing his skull, but he nonetheless got up and made it safely to the chapel.

Explanation and Analysis of the Document

In the image, Herblock has placed the figure of a man with the words "Selma Alabama Special Storm Trooper" on his shoulder patch. The term "Storm Trooper" was employed to call to mind the Nazi

Stormtroopers of the 1930s, whose brutalizing tactics helped enable Adolf Hitler's rise to power in Germany—and to equate Cloud's and Clark's men with them. The figure is washing blood from his billy club, and his expression is one of smug satisfaction—even glee—over the role he has just played. Bragging about how he clubbed one of the female marchers just as she was about to reach the church (Brown Chapel) and safety, the figure sports a gas mask hanging on his belt. On a shelf, he has placed his helmet, while the coil of rope on the bench carries the sinister implication of a lynching. Through the image, Herblock sought to express outrage and to spur action for change.

King called for a second march, which was scheduled for March 9, 1965, the day this cartoon was published, and 2,000 people were present. Again, the marchers went from Brown Chapel to the Edmund Pettus Bridge, even though Judge Frank Johnson Jr. (1918–1999) at the Federal District Court had issued an injunction forbidding it. This time, once King reached the bridge he stopped to pray and then led the marchers back to Brown Chapel—an incident known as Turnaround Tuesday. A third march took place on March 21, 1965, again led by King, this one with Judge Johnson's approval. Since Governor Wallace would not provide protection, President Johnson, in his role as commander-in-chief, ordered some 2,000 regular army troops to supplement Alabama National Guard units, and the marchers, estimated to number some 25,000, would complete the trek on March 25, 1965.

Addressing a joint session of Congress on March 15, 1965, President Johnson urged the introduction and passage of voting rights legislation. Shortly thereafter, the Voting Rights Act of 1965 was proposed. Southern Democratic legislators attempted to water down the bill's provisions through amendments and legislative maneuvering, but these efforts were all voted down. The final draft was approved by the House of Representatives on August 3, 1965, by a 328–74 vote, and the Senate approved it the next day by 79–18. On August 6, 1965, the president signed it into law.

The effect that journalists and cartoonists such as Herblock might have had on the final outcome is hard to measure. Certainly, their work contributed to making the American public aware of the voting rights problem, including the extreme acts of violence that were sometimes used to implement minority voter suppression, and this would in turn have put pressure on legislators to act decisively.

—Raymond Pierre Hylton

Questions for Further Study

1. How effectively does the image convey a message about the "Bloody Sunday" incident? What would that message have been? What more would you add to give the readers a larger picture?

2. How did the Selma movement events contribute to the passage of the Voting Rights Act?

3. The Selma movement was an example of a successful nonviolent campaign. What factors might account for its final success?

Further Reading

Books

Block, Herbert. *The Herblock Gallery*. New York: Simon & Schuster, 1968.

Johnson, Haynes, and Harry Katz. *Herblock: The Life and Work of a Great Political Cartoonist*. New York: Norton, 2009.

May, Gary. *Bending toward Justice: The Voting Rights Act and the Transformation of American Democracy*. New York: Basic Books, 2013.

Meacham, John. *His Truth Is Marching On: John Lewis and the Power of Hope*. New York: Random House, 2020.

Webb, Sheyann, and Rachel West Nelson, as told to Frank Sikora. *Selma, Lord, Selma: Girlhood Memories of the Civil-Rights Days*. Tuscaloosa: University of Alabama Press, 1980.

Websites

Rathbone, Mark. "Selma and Civil Rights." History Review 60 (March 2008). https://www.historytoday.com/archive/feature/selma-and-civil-rights?msclkid=00ae8554cec511ec98e3365bc45c0e36.

Photograph Of Black Panther Party Demonstration

Author/Creator Unknown **Date** 1969 **Image Type** Photographs	**Significance** Depiction of a calm but intimidating demonstration by the Black Panther Party, on the steps of the Washington State Capitol in Olympia, against a state bill that would prohibit the carrying of loaded guns in public for purposes of intimidation.

Overview

The Black Panther Party (BPP), originally formed under the name Black Panther Party for Self-Defense, was cofounded on October 15, 1966, in Oakland, California, by Huey P. Newton (1942–1989) and Bobby Seale (b. 1936); the two had been classmates at Merritt College. The BPP grew from the Black power movement and focused on protecting and improving the lot of urban Black communities. Emphasizing their role in community self-defense, members of the Panthers would patrol the streets carrying rifles and would often shadow and follow police vehicles to discourage acts of abuse—a system they dubbed cop watching. To distinguish themselves visually, they chose for a uniform clothing that most of their members would already own: the men wore black trousers, a black jacket, a blue shirt, dark glasses, and a black beret; the women wore black dresses; and most of the members sported large Afro hairstyles. The method of salute was an arm-raised clenched fist. The BPP's program would expand to include a free breakfast program for children, the operation of medical health clinics, and even the establishment of schools. These were termed liberation schools and emphasized African American studies as well as the fundamentals of English and mathematics. The emphasis was on Black communal self-help and independence.

The BPP's Black power and community defense agenda was merged with a Marxist ideology that saw the party as a component of the global class struggle against capitalism and colonialism. Chapters were formed outside the West Coast as far afield as New York, Philadelphia, and Chicago, and for a while the BPP maintained international ties with Cuba, Algeria, North Korea, North Vietnam, China, and the Palestine Liberation Organization.

The laws of California at that time permitted the open carrying of firearms. Aiming to disarm the Black Panthers, California assemblyman Don Mulford (1915–2000), a Republican, introduced the Mulford Bill in April 1967 to prohibit the carrying of loaded guns in public without a permit. The National Rifle Association supported the gun-control bill, as did both the state Republican and Democratic parties. The Black Panther Party staged a demonstration on May 2, 1967, at the California State Capitol Building—openly displaying their weapons and entering the building—in opposition to it. The bill was soon passed by California legislators and then signed into law by Governor

Document Image

Members of the Black Panther Party protesting at the Washington State Capitol in 1969
(Washington State Archives)

Ronald Reagan in July 1967. This event would inspire the later Washington State Capitol protest depicted here, which occurred on February 28, 1969.

About the Artist

Nothing is known about the photographer, who is unnamed.

Context

The years from 1955 to 1965 marked the high point for the civil rights movement's strategy of nonviolence, as espoused by Dr. Martin Luther King Jr. (1929–1968). The Montgomery Bus Boycott of 1956 had succeeded in integrating the public transit system. The sit-ins of 1960 and

1961 had largely succeeded in integrating restaurants and other establishments. The Freedom Rides and the Birmingham and Selma campaigns had borne fruit in the form of the Civil Rights Act of 1964 and the Voting Rights Act of 1965. Despite these successes, there were indications of limitations to the effectiveness of the movement's nonviolent approach. On August 11, 1965, only five days after President Lyndon Baines Johnson had signed the Voting Rights Act, a series of violent riots took place in the heavily African American Watts area of Los Angeles, California. It was ignited by the arrest of a young Black man, Marquette Frye (1944–1986), on a charge of driving under the influence. Relations between the Los Angeles Police Department and the residents of Watts had long been on edge, and as a scuffle broke out between Frye, the officers, and Frye's mother and brother, Frye was struck over the head by a billy club and started bleeding. A crowd had gathered, and onlookers joined in fighting the police, who called for reinforcements. National Guard units were eventually involved. During the ensuing spree of fighting, rioting, looting, and burning that spread across Watts, thirty-four people died, over 1,000 were injured, and some forty million dollars' worth of damage was done. Though there had been rioting in Harlem and Rochester, New York, and in Philadelphia in 1964, the Watts riot was by far the deadliest up to that time, and the most devastating. It set the stage for even more severe urban riots that occurred from 1965 to 1968.

Many young African Americans, especially, began to gravitate away from nonviolence toward a more militant posture. They found a major source of ideas and inspiration in the words of activist and former Nation of Islam minister Malcolm X (1925–1965), who advocated a more forceful and self-reliant approach ("by any means necessary"). On June 5, 1966, civil rights leader James Meredith (b. 1933) began what he termed a "March Against Fear" across the Mississippi delta to highlight the continuing struggle against discrimination, but he was shot and wounded the following day. Though he survived, Meredith needed time to recover in hospital and was unable to continue. It was then that Dr. King and leaders of other civil rights organizations banded together to complete the march to the Mississippi State Capitol in Jackson. During the course of the march, Stokely Carmichael (1941–1998), the leader of the Student Nonviolent Coordinating Committee (SNCC), broke with the strategy of nonviolence and proclaimed a more forceful direction, which he termed "Black Power." Strongly influenced by the ideas of Malcolm X and the Black power movement, organizations espousing the more forceful approach quickly sprang up, including Seale and Newton's Black Panther Party for Self Defense.

Explanation and Analysis of the Document

The photograph portrays a calm but intimidating demonstration by members of the Black Panther Party, standing on the steps of the Washington State Capitol in Olympia, against a bill that, similar to the earlier California law, would prohibit the carrying of loaded guns in public without a permit. The intent of the photographer is not known—perhaps it was totally neutral. However, depending on one's perspective, two conflicting interpretations are possible. One is to interpret the Black Panthers as representing strength and purpose—a willingness, even a dedication, to protect and care for those in their community, and a counterweight to the police departments they considered biased and therefore enemies, not to be trusted. Another interpretation would see the Panthers, with their rifles and uniforms, as grim, intimidating, and a threat to order and stability.

In the image, on the steps of the Washington State Capitol, seven of the eight participating Black Panther members of the Seattle Chapter, their rifles pointed in the air after they had unloaded them, form a triangular lineup, with Elmer James Dixon III (b. 1950), brother of chapter captain Aaron Dixon (b. 1949), standing front and center, and the Panther member behind him nearly obscured. Behind them, near a column, State Police Captain Robert Ranney with a walkie-talkie stands almost casually talking to a gentleman at his right while eight other individuals, including a young Black teenager, look on. Elmer Dixon and one other Panther member wear bandoliers, and the one furthest to the right has a bag on the step between his feet. The protest notwithstanding, House Bill 123, banning the open display of firearms in Washington, had been passed by the state House and Senate the day before, on February 27, and was signed into law the day of the protest.

The BPP's membership grew during the remainder of the 1960s, and violent confrontations with police occurred with some frequency. On May 1967, the BPP published its Ten-Point Program, defining its mission. In part, the platform demanded "land, bread, housing, education, justice, and peace."

Newton was accused and convicted of killing John Frey, an Oakland police officer, on October 28, 1967, and spent time in prison, igniting "Free Huey" demonstrations across the nation while the legal process was unfolding. Though he was convicted, the conviction was reversed, and Newton was released from prison in 1970. On April 6, 1968, BPP treasurer Robert "Little Bobby" Hutton was killed during a shootout with Oakland police. From a high point in 1970, when national membership is estimated to have been around 2,000, the BPP declined thereafter, targeted by FBI director J. Edgar Hoover's COINTELPRO (counterintelligence program) as an anti-American organization, and weakened by internal disputes, some of them lethal.

On December 5, 1969, a controversial FBI-directed raid on the home of Illinois BPP chair Fred Hampton in Chicago resulted in the fatal shooting of Hampton and fellow BPP official Mark Clark. The FBI's methods in the COINTELPRO campaign were so objectionable that in 1976 Clarence M. Kelley (1911–1997), director of the FBI, acknowledged and apologized for the past injustices the bureau had perpetrated on the BPP and similar organizations.

Eldridge Cleaver (1935–1998), the BPP minister of information who was involved in the 1968 shootout that ended in Hutton's death, fled the United States for Cuba to avoid imprisonment for a rape conviction. In 1971 he would break with Newton the BPP over what he saw as the necessity for an armed liberation struggle and closer ties between the BPP and North Korea. Cleaver was then expelled from the BPP, and the North Korea initiative was abandoned.

In 1974 Newton again felt that his leadership was challenged and acted to expel Bobby Seale and other major BPP figures, triggering another exodus among the membership. Later that same year, Newton was accused of murdering a prostitute named Kathleen Smith and fled the country. He was ultimately acquitted of the charge and returned in 1977. In his absence, Elaine Brown served as chair. Shortly after Newton's return, he and Brown fell into disagreement over the role to be played by women in the BPP, and Brown left the organization. By the 1980s the BPP was reduced to shadow membership and was riddled with allegations of drug trafficking, gang violence, and racketeering. In 1982 the remnants of the BPP disbanded.

—Raymond Pierre Hylton

Questions for Further Study

1. What factors and events came together to lead to the formation of the Black Panther Party? How did all the elements work together in accomplishing this?

2. What were the negative and the positive aspects of the Black Panthers' program?

3. What ideas and feelings might the image of BPP members on the steps of the state Capitol Building have awakened in white communities? In African American communities?

4. Why and how did the Black Panther Party decline and finally go out of existence?

Further Reading

Books

Hilliard, David, and Lewis Cole. *This Side of Glory: The Autobiography of David Hilliard and the Story of the Black Panther Party*. New York: Lawrence Hill, 2001.

Martin, Jetta Grace, Joshua Bloom, and Waldo E. Martin Jr. *Freedom: The Story of the Black Panther Party*. San Francisco: Chronicle Books, 2022.

Seale, Bobby. *Seize the Time: The Story of the Black Panther Party and Huey P. Newton*. Baltimore, MD: Black Classic Press, 1991.

Shih, Bryan, and Yohuru Williams, eds. *The Black Panthers: Portraits from an Unfinished Revolution*. New York: Nation Books, 2016.

Documentaries

The Black Panthers: Vanguard of the Revolution. Stanley Nelson, director. PBS, 2016.

AMERICAN INDIANS OCCUPY ALCATRAZ

AUTHOR/CREATOR Associated Press	IMAGE TYPE PHOTOGRAPHS
DATE 1969	SIGNIFICANCE Documents the occupation of Alcatraz Island during a period of newfound militancy and activism among Native Americans in the late 1960s

Overview

This photograph was published in November 1969 by the Associated Press (AP). Most Americans are likely to be familiar with Alcatraz, nicknamed "the Rock," a twenty-two-acre island in San Francisco Bay that was originally used as a lighthouse but in 1934 became the site of a federal prison. Because of the strong currents and cold water temperatures around the island, escape was virtually impossible, and the prison was one of the most notorious in the United States until it was closed in 1963. It is now a tourist attraction. But not so in 1969, when dozens of Native Americans from various tribes occupied the island and claimed that by treaty it was American Indian territory. The occupation, which lasted nineteen months (from November 20, 1969 to June 11, 1971), attracted widespread national and international attention, and while the occupation ultimately collapsed, it called attention to injustices suffered by Native Americans and was a key event in the growing militancy of Native Americans in the 1960s and into the 1970s. The occupation was called "the cradle of the modern Native American civil rights movement."

About the Artist

It is not known who, specifically, took the photograph. The photo was published by the AP, a news agency that was founded in 1846 and grew to become one of the most prominent news agencies in the country and the world. The AP, along with other news agencies, was on hand to document the events of the occupation, and fifty years later, in 2019, AP renewed attention to the occupation by publishing a number of photos and remembrances of the events of those months.

Context

Alcatraz Island had been designated as "surplus property" by the federal government after its use as a federal prison ended in 1963. As such, it was abandoned and not used for any purpose—that is, until November 20, 1969, when some seventy Native Americans, among them students, married couples, and children, gathered on a dock in San Francisco Bay, boarded boats, and sailed to the island, which they claimed for themselves and for "Indians of all tribes." The occupation was conceived by two men: Adam Nordwall, an Ojibwe businessman from Minnesota, and Richard Oakes, a Mohawk ironworker who had relocated to San Francisco and found work as a bar-

Document Image

The 1969 photograph of American Indians occupying Alcatraz
(AP Images)

tender. The occupiers, in making their claim, cited provisions of the Fort Laramie Treaty of 1868, which stated that unused federal lands could be claimed by Native Americans. The precipitating event was the destruction by a mysterious fire of the San Francisco American Indian Center in October 1969. Oakes and Nordwall thought that Alcatraz would make a perfect replacement, a place to preserve and promote the Native American way of life.

Oakes transmitted a message to the San Francisco Department of the Interior: "We invite the United States to acknowledge the justice of our claim. The choice now lies with the leaders of the American government—to use violence upon us as before to remove us from our Great Spirit's land, or to institute a real change in its dealing with the American Indian. We do not fear your threat to charge us with crimes on our land. We and all other oppressed peoples would welcome spectacle of proof before the world of your title by genocide. Nevertheless, we seek peace."

The occupiers spoke out against what had loosely been termed the "termination policy" of the U.S. government. This policy, launched in 1953 and continued until 1968, consisted of laws to end federal recognition of tribes and their sovereignty, end the government's trusteeship over reservations, and end the exclusion of Native Americans from state laws, including laws governing taxation. The goal was to complete the process, begun in the nineteenth century, of completely assimilating Native Americans into mainstream American culture and society.

The occupiers issued a "proclamation" that was somewhat tongue-in-cheek but served to highlight Native American grievances. The proclamation was addressed to the "Great White Father" (presumably the president) "and All His People." It stated that the occupiers claimed Alcatraz by right of discovery. They proposed a "treaty" offering to pay twenty-four dollars for the island in glass beads and red cloth, citing as precedent the purchase of Manhattan Island by the Dutch from the Lenape Indians for the same amount in 1626. The treaty proposed, somewhat unclearly, that the land would be held in trust "by the American Indian Affairs and by the bureau of Caucasian Affairs."

The proposal went on to state that the purpose of reclaiming the island was to "guide the inhabitants in the proper way of living" and to help its inhabitants "achieve our level of civilization and thus raise them and all their white brothers up from their savage and unhappy state." In a particularly tongue-in-cheek passage, the occupiers stated that the island would be suitable as an Indian reservation according to the "standards" of the white man: The island resembles American Indian reservations because it is isolated from modern facilities and is without adequate means of transportation; it has no fresh running water; it lacks adequate sanitation facilities; it has no oil or mineral rights, industry, educational facilities, or healthcare facilities; its soil is rocky and unproductive; the population exceeds the land base; and the population has "always been held as prisoners and kept dependent upon others."

Oakes functioned as the primary spokesperson for the group. Other leaders included LaNada Means, an activist who later became a law professor and writer, and John Trudell, who became a poet, artist, actor, and musician. American Indians of all tribes were invited to join the occupation. Food and other supplies were donated to support the occupiers. The leaders conducted interviews and news conferences to articulate their vision. They created a school and a radio station ("Radio Free Alcatraz"). A number of celebrities, including Jane Fonda, Anthony Quinn, Marlon Brando, Jonathan Winters, Buffy Sainte-Marie, and Dick Gregory were persuaded to visit the island in support, and the rock band Creedence Clearwater Revival donated $15,000 for a boat to provide transportation. Grace Thorpe, the daughter of legendary Native American athlete Jim Thorpe, was one of the occupiers. So too was actor Benjamin Bratt (then age six) and his family.

Not all went well. Bickering and feuding broke out. Oakes was accused of misappropriating funds donated by famous people who had given little thought to how their donations would be used. In January 1970, thirteen-year-old Yvonne Oakes, Richard's daughter, fell to her death, prompting the Oakes family to leave the island. Some of the original occupiers left to return to school. Many of the new occupiers were whites from San Francisco's drug and hippie culture, who brought with them ample supplies of pot but no bedrolls, jackets, or other provisions, leading to a prohibition against non-Natives staying overnight. The government cut off power and phone service to the island, and in June 1970 a fire destroyed several of the island's buildings. Hundreds of turkeys were donated, but there was no way to cook them, so plastic-wrapped turkeys littered the island. The boat donated by Creedence Clearwater Revival had no captain and was thus of little practical use. Negotiations with the administration of President Richard Nixon went nowhere, although the president was perceived as being sympathetic. By 1971, public sympathy for the occupiers was eroding, and many of the occupiers were leaving the island. On June 11, government officials forcibly removed the last fifteen people. As they were taken away, they gave the "Red Power" salute, a raised fist.

The occupation may have collapsed, but it did not go unremembered. November 20, 2019, marked the fiftieth anniversary of the occupation, when many occupiers and their supporters returned. The U.S. National Park Service recognizes the Alcatraz occupation in a number of regularly offered programs and exhibits on the island, which is visited each year by hundreds of teachers and students who can learn about the occupation and give thought to issues of civil rights. Twice each year the occupation is remembered by sunrise ceremonies on Indigenous Peoples' Day (the second Monday in October) and Thanksgiving Day. Many American Indians return for these events to take part in prayers, dancing, and drumming. Further, the National Park Service collaborates with former occupiers and their families to restore and preserve the messages and political art produced during the occupation.

Native American protests by no means ended with the occupation of Alcatraz. In 1970, Native American activists occupied Mount Rushmore. Also that year they occupied Plymouth Rock in a "National Day of Mourning." In 1972 the Trail of Broken Treaties caravan arrived in Washington, D.C. Perhaps the most noteworthy, and newsworthy, event that took place in the wake of the occupation of Alcatraz was the seventy-one-day occupation of the town of Wounded Knee on the Pine Ridge reservation in South Dakota, the site of an infamous 1890 massacre of Lakota men, women, and children by U.S. Cavalry troops.

Explanation and Analysis of the Document

This widely reproduced photo serves to document the Native American occupation of Alcatraz Island. It depicts ten Native Americans, some in traditional garb, others in modern clothing, standing on a dock above an entryway. Richard Oakes is in the center of the front row. Behind them is a sign with the words "Indians Welcome" and "Indian Land." An existing sign that had been posted by the federal government reads "United States Property," but the occupiers altered the sign by writing the word "Indian" over the word "States." This photo, and numerous others like it, call viewers' attention to the grievances of Native Americans in the face of poverty, government indifference, and prejudice.

—Michael J. O'Neal

Questions for Further Study

1. What were the chief goals of the occupation of Alcatraz?

2. Why should the occupation of Alcatraz be remembered?

3. What impact did the occupation of Alcatraz have, both for Native Americans and for the larger U.S. population?

Further Reading

Books

Blansett, Kent. *A Journey to Freedom: Richard Oakes, Alcatraz, and the Red Power Movement*. New Haven: Yale University Press, 2018.

Fortunate Eagle, Adam. *Heart of the Rock: The Indian Invasion of Alcatraz*. Norman: University of Oklahoma Press, 2008.

Goldstein, Margaret J. *You Are Now on Indian Land: The American Indian Occupation of Alcatraz Island, California, 1969*. Minneapolis: Twenty-First Century Books, 2011.

Johnson, Troy R. *The American Indian Occupation of Alcatraz Island: Red Power and Self-Determination*. Lincoln: University of Nebraska Press, 2008.

Smith, Paul Chaat, and Robert Allen Warrior. *Like a Hurricane: The Indian Movement from Alcatraz to Wounded Knee*. New York: New Press, 1997.

Articles

Johnson, Troy. "The Occupation of Alcatraz Island: Roots of American Indian Activism." *Wicazo Sa Review* 10, no. 2 (Autumn 1994): 63–79.

Miranda, Carolina A. "Indigenous Tribes Took Over Alcatraz 51 Years Ago. Read the 'Holy Grail' of the Occupation." *Los Angeles Times*, November 19, 2020. https://www.latimes.com/entertainment-arts/story/2020-11-19/alcatraz-occupation-indigenous-tribes-autry-museum.

Treuer, David. "How a Native American Resistance Held Alcatraz for 18 Months." *New York Times*, November 20, 2019. https://www.nytimes.com/2019/11/20/us/native-american-occupation-alcatraz.html.

Websites

"Alcatraz Proclamation and Letter, 1969." History Is a Weapon. Accessed August 14, 2022. https://www.historyisaweapon.com/defcon1/alcatrazproclamationandletter.html.

Chavis, Charles L., Jr. "Today in History: 'We Hold the Rock': The Occupation of Alcatraz and the Native American Fight for Sovereignty in the Age of Fracture." PBS, November 16, 2021. https://www.pbs.org/wnet/exploring-hate/2021/11/16/today-in-history-occupation-of-alcatraz/.

Documentaries

Taking Alcatraz. John Ferry, producer, director, and editor. LilliMar Pictures, 2015. https://filmfreeway.com/423513.

United Farm Workers Strike Photograph

Author/Creator Unknown **Date** c. 1970 **Image Type** Photographs	**Significance** Depicts supporters of the United Farm Workers grape and lettuce strikes in California during a time of transition between labor victories of the late 1960s and the start of anti-union sentiment of the 1970s.

Overview

The California grape and lettuce strikes of 1970 were initiated by farm workers, many of whom were Filipino and Mexican immigrants. Workers used strikes and protests in an attempt to gain better wages and working conditions. The lettuce strike of 1970 came after a much longer and more successful campaign to raise wages for grape workers from 1965 to 1970. Workers on strike refused to pick grapes or lettuce, and farm owners lost the crops as a result. An even more effective way of protesting low wages was to enlist the American public in boycotting produce. In solidarity with the striking workers, many Americans refused to buy table grapes in the late 1960s, and labor organizers gave credit to the boycotts for bringing grape growers to the negotiating table. The attempt to replicate the same success with lettuce boycotts in 1970 was not as effective since the lettuce boycott was not taken up by the public to the same extent as the grape boycott.

The strikes won the attention and support of such well-known labor leaders as César Chávez and Dolores Huerta, who were able to rally thousands of workers, keep the movement nonviolent, and make the American public aware of the cause.

This image is significant because it shows a dimension of the 1960s counterculture that is often overlooked. As part of waning postwar abundance, increasing questioning of authority, and rising support for civil rights causes, farm workers found that they could execute a successful strike and boycott that could gain national attention.

About the Artist

The photographer is unknown.

Context

During World War II, the bracero program invited millions of Mexican guest workers into the United States to do the agricultural labor that drafted soldiers had left behind. The program lasted from 1942 to 1964. While men working as part of the program signed short-term contracts—sometimes a series of short-term contracts—that were supposed to end with their return to Mexico when the contract was complete, in

Document Image

Photograph showing supporters of the United Farm Workers strike in 1970
(Smithsonian)

reality, many men illegally sought other types of agricultural work that would pay better than the bracero contracts. The result was that millions of Mexican workers immigrated to the United States and remained permanently, but without the proper documentation allowing them to remain, and many took on a variety of agricultural jobs.

Racism and discrimination were prevalent within the bracero program, as the work offered through the program consisted of the types of jobs that many white Americans would not have chosen. Despite the necessity of these guest workers to keep the U.S. economy moving, many Mexican workers did not fully experience all that the program initially promised. The bracero program, therefore, provides an important backdrop and context for the workers strikes of the late 1960s; minority workers in California had never received fair treatment, wages, or working conditions, and this exploitation fueled the resolve of workers to strike until the growers agreed to their demands.

The agricultural workers' strikes were part of a larger culture of protest that was prevalent in American society in the 1960s and 1970s. Some of the factors that contributed to this atmosphere of protest were increased media attention on what was called the counterculture, characterized by defiance of authority and traditional norms; a growing distrust of government throughout Lyndon Johnson and Richard Nixon's presidencies as the United States became more deeply involved in Vietnam and continued an unpopular draft; and the widespread availability of televisions in American homes and only a few channels, ensuring that most TV-watching Americans were consuming similar programming. All of these factors meant that Americans in the late 1960s were more apt to pay attention to a workers' protest than they might have been before or after that time, and Americans in general would be aware of calls for a boycott on a specific item.

Another important contributing factor was the ongoing civil rights movement. Americans in the 1960s had grown accustomed to wrestling with issues related to race, discrimination, and inequality. While African Americans' struggles often form the main storyline when the history of the 1960s civil rights movement is discussed, other minority groups also appealed for equal rights, participated in marches and protests, and sought majority support. The farm workers in California recognized that the discrimination they faced was based, at least in part, on racism and racial inequality, and they sought to emphasize this component to the nation.

The strikes played an important role in the growing visibility and influence of civil rights activist César Chávez, who had been active in labor organizations in California during the 1960s and took a leadership role in the grape workers' strike and in the establishment of the United Farm Workers (UFW). Chávez led a 250-mile march, or *peregrinación*, from Delano, California, to Sacramento to bring attention to the grape workers' strike. Marches and other publicity tactics, combined with the boycotts, brought the grape workers' strike to a successful conclusion in 1970, with an agreement between the UFW and grape growers.

Explanation and Analysis of the Document

The grape strikes of 1965–1970 set up the grape and lettuce strikes of 1970. The grape strike began in 1965 when grape workers, who were mainly Filipino, stopped working and set up labor strikes in the San Joaquin Valley in California. The grape workers union was called the Agricultural Workers Organizing Committee (AWOC), but the union was small, and the strikers knew that if they did not gain support from other labor organizations, the strikes would end in a matter of weeks. The AWOC, therefore, appealed to a larger organization of Mexican American workers called the National Farm Workers Association (NFWA). The leaders of the NFWA were César Chávez and Dolores Huerta. Chávez and Huerta had founded the NFWA in 1962 to improve migrant workers' status and living conditions. Although the organization was still relatively new in 1965, Chávez and Huerta knew that farm owners often tried to pit one ethnic group against another, so they believed it was necessary for their largely Mexican American group to join in the Filipino grape workers' cause.

When the NFWA agreed to support the strike, the two unions merged into the United Farm Workers. The flag that the man on the right is holding in the photograph is a United Farm Workers flag. The symbol on the sign is a UFW symbol as well.

The UFW's success in the grape strikes led to conflict when lettuce workers went on strike in the summer of 1970. Drivers and packers who were members of the Teamsters Union—in some ways competitors of UFW—led the lettuce strike, which resulted in the price of iceberg lettuce tripling. The strike ended when growers gave the Teamsters Union, not the UFW, the authority to organize lettuce workers. Chávez and the UFW called for strikes and lettuce boycotts until the growers recognized the UFW's jurisdiction in organizing lettuce workers. Many agricultural workers joined the strike in solidarity to the UFW, making the 1970 strike the largest farm worker strike in U.S. history. Chávez himself was arrested, and the bitter disagreement between the unions lasted until March of 1971, when the Teamsters agreed to recognize the authority of the UFW to organize lettuce workers.

This image, therefore, represents a particular moment in the agricultural worker's movement. The UFW and Chávez attempted to set up boycotts of both lettuce and grapes, as the sign in the photograph indicates, but the boycotts were less successful than the earlier grape boycott as American attention to the issue had waned. The image, therefore, captures this transition between the victories of 1970 and the start of anti-union sentiment that would continue throughout the 1970s.

—Elizabeth George

Questions for Further Study

1. Although the photographer is unknown, who do you think is the intended audience for this image? Why?

2. How do the words and symbols on the sign in the photograph relate to the historical context of the farm workers' strikes?

3. If you were an American who had participated in earlier boycotts of table grapes in the 1960s, would you be inclined to boycott grapes (again) and lettuce in 1970? Why or why not?

Further Reading

Books

Feriss, Susan, Ricardo Sandoval, and Diana Hembree. *The Fight in the Fields: Cesar Chavez and the Farmworkers Movement.* New York: Houghton Mifflin Harcourt, 1998.

Flores, Lori A. *Grounds for Dreaming: Mexican Americans, Mexican Immigrants, and the California Farmworker Movement.* The Lamar Series in Western History. New Haven, CT: Yale University Press, 2016.

Websites

"Bracero Agreement." Immigration History website. https://immigrationhistory.org/item/bracero-agreement/.

Carpenter, Lindsay, and Maurice Weeks. "U.S. Farmworkers in California Campaign for Economic Justice (Grape Strike), 1965–70." Global Nonviolent Action Database. https://nvdatabase.swarthmore.edu/content/us-farmworkers-california-campaign-economic-justice-grape-strike-1965-70.

Photograph Of Vietnam War Destruction

Author/Creator
HJ/Associated Press

Date
1971

Image Type
Photographs

Significance
Depicts the U.S. military burning a home that had held Viet Cong ammunition, a tactic that led to resentment among the local population to the presence of American troops

Overview

Rural homes or villages would often be used by communist North Vietnamese or Viet Cong forces to hide munitions, weapons, or foodstuffs during the war. One response to this would be for the United States or South Vietnamese military to burn the home or village to destroy the supplies and to prevent the area from being used again. Over time, such tactics led to resentment among the local population to the presence of American troops.

From January 11 to January 29, 1971, U.S. marines conducted Operation Upshur Stream in the area around Da Nang. The goal was to prevent Viet Cong from utilizing the area to stage attacks on the U.S. air base at Da Nang. This required continuous reconnaissance missions and infantry patrols, with both artillery and air power playing major support roles. In this image, dated January 12 and taken just south of Da Nang in South Vietnam, a group of Vietnamese children watches their house burn just after a joint U.S.-South Vietnamese patrol set it ablaze after finding communist AK-47 ammunition.

About the Artist

The photographer is unknown. The photo is attributed only to HJ/Associated Press.

Context

By the mid-nineteenth century, France had absorbed Indochina into its global empire. Nguyễn Ái Quốc (later known by the pseudonym Ho Chi Minh), born in 1890, would become the leader of the Vietnamese independence movement. He formed the Vietminh in 1941 to fight the French colonial presence.

After World War II, Ho Chi Minh declared independence, but France soon returned. The First Indochina War began in 1946 after attempts at negotiations between the two sides failed. The United States supported France because of common anti-communist goals, and by May 1950 the United States began supplying France in its war. France lost in a surprising yet overwhelming victory for the Vietminh on May 7, 1954, at Dien Bien Phu, marking the end of the war.

The Geneva Conference, which was set to decide various problems in Asia, opened the next day. The

Document Image

Vietnamese children watch their house burn just after a joint U.S.-South Vietnamese patrol set it ablaze.
(AP Images)

conference resulted in the stipulation that Vietnam divide temporarily at the 17th parallel. Although Geneva had called for nationwide elections for president in 1956, the United States and South Vietnamese president Ngo Dinh Diệm were opposed, as it was clear that Ho Chi Minh would win. What had been a temporary partition was now a hard border.

In the spring of 1963, Buddhist groups began a series of demonstrations in response to the killing of eight monks by Diệm's forces. As protests grew, Diệm rejected compromise and responded with force. This culminated in monk Thich Quang Duc committing self-immolation. In response, South Vietnamese special forces raided temples and arrested monks. Frustrated, several generals began to quietly plot against Diệm, who was assassinated on November 2. The United States supported this action.

In late July 1964, the USS *Maddox* sailed into the Gulf of Tonkin, joined by the *Turner Joy*. The two supported covert South Vietnamese raids on North Vietnamese islands. On August 2, the *Maddox* was attacked by North Vietnamese patrol boats. On August 4, a second attack was said to have occurred, although it was later revealed never to have happened. In retaliation for the supposed attacks, the United States bombed North Vietnam, and the Gulf of Tonkin resolution was rushed through Congress. This was not a declaration of war but instead gave the president full authority for action in Southeast Asia.

Operation Rolling Thunder was a massive bombing campaign of the North that lasted for several years. General William Westmoreland, commander of Military Assistance Command, Vietnam (MACV) requested troops to support and defend the American airfields, and on March 8, 1965, 3,500 marines landed at Danang. The war put a massive strain on the U.S. armed forces, and by late 1967, almost 500,000 American soldiers were in Vietnam.

Up to this point in the war, a cease-fire was observed during Tet, the Vietnamese lunar New Year. That changed in 1968. The Tet Offensive was a massive North Vietnamese offensive against cities in South Vietnam. Overall, the Tet Offensive was a military failure for the North, but a political victory. For many Americans, this was proof that the war was not close to an end.

Peace talks begin soon after. Sides did get close as the November presidential election neared, but a breakthrough did not materialize. Republican candidate Richard Nixon did not help matters by urging, through back channels, South Vietnamese president Thieu to refrain from signing an agreement, promising that he would secure a better deal under a Nixon administration. The public, however, was not privy to that electoral subterfuge, and Nixon won close election over Vice President Hubert Humphry.

In July 1969, Nixon announced Vietnamization, his plan to end the war. Vietnamization called for a gradual reduction in American forces, to be replaced with South Vietnamese troops. In April 1970, Nixon announced the expansion of the war into Cambodia, ostensibly to locate and eliminate communist headquarters. Protests peaked in the aftermath, and the nation was witness to tragedy when national guardsmen killed four protesting students at Kent State University and two at Jackson State.

The so-called Christmas Bombings, the heaviest of the war, commenced on December 18, 1972. Half a million civilians evacuated Hanoi during this massive B-52 bombing run that lasted 11 days. A reported 1,318 civilians in Hanoi died. After the bombing, negotiations resumed, and in January an agreement was announced. It was almost identical to the previous version. Prisoners of war were released, and American troops would leave.

Even though U.S. troops were no longer in Vietnam, the war soon reignited. Two years later, North Vietnamese tanks rolled into Hanoi, and the presidential palace was sacked. America's longest war up to that point ended on April 30, 1975. Vietnam once again became one nation, and the American mission of supporting an independent capitalist state in the South had failed.

Explanation and Analysis of the Document

Events and images such as this were not uncommon during the war. While ostensibly there to protect the local population from communist insurgents, U.S. soldiers were ordered to destroy homes and villages where communists or their supplies were hidden, and such tactics naturally fostered resentment and hostility toward the soldiers. "Search and destroy" missions such as the one pictured would be categorized as a success in that weapons were confiscated or destroyed, but in the long run they ran counter to the goal of winning the "hearts and minds" of the Vietnamese population.

The tragedy at My Lai is in many ways connected to these tensions. On March 16, 1968, U.S. soldiers massacred over 500 civilians in a village after receiving poor intelligence about an expected enemy battalion in the area. Soldiers, frustrated with what they viewed as a hostile Vietnamese population, took out their aggression on women, children, and the elderly in one of the great catastrophes of the war. Following orders from superior officers, soldiers shot at random, destroyed crops and animals, and burned buildings. Only one man, Lieutenant William Calley, was convicted, serving three years in house arrest.

In this image, we see a U.S. Marine standing with four children, one of them an infant. It is not clear where the adult family members of the children might be. If a mother or father was a suspected communist, they would be taken and interrogated, perhaps jailed. The marine, his gun held at his side, has likely witnessed similar scenes before. Perhaps he knows some phrases in Vietnamese, but there is likely a language barrier. The children would be confused and scared, unsure what might happen next.

—Matthew Jagel

Questions for Further Study

1. Winning the "hearts and minds" of the local population was the official policy of the United States and was of paramount importance to the American mission in Vietnam. Would events like the one depicted in this photograph help that mission or work against it? Please explain.

2. "Search and destroy" missions were frequently successful in yielding a stash of communist weapons or ammunition. Why might a rural Vietnamese village store such provisions if its destruction could be the result?

3. American soldiers often lamented that they could not differentiate between civilians and enemy soldiers. How does this image fit into that narrative? What does the image tell us about the nature of the war in Vietnam?

Further Reading

Books

Herring, George C. *America's Longest War: The United States and Vietnam, 1950–1975*, 4th ed. New York: McGraw-Hill, 2002.

Karnow, Stanley. *Vietnam: A History*, 2nd ed. New York: Penguin Books, 1997.

Logevall, Fredrik. *Choosing War: The Lost Chance for Peace and the Escalation of War in Vietnam*. Berkeley: University of California Press, 2001.

Young, Marilyn B. *The Vietnam Wars: 1945–1990*. New York: HarperPerennial, 1991.

Websites

"Vietnam War." National Archives. Accessed August 26, 2022. https://www.archives.gov/research/vietnam-war.

"Virtual Vietnam Archive." The Vietnam Center & Sam Johnson Vietnam Archive, Texas Tech University. Accessed August 26, 2022. https://www.vietnam.ttu.edu/virtualarchive/.

Documentaries

Hearts and Minds. Peter Davis, director. BBS Productions, 1974.

Vietnam: A Television History. Judith Vecchione, Austin Hoyt, Martin Smith, and Bruce Palling, directors. WGBH Boston, 1983.

The Vietnam War. Ken Burns and Lynn Novick, directors. PBS Distribution, 2017.

Herbert Block: "National Security Blanket" Cartoon

Author/Creator Herblock (Herbert Block)	**Image Type** Cartoons
Date 1973	**Significance** Called attention to the use of national security to cover up illegal activities by President Richard Nixon

Overview

"National Security Blanket" is an example of an American political cartoon, a type of editorial found in newspapers. These works of art, usually a single drawn panel, provide the cartoonist's views on events, people, laws, and the like in a form more readily accessible than an editorial article. They are usually found on the newspaper's editorial pages.

This particular cartoon is about the growing Watergate scandal that was engulfing the presidency of Richard Nixon in 1973 and Nixon's attempts to cover up his behavior by asserting that national security concerns prevented him from cooperating with investigators. "Watergate" is the generic name given to the multitude of illegal, unethical, and extralegal activities undertaken by Richard Nixon, the White House staff, and the Committee to Re-elect the President (CREEP) during the 1972 election campaign. Nixon's men engaged in a series of illegal and unethical actions, including, among several examples, falsifying State Department cables to implicate former President John Kennedy in the assassination of the president of South Vietnam in 1963, playing dirty tricks on the Democratic candidates for the White House in 1972, and hiring burglars to steal documents and bug the offices of the Democratic National Committee in the Watergate office complex. This last action resulted in the arrest of the burglars and their handlers from CREEP. Nixon and his team then engaged in a massive cover-up, which succeeded through the end of 1972, allowing Nixon to win a landslide reelection victory.

In 1973, the cover-up unraveled thanks to investigations by the Senate, a grand jury, and investigative reporters. As the year progressed, more of Nixon's men began looking to save themselves and cooperated with investigators, revealing the extent of illegal activities. Ultimately, several of Nixon's men would be jailed, and Nixon would resign the presidency on August 9, 1974, to avoid being impeached and removed from office.

About the Artist

Herbert Lawrence Block was a four-time Pulitzer Prize–winning political cartoonist, best known for his work at the *Washington Post* from 1946 to 2001. Working under the pen name Herblock, he was known for his sharp commentary and insights into the major issues and political leaders of the day.

Document Image

The "National Security Blanket" cartoon by Herblock
(Library of Congress)

Block began his career as a cartoonist for the *Chicago Daily News* from 1929 to 1943, winning his first Pulitzer Prize in 1942. He was drafted into the U.S. Army in 1943 and wrote dispatches and drew cartoons for military publications. After discharge he was hired by the *Washington Post*, where he spent the next fifty-five years skewering leaders of both parties, editorializing on major issues, and serving as a sharp commentator on American politics. Block was unafraid to challenge the powerful, and his cartoons criticizing McCarthyism, a term he is often credited with coining, earned his second Pulitzer in 1954. Herblock was known to be a liberal commentator, with cartoons attacking not only McCarthyism but racism, abuse of power, and the growing threat of nuclear weapons.

Richard Nixon was a frequent target of Herblock's work, which most famously portrayed Nixon crawling out of a sewer in a cartoon in 1954, an image that caused Nixon to cancel his subscription to the *Post*. Herblock's series of cartoons about the Watergate scandal brought his third Pulitzer in 1973 and included the cartoon depicted here.

Block continued to contribute his work until August 2001, drawing cartoons about thirteen presidents across seventy-two years of work. Block died of pneumonia on October 7, 2001, at the age of ninety-one.

Context

In 1973, the nation was increasingly gripped by the revelations about what became known as the Watergate scandal. The name of the scandal came from the arrest of a team of burglars who were caught inside the offices of the Democratic National Committee at the Watergate office complex on the night of June 17, 1972. It quickly became apparent that these men were looking to steal documents, tap phones, and otherwise gather intelligence on the Democrats' plans for the 1972 election campaign. The five men captured in the building, along with their immediate supervisors, G. Gordon Liddy and E. Howard Hunt, were indicted for their actions in September. Initially, the men claimed that they had acted on their own without the knowledge of their superiors, a story that held up for the rest of the year.

In fact, the men had received approval and funding for their operation from CREEP, and the intelligence they gathered was reported to the president and his inner circle of advisors. These men, including President Nixon, chief of staff H. R. Haldeman, John Ehrlichman, Charles Colson, and John Dean conspired to cover up White House involvement with the Watergate break-in and several other questionable activities undertaken by the administration in pursuit of Nixon's reelection. These actions included infiltrating the staffs of most of the candidates seeking the Democrats' nomination for the presidency, engaging in an extensive dirty tricks operation to turn the Democrats against each other, illegally pressuring businesses to donate cash secretly to CREEP, paying hush money to the Watergate defendants, and perjury (lying under oath) to the grand jury and in court to maintain the cover-up.

In response, the Senate created a special bipartisan committee to investigate the 1972 campaign. Additionally, the judge overseeing the trial of the Watergate burglars, John Sirica, pressured the defendants to cooperate with the committee and with a new grand jury. Over the course of the year, a number of Nixon administration officials agreed to cooperate, revealing the extent of the actions undertaken by Nixon and his men, the cover-up, and a series of other illegal or questionably legal actions conducted by or at the behest of Nixon and his advisors. Among other things, it was revealed that Nixon had knowledge of the burglars' actions, participated in the paying of hush money, and consistently lied to the public about his actions. It was also revealed that Nixon had installed recording devices in all of his offices and on his phones, so that all of his conversations from February 1971 to June 1973 were recorded and could be used to demonstrate whether Nixon or his accusers were telling the truth. Nixon refuse to turn over the tapes to the Senate committee, the grand jury, or the special prosecutor who was appointed to investigates the matter, claiming executive privilege (the right of the president to have private discussions with aides) and citing national security concerns.

Ultimately, in 1974, Nixon was forced to hand over the tapes by the Supreme Court. The tapes proved Nixon's guilt, and rather than be impeached and removed by Congress, he resigned the presidency.

Explanation and Analysis of the Document

The major image in the cartoon and the title indicate the cartoon's theme. Specifically, President Richard

Nixon is hiding behind the flag, in this case in the form of citing the need to protect national security as justification for his refusal to talk about any of the activities he and his administration were being accused of in 1973. Due to the Cold War with the Soviet Union, Americans grew accustomed to the government citing national security as the reason for maintaining secrets or undertaking actions in the struggle against the communists. For example, President John Kennedy kept secret the presence of Soviet missiles in Cuba for a full week in October 1962 to have time to formulate an appropriate response. His ensuing "success" in what became known as the Cuban Missile Crisis reinforced the idea that the government could justifiably keep secrets from the public for the good of national security.

In this case, however, cartoonist Herblock is attacking the idea that the actions of Nixon and his administration qualify for the protection of national security. In the background of the cartoon, Herblock references several revelations about the actions of the Committee to Re-elect the President (CREEP) and the White House staff that had come to light thanks to the investigations undertaken by the Senate, the grand jury, and reporters. Some of Nixon's aides had testified regarding these activities before the Senate Watergate committee.

In the filing cabinet behind Nixon are three files. The first, labeled "Fake Cables," involved Nixon aide Charles Colson who attempted to pass a phony top-secret State Department cable that he had altered to implicate President Kennedy in the assassination of South Vietnamese president Ngo Dinh Diem. The file labeled "Forged Letters" involved the dirty tricks operation conducted against the Democrats in 1972, specifically the forgery of a letter attributed to Senator Edmund Muskie that cost him the New Hampshire primary.

The file labeled "Stolen Files" is a direct reference to the Watergate break-in, as are the gloves and mask on the floor at Nixon's feet and the burglar's tools in the bag to Nixon's right. The tape recorder and headphones in front of Nixon are a reference to the bugs and recording devices installed by the burglars at the Democratic national headquarters. The roll of tape next to the recorder is a reference to how the burglars were caught. A security guard at the office building saw that the door leading to the Democrats' offices had been held open by a piece of duct tape to prevent it from locking. The guard removed the tape; when he returned a short time later, he found that the tape had been replaced, so he called the police.

The satchel full of cash labeled "Mexico" is a reference to hush money that *Washington Post* reporters Bob Woodward and Carl Bernstein had written about in 1972. The Watergate burglars had in their possession several 100-dollar bills sequentially numbered; Woodward and Bernstein discovered that the money had come from a campaign contribution to CREEP that had been laundered through a bank in Mexico. The other satchel of money and the safe labeled "Political Sabotage Stash" referred to the existence of a sizeable fund of campaign cash that at the time was alleged to be used for the dirty tricks' operations and the break-in.

Nixon refused to cooperate with investigators, refusing to answer questions or turn over any documents. He claimed any cooperation with investigators regarding matters discussed with his aides would be a threat to national security, and thus he would not cooperate. Nixon also cited his belief that all of his conversations with his aides about any topic were protected by the doctrine of executive privilege. Herblock focused on the national security claims in this cartoon, both because they were easier for his readers to understand and because the claim was so out of line with the matters under investigation. Herblock is mocking the idea that illegal activities conducted with the sole purpose of reelecting Richard Nixon are somehow related to the security of the United States. In this way he is challenging readers to dig deeper into the facts and question Nixon's use of national security as justification for his actions and refusal to cooperate with investigators.

—Richard M. Filipink

Questions for Further Study

1. What activities conducted by the Nixon administration is the artist looking to reveal in this cartoon?

2. What does this image tell us about the artist's view of Nixon's claim that his actions are protected by national security concerns?

3. What does this document tell us about the extent of the Watergate scandal?

Further Reading

Books

Block, Herbert. *Herblock Special Report*. New York: Norton, 1974.

Dudley, William. *Watergate: Examining Issues through Political Cartoons*. San Diego: Greenhaven, 2002.

Olson, Keith W. *Watergate: The Presidential Scandal That Shook America*. Lawrence: University Press of Kansas, 2003.

Websites

"Herblock's History: Political Cartoons from the Crash to the Millennium." Online Exhibition, Library of Congress. https://www.loc.gov/exhibits/herblocks-history/index.html.

"REMEMBER WOUNDED KNEE" PATCH

AUTHOR/CREATOR
American Indian Movement (AIM)

DATE
1973

IMAGE TYPE
ARTIFACTS

SIGNIFICANCE
Draws attention to the tragic massacre at Wounded Knee Creek in South Dakota in 1890 and to the occupation of Wounded Knee by American Indian Movement activists in 1973

Overview

Two separate but related historical events are relevant to an understanding of the image of this patch. The earlier historical event took place in December 1890 when U.S. Cavalry troops massacred some 300 Lakota men, women, and children at Wounded Knee Creek, on the Pine Ridge reservation in South Dakota. The massacre at Wounded Knee was one of the worst atrocities committed against Native Americans in the history of the troubled relations between the tribes and the federal government. The later historical event took place in 1973, when some 200 Oglala Lakota, members of the American Indian Movement (AIM), occupied the town of Wounded Knee, the site of the 1890 massacre. The siege was a protest against the U.S. government's treatment of Native Americans, including its abrogation of treaties and seizure of Native lands. The siege lasted seventy-one days, with the area cordoned off by the U.S. Marshals Service, the Federal Bureau of Investigation (FBI), and other law-enforcement agencies. The siege attracted widespread media attention and galvanized Native Americans throughout the country to fight for just treatment.

About the Artist

The patch was created by AIM, or the American Indian Movement, in connection with the siege at Wounded Knee in 1973. AIM traces its origins back to 1968 when 200 members of the Native American community attended a meeting in Minneapolis called by Native American activists led by George Mitchell, Dennis Banks, and Clyde Bellecourt. These men had been frustrated by decades of federal policies with regard to Native Americans. These and other AIM leaders spoke out against high unemployment, slum housing on the reservations, and racist treatment. They later fought to enforce treaty rights and to reclaim tribal land. Perhaps the most famous instance of AIM's militancy was its occupation of Alcatraz Island from late 1969 to mid-1971, when the activists argued that the island belonged to Native Americans. AIM also advocated on behalf of Native Americans in the cities, who suffered from poverty and illness; indeed, most of AIM's membership consisted of Native Americans from urban areas. AIM opened the K–12 Heart of the Earth Survival School in 1972 in Minneapolis, based on the conviction that Native children should be educated in their own communities. Also in 1972, AIM organized the Trail of Broken Treaties march on Washington, D.C., where they occupied the Bureau of Indian Affairs

Document Image

The "Remember Wounded Knee" patch
(Minnesota Historical Society)

in protest. Because of its revolutionary zeal, AIM attracted the attention of the FBI, which tried to suppress the movement. The actions of the FBI sowed the seeds of the 1973 standoff at Wounded Knee.

Context

The 1960s and early 1970s were a time of increased militancy and activism on the part of Native Americans, which culminated in late February 1973, when the American Indian Movement launched a seventy-one-day occupation of the town of Wounded Knee, South Dakota, on the Pine Ridge reservation. What sparked the occupation was the fatal stabbing of a Lakota man, Wesley Bad Heart Bull, in Buffalo Gap. A white man was arrested and pleaded guilty to second-degree manslaughter but was released one day later. Activists clashed with police during a protest at the county courthouse in Custer, South Dakota, where Wesley had been held. Wesley's mother was later found guilty of assaulting a police officer during the melee.

Adding to the grievances of Native Americans in South Dakota was the belief that the tribal chair of the Pine Ridge reservation, Richard Wilson, governed like a dictator—that he bullied and intimidated tribal members by means of a private army, called Guardians of the Oglala Nation, or GOONs, and appointed cronies and relatives to positions of authority. Angry tribal members were unsuccessful in their efforts to oust Wilson, and the federal government was of no help, so they turned to AIM for help, despite AIM's reputation for staging contentious and sometimes violent protests. Wilson sought the help of the U.S. Marshals Service to remove AIM activists from the reservation. Then in February 1973, AIM leaders Dennis Banks, Russell Means, and several hundred AIM members from numerous tribes descended on the town. They fortified the town, took a number of people hostage, and looted a grocery store—provocative gestures intended to draw the attention of the public and of federal authorities.

They did. The FBI, state and federal law enforcement, and some of Wilson's GOONs surrounded the town. Surrounding roads were blocked by armored vehicles. As snipers assumed positions and aircraft circled overhead, the occupiers prepared for an assault. Meanwhile, the media gathered to document the tense standoff, and in the days and weeks that followed, the siege attracted international attention. At the Academy Awards ceremony that year, Marlon Brando, who won the award for best actor, asked a Native American woman to speak on his behalf in declining the award in protest. Tensions at Wounded Knee grew after two Native American men were fatally shot by snipers and several others were wounded.

The FBI was eager to avoid any kind of bloody confrontation, particularly with television cameras rolling, so the agency opened a dialogue with the protestors and promised to address their grievances, in particular the murders of Native Americans and the corruption of Wilson. In exchange, AIM agreed to end the siege. In the aftermath, Banks and Means were indicted for conspiracy and assault, but a federal judge dismissed the case. The end of the siege, however, did not entirely end the tensions at Pine Ridge. Wilson was narrowly reelected as tribal chairman, but the election was marred by beatings, arson, and even murders. After two undercover FBI agents were murdered in 1975 on the Pine Ridge reservation, a member of AIM, Leonard Peltier, was convicted of the slayings and sentenced to life in prison.

AIM was a polarizing organization. Some Native Americans were opposed to the organization's lawlessness, but many others felt that AIM played a useful role in giving Native Americans a voice and that its activities led to the rediscovery of Native American heritage and culture. Further, AIM galvanized Native tribes to seek more control over their resources, government, and education, and by the 1980s, some progress was being made on those issues. Some tribes even regained federal recognition.

The selection of Wounded Knee on the Pine Ridge reservation as a place to make a stand was by no means accidental or coincidental, for it reminded Americans of the massacre that had taken place at Wounded Knee on December 29, 1890, when 500 U.S. cavalrymen slaughtered upwards of 300 Lakota men, women, and children. Incredibly, twenty of the soldiers received the Medal of Honor for their actions at Wounded Knee. The massacre was a reaction against a religious movement among the Plains Indians called the Ghost Dance. This movement, based on the teachings of a Paiute medicine man that an upheaval would lead to the annihilation of white men and the resurgence of Native Americans, spread among the Native tribes in the West starting in the 1870s. The movement had particular significance for the Lakota of North and

South Dakota, who had lost more than 58 million acres of land over the previous decades and who were forced onto five separate reservations, including Pine Ridge. The belief among Ghost Dance adherents was that songs and ceremonies would bring about the conflagration and the restoration of their land. While performing the ceremonies, which involved repetitive songs and mass dances, many Lakota wore special shirts thought to be bulletproof, and many entered a hypnotic state. One of the Ghost Dance's most prominent adherents was Chief Sitting Bull, the leader of the Native American party that had defeated General George Custer at the Battle of Little Bighorn in 1876. Chief Sitting Bull was technically a prisoner, but he had been allowed to travel with Buffalo Bill's Wild West show in 1885.

The U.S. Army was convinced that the Ghost Dance posed a threat. Accordingly, the Army banned all Ghost Dance ceremonies on the reservations. In December 1890, the Army began assembling troops in the region. Their plan was to arrest Sitting Bull, now back in confinement at the Standing Rock reservation, which straddled North and South Dakota. On December 15, 1890, a number of Native police officers employed by the local Indian Agency tried to arrest Sitting Bull. He resisted, and in the skirmish that ensued, Sitting Bull was shot and killed. His followers fled, linked up with his half-brother, Chief Spotted Elk, and headed for Pine Ridge, where they hoped to find refuge. Along the way, they encountered an Army contingent that instructed them to make camp at Wounded Knee Creek.

Overnight, the soldiers surrounded the encampment. The next morning, the troops, under the command of Colonel James W. Forsyth, ordered the Native Americans to lay down their arms. In response, some began to perform the Ghost Dance. Believing that the Ghost Dance was a prelude to war, the soldiers opened fire, some with artillery guns. They chased down those who tried to flee and shot them. Three days later, the Army flung the bodies of the dead Lakota into a mass grave, but not before saving their Ghost Dance garb as souvenirs. The reaction of South Dakota newspaperman L. Frank Baum, who would go on to write *The Wonderful Wizard of Oz*, was typical of reactions in many of the nation's newspapers: "We had better, in order to protect our civilization . . . wipe these untamed and untamable creatures from the earth."

The massacre at Wounded Knee, the last major skirmish in the Indian Wars of the nineteenth century, later became a rallying point for Native Americans, especially after the 1971 publication of Dee Brown's best-selling book, *Bury My Heart at Wounded Knee*. In 1990, the U.S. Congress formally apologized for the massacre. Calls to rescind the Medals of Honor given to the soldiers grew. In 2021 the South Dakota State Senate passed a bill that urged Congress to open an official inquiry into the medals, and members of Congress urged President Joe Biden to revoke the medals.

Explanation and Analysis of the Document

The image is of a patch, such as a person might sew onto a shirt or jacket. It consists of an outer ring, bordered in black, with the words "American Indian Movement." Inside this ring is a second ring, bordered in red, with the words "Remember Wounded Knee" and two dates. One is 1890, the year in which the massacre at Wounded Knee took place; the other is 1973, the year in which AIM protestors occupied the town of Wounded Knee and engaged in a standoff with law enforcement. In the center of the patch is a stylized red image of the head of a Native American. The image includes what appear to be two feathers extending from the head but on closer examination can also be seen as two fingers of a hand in a V configuration, the common symbol of "victory."

—Michael J. O'Neal

Questions for Further Study

1. What historical events does the patch commemorate?

2. Why was the town of Wounded Knee selected as the site of the 1973 protest?

3. How effective was the siege in 1973 at drawing public attention to the plight of Native Americans?

Further Reading

Books

Bancroft, Dick, and Laura Waterman Wittstock. *We Are Still Here: A Photographic History of the American Indian Movement.* St. Paul: Minnesota Historical Society Press, 2013.

Banks, Dennis, and Richard Erdoes. *Ojibwa Warrior: Dennis Banks and the Rise of the American Indian Movement.* Norman: University of Oklahoma Press, 2005.

Brown, Dee. *Bury My Heart at Wounded Knee.* New York: Holt, Rinehart and Winston, 1971.

Greene, Jerome A. *American Carnage: Wounded Knee, 1890.* Norman: University of Oklahoma Press, 2014.

Magnuson, Stew. *Wounded Knee 1973: Still Bleeding: The American Indian Movement, the FBI, and Their Fight to Bury the Sins of the Past.* Arlington, VA: Court Bridge Publishing, 2013.

Matthiessen, Peter. *In the Spirit of Crazy Horse: The Story of Leonard Peltier and the FBI's War on the American Indian Movement.* New York: Penguin, 1992.

Nichols, Roger L. *Massacring Indians: From Horseshoe Bend to Wounded Knee.* Norman: University of Oklahoma Press, 2021.

Websites

Blakemore, Erin. "What Really Happened at Wounded Knee, the Site of a Historic Massacre." *National Geographic*, November 19, 2021. https://www.nationalgeographic.com/history/article/what-really-happened-at-wounded-knee-the-site-of-a-historic-massacre.

Chertoff, Emily. "Occupy Wounded Knee: A 71-Day Siege and a Forgotten Civil Rights Movement." *Atlantic*, October 23, 2012. https://www.theatlantic.com/national/archive/2012/10/occupy-wounded-knee-a-71-day-siege-and-a-forgotten-civil-rights-movement/263998/.

"Primary Sources: Native Americans—American Indians: Wounded Knee Massacre." Christopher Newport University. https://cnu.libguides.com/c.php?g=23203&p=137845.

"Account Given by Indians of the Fight at Wounded Knee Creek, South Dakota, September 29, 1890." *Report of the Commissioner of Indian Affairs* 1 (1891): 179–81. http://images.library.wisc.edu/History/EFacs/CommRep/AnnRep91p1/reference/history.annrep91p1.i0004.pdf.

Documentaries

We Shall Remain. PBS, 2009. https://www.pbs.org/wgbh/americanexperience/films/weshallremain/.

Marty Lederhandler: Photograph Of Gasoline Rationing

Author/Creator
Marty Lederhandler

Date
1973

Image Type
Photographs

Significance
Long lines of cars waiting to buy gas in New York City during the 1973–74 oil crisis, demonstrating America's reliance on foreign oil and the potential costs of the country's interventions in foreign affairs

Overview

This photograph from December 23, 1973, captures a common sight in the 1970s—cars lined up to buy gas, which was both expensive and in short supply.

The gas shortage was linked to the oil crisis that began in 1973 when the United States decided to support its ally Israel in the Yom Kippur War against Egypt and Syria, which were in turn backed by the Soviet Union. The Cold War backdrop to the action in the Middle East solidified American resolve to support Israel, even after Arabian members of the Organization of Petroleum Exporting Companies (OPEC) enacted an oil embargo against the United States. Because the United States imported one-third of its oil from Arab nations, the embargo set off an oil crisis. The oil crisis, in turn, was the beginning of a prolonged downturn in the U.S. economy.

Americans had been accustomed to spending less than forty cents per gallon for gas, and they were shocked when gas quickly doubled in price in 1973. Even for those willing to pay, OPEC members' refusal to export to the United States upended supply chains, leading to shortages.

As gas shortages continued to crop up during the 1970s, leaders started to increase investments in researching and developing alternative energy sources and making cars more fuel efficient. To reduce fuel consumption, a national standard speed limit of fifty-five miles per hour was enforced on all U.S. highways.

The oil crisis also sparked a new movement to conserve energy in homes and businesses. The calls to be more energy aware intersected with the growing environmental movement, represented by the first national celebration of Earth Day on April 22, 1970.

About the Artist

Marty Lederhandler (1917–2010) was a photographer for the Associated Press (AP). In a career spanning sixty-six years, he captured many significant events and personalities in the twentieth century. He began his career with AP in 1936. When World War II began, he was drafted and served as a U.S. Army Signal Corp photographer, recording the D-Day invasion in 1944. Lederhandler photographed every U.S. president from

Document Image

Cars lined up in 1973 waiting to buy gasoline
(AP Images)

Herbert Hoover to Bill Clinton and captured many other world leaders, particularly through his assignments at the United Nations.

The photograph of cars lined up to buy gas in 1973 was taken in New York City. Decades later, Lederhandler was at the AP offices in New York City and witnessed the 9/11 terrorist attacks on the World Trade Center. He photographed the twin towers burning in the background of the Empire State Building. The experience of taking that iconic photograph spurred his decision to retire at age eighty-four.

Context

The oil crisis and ensuing gas shortages hit Americans especially hard within the context of the 1970s economy. By the early 1970s, it was clear that the postwar economic boom, which had fueled the development of suburbs, interstate highways, and a consumption mindset, was over. In its place, inflation was rising and wages were stagnant. These conditions led to the coining of a new term—stagflation—to represent the particularities of the 1970s economy.

At the same time, President Richard Nixon, after a successful first term marked by diplomatic triumphs in the Cold War, was seeing both his presidency and his popularity unravel as he attempted to end U.S. involvement in Vietnam and navigate the Watergate scandal that would ultimately lead to his resignation. Amid all the political variabilities, it was the energy crisis that had the most direct effect on average Americans, hitting them in their wallets and causing a feeling of panic as they waited in long lines to buy fuel. The growing sense that Americans couldn't trust the president or the government led to less confidence that leaders were choosing the correct path through the energy crisis.

It didn't help consumer confidence that the oil crisis was linked to political upheavals in the Middle East; Americans already felt stretched thin through involvement in Vietnam and covert action around the globe. The so-called "Arab oil sheiks" who seemed intent on harming regular Americans were viewed to be as shadowy as any enemy from the Soviet bloc. As in the rest of the Cold War, leaders' desires to maintain the balance of power and contain Soviet influence directed foreign policy. When Israel was at a disadvantage in the early days of the Yom Kippur War, the United States stepped in with an airlift of military supplies, named Operation Nickel Grass, in mid-October 1973. The influx of supplies gave the Israelis the power they needed to negotiate a favorable ceasefire. The cost, however, was OPEC's oil embargo against the United States and other Western nations.

The memory of the 1973 oil crisis contributed to additional fuel shortages in 1978 and 1979. The Iranian Revolution led to decreased oil output from Iran and, more potently, led to fears of a repeat of 1973. Fears of scarcity led Americans once again to line up at the pump and hoard fuel, which led to shortages. The 1978 crisis paved the way for Ronald Reagan to ask Americans, "Are you better off than you were four years ago?" when he ran for president in 1980 and opened the door for Reagan's landslide victory over President Jimmy Carter.

Explanation and Analysis of the Document

This black and white image taken from above shows the long lines at a small gas station in New York City in December 1973. Gas stations used a variety of methods to ration gas. Some used a flag system: green meant the station had gas, yellow meant gas was being rationed, and red meant no gas was available. Americans would drive around town looking for available gas; sometimes they only were able to purchase enough to replenish what they had used while searching. Other people parked in long lines at gas stations, either waiting for the station to open or hoping to be first in line when the station was resupplied.

The viewer cannot see the license plates on the cars, but in some locations customers could only purchase gas on odd or even days, according to license plate number. While these methods may have been necessary to try to cut down on cars lining up at gas stations, they also served to increase panic and a scarcity mindset among Americans.

We can also notice that all of the vehicles appear to be powerful and heavy. Today, we would think of these cars as "gas guzzlers." When the 1960s-era cars in the photograph were built, fuel economy was not important to consumers. One outcome of the gas shortages was that Americans began to pay more attention to their cars' miles per gallon (mpg)—the number of miles they could travel using one gallon of gas—and the standard mpg for cars was raised across the industry.

The photograph emphasizes the number of cars lined up to buy gas and the disruption that searching for scarce fuel caused. The roads surrounding the gas station are blocked by waiting cars, and the scene illustrates the economic slowdown and frustration that many Americans experienced in the 1970s. The photograph does not give any indication of the foreign policy battles that served as the backdrop to the oil crisis, and this lack of a wider context is also appropriate in representing how Americans experienced the financial strain without the galvanizing morale boost of a common cause that they could feel good about or at least rally around. The Cold War had been a constant in American life for over two decades by this point; the Vietnam War had lasted almost as long, and Americans were tired of making sacrifices for causes with ambiguous outcomes.

—Elizabeth George

Questions for Further Study

1. Photographs like this one appeared in newspapers across the country. If you were an American in 1973, how would seeing frequent depictions of gas shortages influence your feelings about politics and the economy?

2. How was the local economy in the United States affected by Cold War politics?

3. The year 1973 saw the ending of U.S. involvement in Vietnam, the investigations into Watergate, and the oil crisis. How would Americans perceive the trustworthiness of the government by the end of 1973? Why?

Further Reading

Books

Jacobs, Meg. *Panic at the Pump: The Energy Crisis and the Transformation of American Politics in the 1970s.* New York: Hill and Wang, 2016.

Merrill, Karen R. *The Oil Crisis of 1973–1974: A Brief History with Documents.* Boston: Bedford/St. Martin's, 2007.

Websites

"Oil Shock of 1973–74." Federal Reserve History. https://www.federalreservehistory.org/essays/oil-shock-of-1973-74.

"Oil Shock of 1978–79." Federal Reserve History. https://www.federalreservehistory.org/essays/oil-shock-of-1978-79.

"Operation Nickel Grass: Turning Point of the Yom Kippur War." Nixon Foundation. https://www.nixonfoundation.org/2014/10/operation-nickel-grass-turning-point-yom-kippur-war/.

"The 1973 Arab-Israeli War." Office of the Historian, Foreign Service Institute, United States Department of State. https://history.state.gov/milestones/1969-1976/arab-israeli-war-1973.

Pyle, Richard. "Marty Lederhandler, AP Lensman for 66 Years, Dies." *San Diego Union-Tribune*, March 26, 2010. https://www.sandiegouniontribune.com/sdut-marty-lederhandler-ap-lensman-for-66-years-dies-2010mar26-story.html.

Photograph Of Anti-Busing Rally In Boston

Author/Creator Spencer Grant	**Image Type** Photographs
Date 1975	**Significance** Illustrates the strong opposition to the desegregation of Boston-area schools through busing

Overview

This photograph shows protestors at a 1975 rally in Thomas Park in South Boston. The apparently all white protestors were gathered at the rally to express their dissatisfaction with the decision to integrate Boston's public schools by busing some students to schools outside their home districts to even out the ratios of Black students to white students in each school. Throughout the 1974–75 school year, anti-integration protestors rallied at schools and public locations to protest the new policies.

Busing students among neighborhoods was a result of Federal Judge Wendell Arthur Garrity Jr.'s decision in *Morgan v. Hennigan* that the Boston School Committee had failed to comply with the Racial Imbalance Act of 1965. Judge Garrity ordered the Boston School Committee to implement the busing plan in compliance with the Massachusetts State Board of Education.

Even though Black parents and students had organized, protested, and boycotted for over a decade to demand change, it was the white protestors who resisted integration in 1974 and 1975 who garnered the most media attention. Many Black civil rights leaders saw the coverage and popularity of the anti-busing protests as evidence of the backlash against integration, even twenty years after the landmark *Brown v. Board of Education* decision. The photograph is significant, therefore, for capturing whites demonstrating for their right to segregation, which served as a startling check to the advances toward equality that Black Americans had won in the 1950s and 1960s.

About the Artist

Spencer Grant was born in Brooklyn, New York, in 1944 and graduated from Boston University in 1966. Grant worked as a stock photographer for Stock Boston in the early 1970s, when he took this photograph at Thomas Park in South Boston. Grant worked in and around Boston from the 1960s to the 1990s. He also worked as a freelance photographer for United Press International (UPI), the *Boston Globe*, *Time* magazine, *Boston* magazine, and *Esquire*.

Context

In 1855, Massachusetts became one of the first states to outlaw segregation in schools. Even before the Civil War, public opinion in Boston and throughout Massachusetts favored integrated schooling between white and minority students. Opinion changed starting

Document Image

A 1975 anti-busing rally in Thomas Park in South Boston
(Spencer Grant)

around the 1930s, however, and schools gradually became more segregated by race. This was not always the result of overt discriminatory policies; "redlining," or banks denying home mortgages to minority applicants who wanted to buy in specific neighborhoods, became increasingly prevalent. After World War II, public housing officials began to allocate housing based on race. This choice created segregated neighborhoods by default, contributing to the problem of segregated schools. The situation was compounded as white Americans increasingly moved out of cities and into the suburbs—an exodus called "white flight"—while Black Americans moved into cities. All of these factors created *de facto* segregated schools, even if leaders had not made a specific decision to bar Black students from white schools. When the landmark 1954 decision in *Brown v. Board of Education* outlawed segregation in schools, therefore, most schools in Boston—as well as many other locations in the northern states—were not in compliance with the law due to the housing patterns.

Throughout the 1950s and 1960s, the civil rights movement won many victories for Black Americans, who were experiencing many forms of discrimination, from where they were allowed sit on a bus to how much they were paid and whether they could vote. Many white Americans supported the movement, and leaders such as Martin Luther King Jr. appealed equally to white and Black Americans. Black parents and students in Boston and other northern cities began to organize and protest against the poor conditions in their schools, citing inadequate funding, facilities that were unequal to predominately white schools, and lack of adequate staff and equipment, among other concerns.

In 1965, the Massachusetts State Board of Education passed the Racial Imbalance Act, which decreed that any school with more than 50 percent nonwhite students was racially imbalanced. The Boston School Committee appealed the definition of an imbalanced school and refused to make any changes. Black Bostonians continued to rally and protest to try to spur the Boston School Committee to action, to no avail. In 1972, a parent named Tallulah Morgan, along with a coalition of fourteen other parents of Black students, filed a lawsuit under the direction of the National Association for the Advancement of Colored People (NAACP). The parents sued James Hennigan, president of the Boston School Committee, for failing to comply with the Racial Imbalance Act.

The case of *Morgan v. Hennigan* took two years to wind its way through the court system. Finally, Federal Judge Garrity rendered his decision that Boston schools were out of compliance and, to receive funding, had to enforce a system of busing to meet the 50 percent threshold. While the decision was a victory for the Black Bostonians who had worked for changes to predominately Black schools for decades, the reaction and resistance of white Bostonians became the major storyline, particularly during the 1974–75 school year.

There were other factors influencing the atmosphere as well. Many of the students who were subject to busing were from poor neighborhoods and ethnic enclaves. Critics claimed that all Bostonians were not sharing equally in desegregation and that Boston's leaders never addressed the poor quality of all schools in low-income neighborhoods, whether predominately Black or white.

The busing program lasted for thirteen years, and white parents and students continued to contest it bitterly. Critics of the program argue that the program did more to foster racial division than it did to achieve educational equality.

Explanation and Analysis of the Document

When looking at the image, the eye is drawn immediately to the cardboard sign proclaiming "Whites" "Have" "Rights." It is the only indication that the gathering is a protest, aside from the large button that the woman at the front is wearing, proclaiming "No we won't go." Looking closer, one notices the American flag and that the crowd seems to be uniformly white. The photographer, Spencer Grant, seems to be positioned up on a stage or platform that the crowd is facing. Many people in the image seem to be applauding or cheering in response to activity on the stage.

Exploring the phrase "Whites Have Rights" uncovers the many facets of this protest and its historical context. On one level, and considered with the phrase "No we won't go" on the button, the protestors seem to be arguing that they have the right not to be bused to schools far from their homes; that is, whites have the right to attend the better schools within walking distance in their own neighborhoods. In support of this idea, many mothers of white students in South Boston formed a group called Restore Our Alienated Rights

(ROAR) and led protests at schools, going as far as throwing rocks and bricks at buses, yelling racial slurs at children as they attempted to enter their assigned schools, and attacking police who were charged with keeping the peace.

Many Black Americans, however, noted that it was not the inconvenience of busing that was the real issue. In March 1982, civil rights leader Jesse Jackson wrote an opinion peace in the *New York Times* titled "It's Not the Bus. It's Us," in which he noted, "The central issue is not transportation; it is equal protection under the law. 'Antibusing' is a code word for racism and rejection." Supporters of integrated schools saw the anti-busing rallies as an explicit rejection of *Brown v. Board of Education* and twenty years of advances. When protestors were able to focus their ire on busing rather than integration, they felt justified in responding violently to Black students who were trying to receive an education equal to their peers.

In the end, many whites exercised their right to move, and the proportion of white students in Boston schools declined from more than 60 percent in 1970 to less than 15 percent after 1975. The controversy and the upheaval did not improve the quality of education in Boston, nor did it mend race relations or address income and housing disparity. Like many other problems connected to civil rights and equality, the interconnected nature of the issues meant that it was difficulty to attempt to solve only one. The image demonstrates the belief that rights for one group meant exclusion for another group, rather than equality for all.

—Elizabeth George

Questions for Further Study

1. What civil disobedience strategies did white protestors borrow from the civil rights movement? How did those strategies affect public perception of the protests?

2. What factors led to the segregation of public schools in Boston? How was busing meant to address those factors?

3. To what extent did the phrase "It's not the bus. It's us" describe the complexities of the controversies over busing?

4. Was busing an effective solution to segregated schools in Boston? What other strategies could leaders have used?

Further Reading

Books

Delmont, Matthew F. *Why Busing Failed: Race, Media, and the National Resistance to School Desegregation*. Berkeley: University of California Press, 2016.

Formisano, Ronald P. *Boston against Busing: Race, Class, and Ethnicity in the 1960s and 1970s*. Chapel Hill: University of North Carolina Press, 1991.

Patterson, James T. *Brown v. Board of Education: A Civil Rights Milestone and Its Troubled Legacy*. New York: Oxford University Press, 2002.

Websites

Cannato, Vincent. "The Controversy over Busing." Bill of Rights Institute. https://billofrightsinstitute.org/essays/the-controversy-over-busing.

"Desegregation Busing." *Encyclopedia of Boston*. Boston Research Center. https://bostonresearchcenter.org/projects_files/eob/single-entry-busing.html.

"Morgan v. Hennigan." *Encyclopedia of Boston*. Boston Research Center. https://bostonresearchcenter.org/projects_files/eob/single-entry-morgan.html.

Spencer Grant Collection. Boston Public Library. https://www.digitalcommonwealth.org/collections/commonwealth:x920fw84d.

Warren K. Leffler: Photograph of Phyllis Schlafly at White House Demonstration

Author/Creator Warren K. Leffler	**Image Type** Photographs
Date 1977	**Significance** Exemplifies the presence of women in opposition to the Equal Rights Amendment

Overview

This photograph depicts Phyllis Schlafly during a protest rally held by her supporters in the STOP ERA movement outside of the National Women's Convention of 1977. When the Nineteenth Amendment, recognizing women's right to vote, passed Congress and the states in 1920, the next step for the women's movement appeared to be to work on another amendment, this one guaranteeing the same equality for women that had gone into the Thirteenth, Fourteenth, and Fifteenth Amendments for African Americans. When it came to ratification, however, the Equal Rights Amendment (ERA) faced a radically unusual opponent: Schlafly, who advocated against the equality of men and women before the law. With her legal education and conservative Christian moral principles, Schlafly cut an unusual image in the 1970s, often referred to as the "Me Decade." As it turned out, her opposition to the ERA was ahead of its time—the 1980s would be a conservative decade, one in which the very definition of what it meant to be conservative happened to bend in the same direction that Schlafly wanted to carry the country. Though the ERA would pass Congress in 1972, it only managed to pass through 37 of the 38 necessary state legislatures in the allotted seven-year time limit for passage, and the amendment failed. Schlafly would become the very image of women's inequality in the United States, a reviled figure for women's rights groups but a hero to conservatives all the way until her death in 2016.

About the Artist

Photographer Warren K. Leffler was one of five staff photographers for *U.S. News & World Report* in the 1960s and 1970s. He made his reputation during the civil rights movement as a chronicler of his times; however, he would never publish a collection of his work, an unusual move in such historical times. The magazine and Leffler were based in Washington, D.C. *U.S. News & World Report* was an independent news magazine, founded with the merger of a pair of two older news magazines in 1948. The magazine was owned by employees like Leffler, and it tended to cover more health, education, and welfare issues than other magazines, hence its interest in the women's movement. Its competitors *Time* and *Newsweek* were jointly owned by the Time-Life Corporation and thus had a larger pool of financial resources to work with. *U.S. News & World Report* was known to have a slightly more conservative perspective on events than its two rivals, hence its likelier status as a place where Phyllis Schlafly would find an image and a voice. Always behind *Time* and *Newsweek* in its readership numbers, in

Document Image

Phyllis Schlafly
(Library of Congress)

1983 *U.S. News & World Report* began an annual ranking of the nation's best colleges and universities, a tactic that worked—the college rankings issue became a best-selling and influential edition of the journal every year following. Gradually, *U.S. News & World Report* began to emphasize rankings of other entities, such as hospitals, cars, and states to live in, over its weekly news offerings; by 2009, it had ceased publishing a print edition and is today known almost exclusively for these rankings.

Context

The idea of equal rights for women dated back as far as the establishment of the Constitution itself, but it finally began to be taken seriously after the 1848 Seneca Falls Convention, which launched the women's rights movement. This first wave of feminism culminated in the Nineteenth Amendment to the U.S. Constitution, recognizing women's right to vote, in 1920. Almost immediately, a second wave began with the promulgation of the "Lucretia Mott Amendment," which would later come to be called the Equal Rights Amendment (ERA). It declared: "Equality of rights under the law shall not be denied or abridged by the United States or by any state on account of sex. The Congress shall have the power to enforce, by appropriate legislation, the provisions of this article." The amendment was first introduced to Congress in 1923 and was reintroduced every year thereafter; it even passed the U.S. Senate in 1950.

Change remained gradual but seemed inexorable. Title VII of the 1964 Civil Rights Act prohibited discrimination of persons on the basis of sex. Women's rights in general were prioritized in government in the early 1970s. A set of amendments to the Higher Education Acts of 1965 included Title IX, which prohibited discrimination on the basis of sex in any educational institution that took federal aid money. Birth control was made legally obtainable by single women, and abortion was recognized as legal by the Supreme Court by 1973. The Equal Rights Amendment was brought to the floor of the House of Representatives in 1970 by Representative Martha Griffiths (D-Mich.). It won bipartisan support over the next two years and passed both the Senate and House of Representatives in March 1972 with overwhelming majorities. According to the rules of the Constitution, it then had to pass three-quarters of the state legislatures—38 out of 50 states—and Congress imposed a seven-year time limit for it to pass through all 38 states. The ERA appeared well on its way to ratification through 1972, 1973, and 1974. Yet at the point where the ERA seemed on the verge of succeeding, it ran into an unexpected opposition.

Phyllis Schlafly was an active Missouri Republican who had run for Congress twice and lost. A college graduate with a master's degree from Radcliffe College, she wrote twenty books over the course of her lifetime, published regular newspaper columns, and appeared regularly on both television and radio as a political commentator. In short, she was seemingly the model woman the ERA was designed to promote—politically activist, intellectual, and ambitious. She would even get a law degree from the University of Illinois and pass the bar in 1978. Yet she was implacably opposed to the Equal Rights Amendment as a step toward the moral dissolution of American society, and she organized a campaign called STOP ERA—STOP being an acronym for "stop taking our privileges"—to do everything in her power to keep the amendment from passing its final five states.

According to Schlafly, the Equal Rights Amendment protected no law that was not already on the books in the states or in the federal government. Its seeming redundancy in her eyes was not enough to oppose its ratification, however; as a feminist cause, the ERA promoted the cultural equalization of men's and women's roles and thus reduced women's traditional role as the moral arbiters of Christian society. The Supreme Court's decision on *Roe v. Wade* in 1973, which determined that the Constitution guaranteed women the right to obtain legal abortions, was to Schlafly a typical step in the wrong direction. Passing the Equal Rights Amendment would lead to same-sex marriage, women being drafted into the military, and women being responsible for alimony payments in a divorce—to her eyes, all signs of the decline and fall of American civilization.

Moral opinion meant nothing without grassroots organization. Schlafly was a brilliant debater, well-versed at making supporters of the ERA look as if they were the real radicals—the journalist Betty Friedan said Schlafly should be burned at the stake. She convinced a large number of women that the ERA would make abortion available on demand, thus sparking the anti-abortion lobby in the United States. She was especially able to convince women—to the bewilderment of the feminists in support of the ERA—that being a stay-at-home housewife was a privilege that the ERA would take away from them. The illogical nature of this argument made little difference. Schlafly was ahead of her time in organizing conservative activists around an issue and getting them to go to the polls and vote, regardless of the issue's validity, mostly because said issue was supported by liberals and therefore had to be undermined. Especially important was that she understood that the way to win political points was at the level of state legislatures, as opposed to in Congress, a tactic Republicans would use to dramatically shift U.S. courts, congressional districts, and political issues in their favor.

Momentum for the ERA slowed in the states in 1975, when 35 out of the necessary 38 states had approved of its ratification. Schlafly's STOP ERA Movement (later renamed the Eagle Forum as it expanded its political ambitions) attracted volunteers, almost all of them Christian churchgoing women, to pressure state legislators and hand them apple pies as innocuous and highly symbolic nudges for their votes. Over the next five years, despite the deadline to pass the ERA being extended to 1982, five states even voted to rescind their approval of the amendment. The passage of the ERA became associated mostly with the pro-choice movement, and thus legislators felt justified in voting against it and in favor of what they believed to be the lives of unborn children. The ERA died in June 1982 and remains unratified to this day, even though many of the other issues Schlafly emphasized as immoral—such same-sex marriage and women in the military—have become commonplace and the country's morality has not collapsed as a result. Schlafly died at age ninety-two in 2016.

Explanation and Analysis of the Document

Leffler's photograph of Phyllis Schlafly came from a protest rally held by her supporters in the STOP ERA movement outside of the National Women's Convention of 1977. The movement was there to protest the involvement of First Lady Rosalynn Carter at the convention, a fact Schlafly claimed was evidence that her husband, President Jimmy Carter, was exploiting his wife to win feminist votes. In appearance, a photo like this one promoted the image Schlafly wanted to project of what a proper, moral, Christian woman should look like. She wore pearl necklaces and simple earrings as her jewelry of choice and maintained an outdated 1950s hairdo, swept back in a bun and sprayed in place. Her perfect posture was entirely contained in a wool coat buttoned up to its neckline, and her smile was permanent in public. Schlafly appeared prim, friendly but unglamorous, and therefore representative of the values she promoted. She clearly denoted a pre-feminist—and what she hoped would be a post-feminist—United States.

—David Simonelli

Questions for Further Study

1. Phyllis Schlafly herself presents the image of what she considered the proper American homemaker to look like. What is the image presented by the women surrounding her? How do they reflect her conservative values?

2. Why in particular do you think it would be important for Schlafly to regularly be depicted smiling?

3. Warren Leffler, the photographer, was working for *U.S. News & World Report* magazine. Why would this magazine be more likely than other magazines to have a photographer in front of the White House covering Schlafly's protest?

Further Reading

Books

Critchlow, Donald T. *Phyllis Schlafly and Grassroots Conservatism: A Woman's Crusade*. Princeton NJ: Princeton University Press, 2005.

Felsenthal, Carol. *The Biography of Phyllis Schlafly: The Sweetheart of the Silent Majority*. Chicago: Regnery Gateway, 1982.

Spruill, Marjorie. *Divided We Stand: The Battle over Women's Rights and Family Values That Polarized American Politics*. New York: Bloomsbury, 2018.

Websites

Cohen, Alex, and Wilfred U. Codrington. "The Equal Rights Amendment Explained." Brennan Center for Justice website, January 23, 2020. https://www.brennancenter.org/our-work/research-reports/equal-rights-amendment-explained.

"Equal Rights Amendment." Alice Paul Institute website, 2018. https://www.equalrightsamendment.org/.

Herbert Block: "Strange How Some Choose To Live Like That" Cartoon

Author/Creator Herblock (Herbert Block)	Image Type Cartoons
Date 1984	Significance Commentary on President Ronald Reagan's seeming indifference to the poor during his administration

Overview

Since his tenure in office ended, Ronald Reagan gained a reputation as a great president for his role in helping to bring the Cold War to an end and his ability to sell a vision of American life to the U.S. voter that was inspiring. Since the 1980s, the U.S. economy has experienced recessions but has rarely experienced the inflation, unemployment, and high taxation that Reagan inherited. On the other hand, the impact of Reagan's policies on the United States at the time tends to be forgotten. Reagan believed in "supply-side economics"—in short, the notion that if the government put more money into people's pockets instead of taking it out in taxes, taxpayers would spend more money and boost the economy. However, Reagan's tax cuts went almost entirely to the wealthy during his eight years in office. Furthermore, unemployment never dropped to its normal level of 5 percent, mostly hovering around 10 percent throughout his presidency. The homeless population in the country exploded, and for all his efforts to sell a Hollywood-happy version of the United States and its socioeconomic life, Reagan could not hide the poverty and desperation that went unalleviated by his policies. In this cartoon, one of Reagan's harshest critics, the political cartoonist Herblock (Herbert Block), damns Reagan's apparent indifference to the plight of the poor in the United States under his watch.

About the Artist

Herbert Lawrence Block, known to his audience as Herblock, was the most acerbic, pointed, and celebrated political cartoonist of the twentieth century. Sketching out his first dark-penciled drawing for the *Chicago Daily News* in 1929, he drew his last political cartoons for the *Washington Post* in mid-2001. His career spanned a third of the United States' existence, from the Great Depression to the verge of the terrorist attacks of September 11, 2001.

Herbert Block was born in Chicago on October 13, 1909, and showed a talent for drawing at a young age; his father had likewise contributed drawings to early humor magazines like *Life*, *Puck*, and *Judge*. Herbert won a scholarship to the Art Institute of Chicago, where he took classes at night while attending high school. He attended Lake Forest College in Chicago but dropped out after two years when he landed his first job on the *Chicago Daily News*. His cartoons were clean, heavily shaded, and "blocky" in coincidental deference to his name—a Herblock cartoon was instantly recognizable as his production. Though he was a fan of the New Deal—it taught him "what govern-

Document Image

The "Strange How Some Choose to Live Like That Instead of Choosing to Be Rich Like Us" cartoon
(Library of Congress)

ment could do"—he did not hesitate to criticize President Franklin Delano Roosevelt for his efforts to pack the U.S. Supreme Court in 1937. His talent got him syndicated very quickly, first with the Newspaper Enterprise Association (NEA) out of Cleveland, and he won his first Pulitzer Prize in 1942. Block served in the U.S. Army's Education Division from 1943 to 1945 during World War II. He was recruited to the *Washington Post* in 1946 specifically to add his already-well-known drawings to its editorial page and make the *Post* a stronger competitor in the Washington, D.C., market.

In the 1950s, Herblock came into his own as a political commentator, taking on the powerful and puncturing their pretensions in the name of the average person. A strong believer in civil liberties, he directed cartoons against the House Committee on Un-American Activities. He coined the term "McCarthyism" to describe the cruel, bullying political tactics of Senator Joseph McCarthy, and from an early period he distrusted Richard Nixon, seeing both of these men as demagogues using anti-communism to advance their own careers. Far from suffering for his attacks on these figures, as so many others had in the United States during the Red Scare, he won his second Pulitzer in 1954. Later, with Nixon's presidency, he was again an early critic and publicist for the Watergate scandal, sharing another Pulitzer with the rest of the *Washington Post* staff for his coverage. He won a fourth Pulitzer in 1979. Later, Ronald Reagan earned Herblock's wrath for his seeming indifference to the plight of the poor and downtrodden populations of the United States. As a journalist who had come of age during the New Deal, Herblock believed government's role was to solve problems for large groups in society, the exact opposite philosophy that Reagan espoused.

By the last decade of his life, Herblock had become a political institution himself. He was awarded the Presidential Medal of Freedom in 1994, and in the year 2000 the Library of Congress put on a retrospective of his work, one of whose cartoons is represented here. He drew his last cartoon on August 26, 2001, and he died in October of the same year.

Context

When Ronald Reagan attained the office of the presidency in 1981, he inherited a sluggish economy that had sapped voters' faith in the future of the United States as an economic power. The final years of the 1970s had been characterized by high unemployment and high inflation—an unusual economic situation dubbed stagflation. The "misery index," as President Jimmy Carter had called it four years earlier, was at a staggering 21 percent. The Vietnam War's ending, problems with the world's oil supply, and the decline of U.S. industry and its productivity were the most permanent reasons for stagflation.

Reagan's answer to the problems of the U.S. economy lay in what was referred to as supply-side economics. Rather than relying on the old New Deal/Keynesian answers to a sluggish economy—a government spending itself into debt to create jobs—supply-side economists concentrated on subsidizing businesses, investments, and labor, most efficiently by cutting taxes. Instead of the government getting into debt by spending money, it would get into debt by giving money back to the private corporations and individuals that created jobs in the economy, and it would eliminate regulations to stimulate economic growth. Basically, Reagan believed that jobs would be created and inflation could be solved by putting money into the hands of wealthy people, who presumably would spend large amounts of money and invest in creating jobs for people. The fact that it would take time for such programs to work—time that the poor and homeless did not have—was not a part of supply-side calculations.

During his presidency, supply-side economics came to be associated with Reagan, gaining the nickname Reaganomics. Reagan's first budget nearly failed to pass the Congress in spring of 1981; then, when the president was shot, widespread sympathy and admiration for the president's pluck allowed the Economic Recovery Tax Act to pass in August 1981. It reduced personal income tax rates for the highest earners from 70 to 50 percent and cut corporate taxes. At first, the economy went into recession, and unemployment rose to almost 11 percent of the workforce. Homeless people became ubiquitous in American cities, and the industrial heartland saw factory after factory close its doors. But a slow recovery began at the end of 1982, and by 1984—an election year—the United States was well on its way to sustained growth that would last for most of the 1980s.

Yet for all the economic improvement, the "trickle-down" aspect of supply-side economics simply did not work. While the economy grew at an annual rate of 3 percent, unemployment remained stubbornly high, between 7 percent and 11 percent, throughout the decade; wealthy people simply did not make jobs for the average person as Reagan expected. Middle-class Americans mostly lived with this problem, and the stock market grew dramatically. Young urban professionals, or "yuppies," attracted media attention because of their conspicuous consumption of designer clothes, gourmet foods, and luxury automobiles. A new television show, *Lifestyles of the Rich and Famous*, provided glimpses into the opulent lives of celebrities; Donald Trump, heir to a family fortune, was a perpetual star of the era for his displays of wealth, in part secured at the expense of paying his bills to the poorer people whom Reaganomics was supposed to care for. Most of all, the national debt became massive as lower-income taxpayers could not make up for all Reagan's tax cuts to the wealthy; the debt at the end of his presidency increased by more than it had in all previous administrations combined.

Explanation and Analysis of the Document

Wealth inequality was not a problem that started with Ronald Reagan's presidency, but it was certainly exacerbated by it. The idea of the "1 percent" who held all the wealth in the United States began in the 1980s. Herblock was particularly incensed by the problem of growing wealth inequality. In this cartoon, he shows Reagan riding with one of his California advisors in the White House, Edwin Meese, commenting that homeless people had made a choice to be homeless. The day before this cartoon ran in the *Washington Post*, Reagan had been interviewed on ABC's *Good Morning America*, where he was asked about the "misery" his policies caused. Reagan responded—rightly—that his administration was spending massive amounts of money on welfare programs, and he asserted that certain people were "sleeping on the grates, the homeless who are homeless, you might say, by choice."

—David Simonelli

Questions for Further Study

1. Describe the gist of this cartoon.

2. Why would you guess that the co-rider with Reagan in this cartoon would be Edwin Meese? What do you think his role was in the White House, that Herblock would see it as appropriate to include him in this cartoon?

3. How do you think Reagan's attitude toward the homeless population made an impact on his reelection in 1984, if at all? Why?

Further Reading

Books

Lanoue, David J. *From Camelot to the Teflon President: Economics and Presidential Popularity since 1960.* New York: Greenwood Press, 1988.

Schaller, Michael. *Reckoning with Reagan: America and Its President in the 1980s.* New York: Oxford University Press, 1992.

Spitz, Bob. *Reagan: An American Journey.* New York: Penguin Press, 2018.

Documentaries

"Reagan: Chapter 1." *The American Experience.* Public Broadcasting Service, 2020. https://www.pbs.org/wgbh/americanexperience/features/reagan-chapter-1/.

"Reagan: Chapter 2." *The American Experience.* Public Broadcasting Service, 2020. https://www.pbs.org/wgbh/americanexperience/features/reagan-chapter-2/.

Pat Oliphant: "There He Goes Again" Cartoon

Author/Creator Pat Oliphant	**Image Type** Cartoons
Date 1984	**Significance** Commentary on President Ronald Reagan's popularity despite social and political problems during his presidency

Overview

Ronald Reagan, Republican President of the United States from 1981 to 1989, was famous for his ability to negotiate foreign and domestic policy issues without ever seeming to forfeit his popularity with the American public. Good-natured, with a quick sense of humor and a well-earned reputation as a good public speaker, Reagan seemed to many informed observers to use his public image to cover up the problems besetting the United States in the 1980s during his presidency—and possibly, because of his presidency. In this cartoon, the eminent political cartoonist Pat Oliphant highlights Reagan's ability to navigate one political issue after another without doing damage to his popularity, while his opponents simply remain sidelined, unable to turn any of these issues to their own political advantage.

About the Artist

Pat Oliphant was born near Adelaide, Australia, in 1935. Interested in becoming a journalist, he took courses at the Adelaide School of Art and recognized a talent in himself for drawing. He began working various jobs at newspapers in Adelaide as a teenager before alighting on a career as a political cartoonist at age twenty. Generally a liberal in his political outlook, he became frustrated with the conservative bent of Australian newspapers and moved to the United States in 1964 to work at the *Denver Post*. His style—lavish drawings in the style of Britain's humor magazine *Punch* and artist Ronald Searle, combined with a sharp political wit influenced by *Mad* magazine—gained him a quick audience beyond Denver, and by 1967 he had won a Pulitzer Prize.

Typical of his acerbity, Oliphant criticized the Pulitzer board for choosing his cartoon as a prizewinner because he did not consider it particularly high quality. In a career spanning more than fifty years and ten presidents, Oliphant occasionally drew outrage for his skewering of subjects like the Catholic Church or U.S. foreign policy related to Israel. He also covered Watergate and Vietnam—Richard Nixon became a stock figure of evil in his cartoons—the fall of the Soviet Union, the Gulf War, the coming of the Iraq War, and Donald Trump's presidency. Soon after winning the Pulitzer, he moved on to the *Los Angeles Times*, and his cartoons were syndicated, bringing them to a nationwide audience and making him one of the two or three most influential political cartoonists of his generation. By 1981, he was popular enough that he was

Document Image

"There He Goes Again"
(Library of Congress)

able to become independent of a newspaper, syndicating his cartoons himself to 500 newspapers across the country. From early on, he also drew a small penguin he called Punk into his cartoons as a sort of corner-panel commentator, allowing Oliphant to supplement his opinions.

Oliphant was naturalized as an American citizen in 1979. Over his career, he won two Reuben Awards from the National Cartoonists Society and Germany's Thomas Nast Prize, along with awards from the Society of Professional Journalists, the National Cartoonists Society, the National Wildlife Federation, the American Civil Liberties Union, and the *Washington Journalism Review*. After coming out of retirement for Donald Trump's presidency, he stopped producing cartoons in 2021, preferring to work in bronze sculptures at his home in Santa Fe, New Mexico.

Context

Ronald Reagan was a politician who came to his career via Hollywood. He began as a Hollywood actor in the 1940s and 1950s, usually second-billed and playing characters not far from his own personality. He began his political career as the president of the Screen Actors Guild during the communist scares of the era, where he built a strong resumé as being an anticommunist. Later, after supporting Barry Goldwater for the presidency in 1964, Reagan was elected the Republican governor of California for two terms, from 1967 through 1975, making a reputation for himself as an extremist right-wing opponent of student protests and Great Society programs, famously saying of both that the country should "put the bums to work."

Yet despite his harsh rhetoric, Reagan nearly won the Republican nomination for the presidency from incumbent Gerald Ford in 1976, and he successfully captured it in 1980. Despite his politics, which were considered radical at the time, Reagan had a reassuringly affable personality, was quick to crack a smile and a joke, and appeared emotionally accessible in public. His training as an actor came in handy as a presidential candidate. Unlike most other politicians, Reagan understood what it meant to be available to cameras from every angle and how to avoid looking tired, depressed, bored, or lost. In short, according to the famous standard, Reagan seemed like a guy who was a little smarter than the average voter but also a good guy to sit around and have a beer with.

Reagan's first demonstration of his ability to avoid negative assessment came during his campaign against incumbent Democratic President Jimmy Carter in 1980. Reagan was known to believe that a nuclear war with the Soviet Union might be winnable, that government welfare programs for the poor should be drastically cut, and that unions had destroyed the American industrial base. Carter repeatedly tried to remind the American people of Reagan's reactionary conservatism during the election campaign, but in the face of Reagan's affability, Carter came across as nannyish. During the presidential debates, Reagan even threw this tactic back in Carter's face, responding to one of his accusations by saying, "There you go again."

Once in office, Reagan's conservative allies expected him to operate in the tradition of a conservative Republican from the past—to balance the federal budget, cut taxes, stay out of foreign entanglements, and repair the competitiveness of American industry. Reagan did none of these things successfully. While he attempted to cut taxes for the wealthy and cut welfare programs, in the long run his policies ran up a massive government budget deficit. Military spending exploded during his time in office, driving the deficit up even worse. He agreed to send troops to Lebanon to run a United Nations peacekeeping mission and saw them blown up in their barracks by an Iranian terrorist in October 1983. Reagan was obsessed with stemming the tide of communism in Central America and funded the right-wing government of El Salvador and a terrorist organization referred to as the Contras, who were fighting the Sandinistas of Nicaragua. Reagan effectively redefined what it meant to be a conservative in the 1980s: it was no longer important to reduce the size of government but rather to determine what a government spent its money and energies on.

None of this seemed to matter when it came to Reagan's popularity, however. Despite the economic difficulties of his early presidency—during which he weathered unemployment rates as high as 11 percent—Reagan's sunny disposition meant it was difficult for the American people to disapprove of him. History has been kinder to Reagan than critics in his time, yet his approval rating never dropped below 45 percent through his entire presidency, despite the fact that he angered his political opponents and disturbed his political supporters with his policies. He gained the nickname the "Teflon president" for his ability to have no major issue sully his poll ratings. By 1984, the economy was improving, recent foreign policy crises were in the past, and Reagan's popularity rating soared at exactly the right time: the 1984 election campaign.

Explanation and Analysis of the Document

Oliphant's cartoon shows President Ronald Reagan wearing a tuxedo and dancing across ice floes labeled "Beirut," "Education," "Deficit," "Nuclear Arms," and "Central America"; in the background, former Democratic Vice President Walter Mondale, Senator Gary Hart (D-Col.), Senator John Glenn (D-Ohio), Senator Ernest Hollings (D-S.C.) and other Democratic presidential candidates struggle to keep their feet. Reagan is dressed like the classic movie star and dancer Fred Astaire, emphasizing the deftness and grace with which he navigates across what should be slippery and difficult issues that are sinking the prospects of the Democrats. Walter Mondale seemingly says, in despair, "There he goes again," a reference to Reagan's famous put-down of President Jimmy Carter in 1980. Reagan promised to make education and the deficit the focus of his second term as president if he won in 1984. The Democrats hammered away at Reagan for creating both problems in the first place by spending so much money on defense and cutting education programs like Head Start. However, nothing seemed to have an impact on Reagan's poll numbers in February 1984. While the Democratic candidates railed away at each other in their primary campaigns, Reagan had an approval rating of 57 percent and climbing. The "Teflon president" would go on to win a historic electoral college victory, sweeping every state except Mondale's home state of Minnesota in November.

—David Simonelli

Questions for Further Study

1. Why would dressing Reagan as Fred Astaire, an old Hollywood movie star, be useful in conveying the message in this cartoon?

2. Of the Democratic candidates struggling to make their way across the ice floes as issues, the figure representing Senator Gary Hart is actually in the water, hanging on to one of the floes. What do you think Oliphant was trying to represent about his campaign as opposed to that of the other candidates?

3. Reagan was viewed as the "Teflon president," but his average poll numbers actually were not as high during his presidency as those of his immediate successors, George H.W. Bush and Bill Clinton. What do you think that says about the poll numbers of Reagan and his immediate predecessors, Jimmy Carter, Gerald Ford, and Richard Nixon?

Further Reading

Books

Lanoue, David J. *From Camelot to the Teflon President: Economics and Presidential Popularity since 1960.* New York: Greenwood Press, 1988.

Schaller, Michael. *Reckoning with Reagan: America and Its President in the 1980s.* New York: Oxford University Press, 1992.

Spitz, Bob. *Reagan: An American Journey.* New York: Penguin Press, 2018.

Websites

"1984 Democratic Presidential Candidates Debate: Jesse Jackson Walter Mondale Gary Hart." YouTube, 2020. https://www.youtube.com/watch?v=SfBufBVQbVs.

Documentaries

"Reagan: Chapter 1." *The American Experience.* Public Broadcasting Service (2020) https://www.pbs.org/wgbh/americanexperience/features/reagan-chapter-1/.

"Reagan: Chapter 2." *The American Experience.* Public Broadcasting Service (2020) https://www.pbs.org/wgbh/americanexperience/features/reagan-chapter-2/.

"SILENCE = DEATH" FLYER

AUTHOR/CREATOR
Silence = Death Project: Avram Finkelstein, Brian Howard, Oliver Johnston, Charles Krelff, Chris Lione, and Jorge Soccarás

DATE
1987

IMAGE TYPE
FLYERS

SIGNIFICANCE
Featuring the gay-affirming symbol of the pink triangle, linked a message of gay pride with a call to action to secure dignified healthcare and an end to discrimination against those who contracted HIV/AIDS

Overview

The first known cases of HIV/AIDS in the United States occurred in 1981. Initially the disease and the cause of transmission were unknown, but it seemed to be affecting gay men disproportionately. Communities of young gay men, especially in New York City and San Francisco, were devastated by the disease, which attacked a person's immune system and caused a rapid decline and death.

The response from the National Institutes of Health (NIH) and the Centers for Disease Control and Prevention (CDC) was slow, stalling research on the virus and treatments, and preventing AIDS patients from accessing potentially life-saving care. Some traveled to Mexico to purchase drugs such as azidothymidine (commonly called AZT) in hopes of prolonging their lives. By 1990, more than 100,000 people in the United States had died of AIDS.

To draw attention to the silence of medical and legislative leaders while also inspiring affected communities to activism, the Silence = Death Project was formed. Six men produced a provocative poster to give voice to the suffering that AIDS caused and to spark the curiosity of people who might want to join in the fight. The "Silence = Death" poster became a symbol of AIDS activism and remains a visible reminder of the ongoing quest for access to medication for those living with HIV/AIDS even today.

About the Artist

A collective of six men in the Silence = Death Project developed the poster in 1987: Avram Finkelstein, Brian Howard, Oliver Johnston, Charles Krelff, Chris Lione, and Jorge Soccarás. These men eventually joined forces with the AIDS Coalition to Unleash Power (ACT UP), and the poster became a hallmark of their activist work. ACT UP was a radical, grassroots organization formed in New York City in March 1987. Led by Larry Kramer, the organization mobilized around the HIV/AIDS crisis, which disproportionately affected gay men. The movement grew out of the Lesbian and Gay Community Services Center in New York City and politicized the issue of healthcare—or lack thereof—for those suffering from AIDS.

ACT UP is known for its commitment to direct action. Borrowing strategies from Black civil rights organizers

Document Image

The "Silence = Death" flyer
(Wellcome Collection Gallery)

from the 1940s through the 1970s, ACT UP aimed to be visible through marches and acts of civil disobedience. In October 1987, ACT UP became nationally recognized for its participation in the Second National March on Washington for Lesbian and Gay Rights, also known as the Great March. Demonstrators held a mass gay wedding, protested the U.S. Supreme Court for upholding sodomy laws, and unveiled the AIDS quilt, a community folk art project devoted to memorializing the lives lost to AIDS. After the march, ACT UP chapters popped up in cities across the United States.

One example of the direct-action strategies of ACT UP was Stop the Church. The Catholic Church condemned homosexuality and comprehensive sex education that offered information about condom use. On December 10, 1989, members of ACT UP and Women's Health Action and Mobilization (WHAM) arrived during a Catholic mass at St. Patrick's Cathedral to host a "die-in" to protest Cardinal John O'Connor's opposition to sex education and condom distribution. Lying in the aisles during service, activists refused to move. Some yelled out chants and slogans like "you're killing us," and others chained themselves to pews. Tom Keane chewed up a Eucharist wafer and spit it out. Meanwhile, the organist continued to play, and the cardinal urged people to ignore the demonstrators. Protesters were arrested, and the demonstration received wide criticism in the media in subsequent days.

ACT UP continued with creative direct-action strategies. Some, like the protest at CBS studios in which activists shouted "AIDS is news. Fight AIDS not Arabs!" generated attention to the cause; others, like the 1991 protest of Macy's in which people dressed up like Santa Claus to protest the company's refusal to hire an HIV-positive Santa, highlighted discrimination. In 1990, more than 1,000 people stormed the National Institutes of Health campus to urge Anthony Fauci, then the director of the National Institute of Allergy and Infectious Disease, to accelerate the process of developing treatments for HIV/AIDS.

The central aim of ACT UP chapters was to break the silence around HIV/AIDS and to convince politicians and the public both to witness the humanity and tragedy of the AIDS pandemic and to support public policy that funded research on AIDS and healthcare for HIV/AIDS patients.

Although the height of ACT UP influence was in the 1980s and 1990s, some chapters of ACT UP, including in New York, continue the work to secure treatment for people with AIDS.

Context

In the 1970s, the gay liberation movement encouraged sexual minorities—who grew to be known by initialisms such as LGBTQA+, or lesbian, gay, bisexual, transgender, queer, asexual—to "come out." Activism in the movement was based on the premise that gay and lesbian people were everywhere, and that increased visibility would pressure legislators to strike down sodomy laws that criminalized gay sex and pass anti-discrimination laws that made sexual minorities a protected class. By 1974, activists successfully convinced the American Psychiatric Association to remove homosexuality from the Diagnostic and Statistical Manual of Mental Disorders. Mainstream feminist movements, which had previously ignored sexuality, began to openly include lesbians within their ranks.

Meanwhile, a growing conservative backlash against the civil rights gains of the 1960s and 1970s focused on "family values" and identified LGBTQA+ people as a threat to American morality. In Florida, for example, orange juice spokesperson Anita Bryant launched the Save our Children campaign, which endeavored to identify and eradicate gay and lesbian teachers from public schools. Powerful conservative voices also denounced public funding for social services, gaining favor with voters by promising lower taxes, smaller government, and greater personal freedom. This view is captured in President Ronald Reagan's 1981 inaugural address, in which he famously said: "Government is not the solution to our problem. Government is the problem." Vocal Christian conservatives argued that the illness was God's punishment for so-called sinful sexual practice. The combination of homophobic sentiments and anti-government politics caused Reagan and many elected officials to ignore the HIV/AIDS crisis.

In addition, medical professionals were unclear at first about the origin of HIV/AIDS or the methods of transmission. Confusion bred hysteria and fear, and those afflicted with the disease quickly became stigmatized. The disease was first dubbed a "gay cancer" and then Gay-Related Immune Deficiency (GRID) because most reported cases were gay or bisexual men. Some politicians supported quarantining those infected with the virus, and some states attempted to pass measures to isolate HIV/AIDS patients. The government did little to support research on the illness, and media coverage was scant. By 1984, more than 4,250 deaths from AIDS had been reported. Meanwhile, President Reagan cut funding to the Centers for Disease Control (CDC) and National Institutes of Health (NIH).

As people died, many of them young men, LGBTQA+ communities suffered triply under the grief of loss, the pain of illness, and the inaction from their government. President Reagan remained silent on the issue of AIDS until, in 1985, his friend and fellow Hollywood start Rock Hudson contracted the virus and died. Thousands of people across the United States needed medical care by then, including access to life-saving treatments for HIV/AIDS, and agencies needed funding for research. On October 11, 1987, ACT UP New York led a march on Washington, D.C., to demand the federal government address the devastation in their communities.

At the same time, in lieu of government support, activists took measures into their own hands, forming campaigns to educate the public about condoms to prevent the transmission of HIV/AIDS, to care for sick and dying people, and to push back on stigma and discrimination.

Explanation and Analysis of the Document

The simple fact of the poster is important to the analysis of the "Silence = Death" campaign. In a time when mainstream media and government outlets refused to acknowledge the AIDS crisis and the suffering of people across the United States, a poster was a powerful way to reach the public. They were plastered near commercial advertisements using a flour and water mixture to hang them—a process known as wheatpasting. Artists and activists collaborated to find effective ways to grab people's attention with provocative combinations of words and images, and the poster became an important medium for the AIDS movement in the 1980s and 1990s.

The upside-down pink triangle was first used by Nazis in Germany in the 1930s and 1940s to label gay men and others considered to be sexual deviants in concentration camps. Gay activists in the 1970s reclaimed the symbol, inverted it, and proclaimed it a symbol of pride and the LGBTQA+ rights movement. People of all genders wore it in the 1980s as a sign of self-identity and also as code to communicate with other queer people.

In the poster, the use of the inverted pink triangle represents a rejection of the victimhood of AIDS and an invitation to the LGBTQA+ community to reclaim power over one's circumstances. The font was a trendy one at the time, and the black background would stand out in the midst of all the other advertisements on the streets of Manhattan.

The phrase "Silence = Death" had two audiences and a separate purpose for each of them. For the LGBTQA+ community, the phrase was intended to inspire people to become politically active around the issue of AIDS. While queer people certainly already knew about AIDS, knew people were suffering, and knew that AIDS patients were not justly treated, they didn't yet know what to do about any of that. The poster was to serve as a rallying cry, to inspire people to lift their voices and demand justice. For non-LGBTQA+ people, the phrase presented a coded message of authority and power to suggest that people were already organized around the issue of AIDS, even though they weren't. As a result, the wording was deliberately ambiguous, designed to instill in all audiences a sense that a powerful social movement was emerging in response to AIDS.

The language of the poster is purposely intense, and at first glance it does not appear to be about HIV/AIDS. For viewers who understood the meaning of the pink triangle, the poster would have been immediately recognizable as a message about LGBTQA+ people. By using the coded symbol and provocative language, the poster pushed viewers to be curious and want to learn more about HIV/AIDS activism.

The posters were wheatpasted on the streets of New York City next to advertisements for commercial products, so people saw them as they passed by. For those traveling in a car or bus, the message was brief enough to make an impression. Though it is not present on the image reproduced here, there was small print at the bottom visible only to people who walked by and saw the poster up close. The small print urged people to "Turn anger, fear, grief into action."

After the debut of the "Silence = Death" poster, ACT UP was founded, and a movement was born. While these two events were coincidentally related, the poster quickly became a symbol of HIV/AIDS activism and the LGBTQA+ movement.

—Mallory Szymanski

Questions for Further Study

1. Why did AIDS activists target "silence" in their public education campaigns?

2. Assess the effectiveness of the poster design. What emotions or responses might this poster have elicited from viewers?

3. Why did activists take up the responsibility of educating the public about HIV/AIDS in the 1980s? Consider examples of other widespread and controversial health issues, such as tobacco use, obesity, and COVID-19. What are some sources of information about public health issues that you have noticed? What were their messages? Were they effective?

Further Reading

Books

Beam, Joseph. *In the Life: A Black Gay Anthology*. Boston: Alyson Publications, 1986.

France, David. *How to Survive a Plague: The Story of How Activists and Scientists Tamed AIDS*. New York: Knopf Doubleday, 2016.

Schulman, Sarah. *Let the Record Show: The Political History of ACT UP*. New York: Farrar, Straus and Giroux, 2021.

Websites

ACT UP: NY Archive. https://actupny.org/.

AIDS Community Research Initiative of America (ACRIA). https://acria.org/.

AIDS Education Posters, University of Rochester River Campus Libraries Special Collections. https://aep.lib.rochester.edu/.

AIDS, Posters, and Stories of Public Health, National Library of Medicine, Digital Exhibition. https://www.nlm.nih.gov/exhibition/aids-posters/index.html.

Out History. https://outhistory.org/.

"A Timeline of HIV and AIDS." HIV.gov. https://www.hiv.gov/hiv-basics/overview/history/hiv-and-aids-timeline.

Documentaries

How to Survive a Plague. David France, director. Public Square Films, 2012.

United in Anger. Jim Hubbard, director. Bronx Documentary Center, 2012.

Vito. Jeffrey Schwarz, director. HBO Documentary Films, 2011.

Photograph Of Berlin Wall Teardown

Author/Creator Associated Press	**Image Type** Photographs
Date 1989	**Significance** Illustrates the literal and symbolic fall of communism and reopening of exchange between East and West

Overview

This document is an example of a mass media photograph, commonly used in the twentieth and twenty-first centuries. The first photograph to have a human in it was "Boulevard du Temple" by Louis Daguerre, taken in 1838 in Paris. By the twentieth century, the use of news-related photography was commonplace and helped to influence public opinion worldwide on numerous occasions, including throughout both world wars, when images shocked the world by bringing the reality of those events to the forefront of people's daily lives.

This particular photograph is from the fall of communism in East Germany in November 1989, specifically the tearing down of the Berlin Wall, which had separated East Berlin and communist East Germany from West Berlin and democratic West Germany since 1961. The wall was a symbol for both East and West Germans, as well as the focal point of the Cold War between the United States and its allies and the Soviet Union and its allies.

At the end of World War II, the victorious Allied powers divided defeated Germany into four zones. Each was occupied by either the United States, Great Britain, France, or the Soviet Union. The same was done with Germany's capital city, Berlin. The relationship between the Soviet Union and the other three Allied powers quickly disintegrated, and in 1961, the wall was erected.

The Berlin Wall was both practical and symbolic. It served as a deterrent for would-be escapees—though many still tried, and some succeeded—and it was directly linked to the deaths of at least 140 people who were trying to escape East Berlin in some manner. At least another 100 died by accident or were shot or killed trying to flee through other border fortifications. The East German guards were given orders to shoot on sight and were even rewarded per kill. They were paid 150 East German marks per escapee shot and killed, and they were punished if they refused to shoot or were deemed to have purposely missed.

After more than forty years of East German communist rule and Soviet domination, democratic revolutions began to spread across Central and Eastern Europe, finally reaching Berlin in November 1989. The Berlin Wall, which had separated Berlin and German families and friends for almost three decades, was the obvious point of conflagration.

Document Image

Protestors tearing down the Berlin Wall in 1989
(AP Images)

About the Artist

This photograph was taken by an unknown Associated Press photographer on November 11, 1989, twenty-eight years after the wall was erected in Berlin.

Context

By 1989, the Cold War had gripped the world, especially Eastern and Central Europe, for close to forty-five years. Germany and Berlin were at the center of this ideological struggle between the United States and its allies and the Soviet Union and its allies. Though these two nations were never officially at war with each other, they were close, and the Berlin Wall, erected in 1961, was often viewed as a potential ground zero.

The Berlin Wall was also a propaganda tool, used by both communists in the East and the democracies in the West. It was detested by West Germans and their allies, a sign of an oppressive communist regime that had divided a city and a people. The West Berlin city government sometimes referred to it as the "Wall of Shame," a term coined by mayor Willy Brandt in reference to the wall's restriction on freedom of movement. The East Germans often referred to it as the Anti-Fascist Protection Rampart, trying to convince their citizens, and the world, that the barrier was there to protect East Germans from the supposed evils of the outside world.

Before the wall's construction, more than 3.5 million East Germans circumvented Soviet migration restrictions and defected from East Germany, many by crossing over the border from East Berlin into West Berlin. From West Berlin they could then travel to West Germany and to other Western European countries. Between 1961 and 1989, the wall prevented almost all emigration. During this twenty-eight-year period, more than 100,000 people attempted to escape, and over 5,000 people succeeded. Unfortunately, somewhere close to 200 died.

In 1989, a series of revolutions in nearby Soviet-allied Eastern Bloc communist countries, particularly Poland and Hungary, led to a chain reaction that reached East Germany, eventually bringing down the Iron Curtain—the ideological divide between East and West. As pressure mounted, the communist leaders began to make concessions.

After several weeks of civil unrest, the East German government announced on November 9, 1989, that all East Germans could visit West Germany and West Berlin. Crowds of East Germans crossed and climbed onto the wall, joined by West Germans on the other side, in a celebratory atmosphere, which was captured in numerous photographs, such as the document studied here.

Over the next few weeks, East and West Germans chipped away parts of the wall and kept or sold them as souvenirs. The Brandenburg Gate, a few feet from the Berlin Wall, was opened on December 22, 1989, and the demolition of the wall officially began on June 13, 1990; it was completed in 1994. The "fall of the Berlin Wall" paved the way for German reunification, which formally took place in October 1990.

Explanation and Analysis of the Document

The photograph shows a section of the Berlin Wall being removed in November 1989. One of the first aspects of this photograph that likely strikes the viewer is that the photographer has captured the removal of a portion of the wall in action. A piece of one the most symbolic, yet concrete, barriers of the Cold War is being removed as Berliners, East and West, watch.

Another remarkable aspect of the photo is the glimpse of East German border guards or soldiers standing in the space vacated by the piece of the wall that is being removed. For close to thirty years, these guards, as members of the East German military, were hated, feared, and also pitied by the populace. They had the unenviable task of being forced to try to stop their own countrymen from escaping the communism of East Berlin by fleeing over, under, through, or around the wall and into freedom in West Berlin. From the construction of the wall in 1961 to its destruction in 1989, border guards were given daily verbal orders to "track down, arrest or annihilate border violators."

The faces of the soldiers are worth examining and noting. They are staring the scene as if intrigued, curious and perhaps in awe of the situation. They, like everyone else at the moment, do not know what to make of this historic incident. They were staring at history, whether they realized it or not.

The graffiti on the Berlin Wall shows how West Berliners treated and viewed the wall for decades and illustrates their contempt for the East German regime.

—Seth A. Weitz

Questions for Further Study

1. What prompted thousands of East Germans to go to the Berlin Wall on the night of the opening, forcing the borders to open peacefully?

2. What can this picture tell us about the history of the Berlin Wall?

3. What does this photograph show us about the power of protest?

Further Reading

Books

Sarotte, Mary Elise. *The Collapse: The Accidental Opening of the Berlin Wall*. New York: Basic Books, 2015.

Taylor, Frederick. *The Berlin Wall: August 13, 1961–November 9, 1989*. New York: Harper Perennial, 2020.

Websites

"Berlin Wall." History.com. https://www.history.com/topics/cold-war/berlin-wall.

Documentaries

Behind the Wall. Michael Patrick Kelly, director. Aquapio Films, 2011.

Tom Olin: "Wheels of Justice" March Photograph

AUTHOR/CREATOR Tom Olin	IMAGE TYPE PHOTOGRAPHS
DATE 1990	SIGNIFICANCE Documentation of a disability rights movement demonstration before the passage of the Americans with Disabilities Act (ADA) in 1990

Overview

The year 1990 saw the culmination of a fifty-year battle for equal access to government and private institutions with the passage of the Americans with Disabilities Act. Preceding the act's passage were a series of demonstrations in Washington, D.C., where this photograph was taken. The most famous section of the demonstrations was the "Capitol Crawl," when physically disabled participants pulled themselves bodily up the Capitol steps to show the world the barriers to their access to government institutions and their determination to gain access anyway. Three months after the demonstration, on July 26, 1990, President George H.W. Bush signed the Americans with Disabilities Act into law. The law prohibited employment discrimination against the disabled and demanded their physical and institutional accommodation in both public and private institutions. The ADA changed the United States dramatically, making disability accommodation an accepted aspect of public and private life and beginning a still-unfinished road to equality for all citizens of the United States.

About the Artist

Tom Olin has been as important as any other figure in the disability rights movement, largely because he was its documentarian. As a photographer, he made the movement known through his pictures on the pages of U.S. newspapers and therefore made the issue of disability rights one with which the average American had some familiarity. His own disability leant him empathy with the physically disabled—being dyslexic, he could not gain acceptance into any higher education institution outside of community colleges. In the 1970s he moved to Canada to avoid being drafted into the Vietnam War. Olin became interested in disability rights while working as an orderly at a rehabilitation hospital when he moved to Grand Rapids, Michigan. Later, he moved to Berkeley, California, and worked near the university as an attendant for people with disabilities. He became interested in photography and got work at a video production company around the same time; his first photographic subjects were many of the people he worked with who had disabilities. His first professional photojournalism on the subject of people with disabilities was in Los Angeles in 1985, and he became the unofficial documentarian of the disability rights movement thereafter. Besides the Wheels of Justice March, he worked for *Mouth Magazine*, a disability rights magazine, from 1995 to 1999. He has been

Document Image

The "Wheels of Justice" march in 1990
(Tom Olin)

accorded the status of a hero to the movement for his willingness to take it on as a permanent subject; his work has appeared in documentaries, newspapers, Centers for Independent Living, magazines, textbooks, web pages, museums, and art shows worldwide.

Context

The disability rights movement in the United States was more complicated than other civil rights movements in that the definition of a disability changed dramatically over time. Those with visual or obvious physical disabilities usually led the way, beginning with the presidency of Franklin Delano Roosevelt. Roosevelt's inability to use his legs was hidden in his public and presidential appearances but not a completely ignored aspect of his humanity. In some respects, his paralysis was inspiring, and in others dispiriting, but most of all, the government he led was not accommodating; he and others like him with physical disabilities simply had to find ways of making their own way through a world designed to accommodate able-bodied people.

The African American civil rights movement of the 1960s inspired many other movements to push for full and equal access to government accommodation, and those with disabilities joined in the effort. Friendships were formed across disabilities as people who were deaf, blind, disabled, and had otherwise compromised bodies found they had a great deal in common in their lack of access to government, either in compensation that was not forthcoming for their disabilities or simply physical access to buildings. At the University of California, a student in a wheelchair named Ed Roberts created a plan for a Center for Independent Living, an accessible building run by the students themselves to allow them to live independently on campus. The idea spread to other institutions in the 1960s and 1970s. At the same time, already-existing institutions came to be seen as a national disgrace for their lack of facilities, funding, and management to accommodate the disabled. The archetype was Staten Island's Willowbrook State School, described by the reporter who exposed it on television in 1972 as a "badly run kennel for humans." In general, mental illness asylums were places where patients were exposed, ignored, beaten, and restrained physically and chemically, all largely to make the lives of the staff easier.

In 1973 Congress passed the Rehabilitation Act of 1973, which tasked the Department of Health, Education, and Welfare with making certain that recipients of federal aid did not discriminate against anyone with a disability. There were many facets of the law, but the section that received the most focus was section 504, which read, "No otherwise qualified individual with a disability in the United States shall, solely by reason of her or his disability, be excluded from the participation in, be denied the benefits of, or be subjected to discrimination under any program or activity receiving federal financial assistance." In essence, this was taken to mean that there should be open access to federally funded institutions, and that those institutions should take into account the fact that people who wished to enter them needed various forms of access. In 1975 the Individuals with Disabilities Education Act was passed by Congress, requiring public schools to provide equal access to education and one free meal a day to children with disabilities. In some respects, this was the disability movement's *Brown v. Board of Education* ruling—it implemented section 504 in public schools and thus inspired others to want to implement it in all other public institutions.

In April 1977 demonstrators across the United States performed sit-ins in courtrooms, libraries, administrative buildings, police departments, the Department of Health, Education, and Welfare itself, and other government buildings, illuminating the problem of physical access to institutions that were allegedly accessible to all citizens of the United States. In San Francisco, Atlanta, Boston, Chicago, Denver, Los Angeles, Washington, D.C., Philadelphia, and Seattle, demonstrators occupied public buildings for days. In some cases, they found that the officials running these institutions had no idea that a Rehabilitation Act existed, nor what section 504 meant. In other cases, local officials brought them food, mattresses, and other supplies to keep the protests going. Future protests included people in wheelchairs lying down in busy intersections in Denver. The 504 Sit-Ins, as they were referred to, gave the civil rights movement for the disabled a national profile.

Access to public government-related institutions was one matter; access to the much-larger private sector of the U.S. economy, infrastructure, and employment market was another. In March 1988, a series of student protests began at Gallaudet University in Washington, D.C., when the board of trustees appointed a non-hearing-impaired president to the vacant post over two deaf candidates. Gallaudet was the world's only university for the deaf, and the students began a protest called Deaf President Now, demanding that the new president resign, that the board of trustees select one of the deaf candidates, that the chair of the board of trustees resign, and that a majority of trustees be appointed who were deaf. After a week of demonstrations, the trustees met all of the students' demands. The stage was now set for the disabled community to demonstrate in favor of similar accommodations in both public and private institutions across the United States.

Explanation and Analysis of the Document

The "Wheels of Justice" March was held in Washington, D.C., on Monday, March 12, 1990, organized by the American Disabled for Attendant Programs Today movement (ADAPT). The March was to promote the goal of forcing Congress to act upon the need for an Americans with Disabilities Act, a catch-all law to demand equal access under law for all Americans to any institution in the country. At the time, the bill was stalled in committee. The march began early in the morning and eventually encompassed some 700 people. They gathered in front of the White House, from where this picture was taken, to begin the "Wheels of Justice" march to the Capitol Building up Pennsylvania Avenue. The march was large enough to have an impact on traffic, and loud enough—chanting "What do we want?" "Our ADA!" "When do we want it?" "NOW!!"—to attract local and national media attention. From the west side of the Capitol, marchers listened to speeches from sympathetic congresspeople, Gallaudet University president I. King Jordan, some members of the executive branch dedicated to disability rights, and Mike Auberger, cofounder of ADAPT. Soon after the speeches, some of the people in wheelchairs began—without any planning—to crawl up the Capitol steps, emphasizing how difficult it was for them to access a governmental body supposedly designed to represent their interests. There could be no more dramatic display of exactly what the ADA was meant to accomplish. Three months later, in July 1990, President George H.W. Bush would sign the Americans with Disabilities Act into law.

—David Simonelli

Questions for Further Study

1. Describe this photograph and how its context represents a cross-section of Americans with disabilities. Why would such a cross-section be important in the pressure that ADAPT wanted to place on Congress?

2. The man on the far left of the photograph is carrying a sign saying "We Shall Overcome." To what was he trying to link the cause of disability rights by carrying this sign?

3. What evidence is there in the photograph that the march would gain some of the publicity it was seeking?

Further Reading

Books

Clark, Erin. *If You Really Love Me, Throw Me Off the Mountain*. Gainesville, GA: EyeCorner Press, 2020.

Equal Access, Equal Opportunity: 25th Anniversary of the Americans with Disabilities Act. Tampa FL: Faircount Media Group, 2015.

Lehrer, Riva. *Golem Girl*. New York: Penguin Books, 2020.

Nijkamp, Marieke, and Manuel Preitano. *The Oracle Code: A Graphic Novel*. Burbank, CA: DC Comics, 2020.

Shapiro, Joseph, P. *No Pity: People with Disabilities Forging a New Civil Rights Movement*. New York: Times Books, 1993.

Wong, Alice, editor. *Disability Visibility: First-Person Stories from the Twenty-First Century*. New York: Random House, 2020.

Greg Gibson: Photograph Of Anita Hill Testifying Before The Senate Judiciary Committee

Author/Creator
Associated Press/Greg Gibson

Date
1991

Image Type
Photographs

Significance
Symbolic representation of Anita Hill's unwarranted exposure to press, Congress, and the public for her testimony against the nomination of Clarence Thomas to the Supreme Court

Overview

In July 1991, President George H.W. Bush nominated Clarence Thomas, a conservative African American judge for the U.S. Court of Appeals in Washington, D.C., to replace Justice Thurgood Marshall on the Supreme Court. While his confirmation hearings were ongoing, a former aide of Thomas's named Anita Hill publicly accused him of sexual harassment during the time they had worked together in the 1980s. Hill claimed that Thomas had repeatedly made sexually crude and offensive comments to her and about her, calling into question Thomas's judgment and fitness to be a Supreme Court justice. For four days in October 1991, the Senate Judiciary Committee, led by Senator Joe Biden, held televised hearings on Hill's charges. This photograph by Greg Gibson was taken during the hearings. Thomas denied the charges, and several Republican senators not only defended his character but cast doubt on Hill's veracity and her mental health. Hill's testimony was shocking and explicit, and many Americans noted the uncomfortable image of a lone woman confronted by an all-male government committee that lacked empathy even from the most open-minded questioners, as demonstrated in the photograph reproduced here. On October 15, the Senate voted 52 to 48 to approve Thomas's confirmation. The hearings fostered a greater public awareness of the problem of sexual harassment in the workplace and about the dangers and exposure faced by women who dared to come forward to explain their experiences.

About the Artist

Greg Gibson is one of the most accomplished photographers in the United States. Beginning his career in college in 1980, he shot high school and college sports for the *Raleigh News and Observer*. Upon graduation from North Carolina State University, he became the youngest state photo editor in wire service history when he was hired by United Press International at age twenty-two as photo editor in North Carolina. Within a year, he had won an award as North Carolina Photographer of the Year by the North Carolina Press Photographer's Association. In 1989 he was hired by the French news agency Agence France-Presse (AFP) to be its stringer out of Washington, D.C. There, he began coverage of the White House, Capitol Hill, and international travel, and caught the interest of the Associated Press (AP), the largest syndicated news

Document Image

Anita Hill testifying before the Senate Judiciary Committee in 1991
(AP Images)

organization in the United States and the world. He became a staff photographer in the AP's Washington Bureau, which was his role when he took the picture displayed here.

Over the course of his career with the AP, Gibson's photos appeared in the *Washington Post*, the *New York Times*, *USA Today*, *Time*, *Life*, *Newsweek*, *People*, and *Vanity Fair*, amongst other journals and newspapers. In 1993 he won a joint Pulitzer Prize with his other AP colleagues for coverage of the 1992 presidential campaign. With the proliferation of the internet, he became founder and president of Press Room Online Services, one of the first online communities for journalists and their scheduling, email, and networking needs. He won a second Pulitzer in 1999 for coverage of President Bill Clinton during the scandal involving White House intern Monica Lewinsky. In 2000, Press Room Online Services was acquired by a larger service, Frontline Communications, and Gibson became its regional director for the Washington, D.C., area. In the same year, he retired as an AP stringer, concentrating instead on documentary, portraiture, and wedding photography. In 2020 he returned to national prominence as the founder of Real Picture Live, a production company photographing coordinated events for members of Congress, government officials, and CEOs.

Context

In June 1991, Supreme Court Justice Thurgood Marshall announced that he would retire as the first and only black justice in the history of the U.S. Supreme Court. After a short vetting process, President George H.W. Bush nominated the forty-three-year-old Clarence Thomas for the court in August. Like Marshall, Thomas was African American, but he was known for his conservative views and had worked in the previous Reagan administration in the Department of Education's civil rights division and then moved on to the Equal Employment Opportunity Commission. In 1991 he was a judge on the D.C. Circuit Court of Appeals. His confirmation hearing before the Senate Judiciary Committee, led by Senator Joe Biden (D-Del.), began in September, and it appeared at the time that his confirmation was a foregone conclusion.

From the moment of Thomas's nomination, however, rumors circulated that Thomas had repeatedly sexually harassed and propositioned his female staffers; as a later statement would put it, "if you were young, black, female and reasonably attractive, you knew full well you were being inspected and auditioned as a female" by Thomas while working for him. In particular, a former staffer named Anita Hill had allegedly endured unwanted attention from Thomas, having been pressured for dates and subjected to lewd comments and inappropriate conversations about sex, pornography, and his own sexual prowess.

By 1991, Hill was a professor of law at the University of Oklahoma. Biden's committee asked the FBI to look into the allegations. Hill herself confirmed the allegations but was unwilling to testify before the committee against Thomas's nomination. Nevertheless, the FBI's report was leaked to reporters for NPR and *Newsday* and therefore became public. Corroborating witnesses came forward as well, and Hill changed her mind. She held a press conference to say she was willing to testify to the Senate committee. Hearings were scheduled for early October 1991 to look into Anita Hill's charges of sexual harassment and Clarence Thomas's character.

The hearings were televised. African American law professor Anita Hill appeared alone before the committee, without counsel, to be questioned by an all-white, all-male Senate Judiciary Committee about her claims of sexual harassment against African American Supreme Court nominee Clarence Thomas. Interested Americans were mesmerized by the testimony of these two people, especially considering its graphic nature. Hill had to repeatedly discuss Thomas's efforts to get her to go on a date with him, his graphic and offensive references to large breasts and large penises, his interest in pornography, and even Thomas's suggestion that Hill had left a pubic hair on his Coke bottle. Hill kept her cool despite the uncomfortable nature of the testimony and the questioning by senators. Thomas himself began his own testimony by saying he was being subjected to "a high-tech lynching," and Republican senators leapt to his defense, accusing Hill of lying, being obsessed with Thomas, being mentally unbalanced, or some combination of all three. Hill took and passed a lie detector test, but committee members dismissed its validity. More than a dozen witnesses were called to defend Thomas's character; four corroborating witnesses for Hill's testimony were not heard because, according to committee leader Biden, there was not enough time in the hearing's schedule. Hours after the last of the hearing's testimony had been heard, the Senate voted to confirm Thomas 52–48, a narrow margin but enough to place Thomas on the Supreme Court.

Anita Hill and Justice Thomas's confirmation hearings had a deep impact on future politics, the handling of claims of sexual harassment, and judicial hearings. The National Women's Law Center and the Equal Employment Opportunity Commission took in a flood of claims of sexual harassment in the workplace over the next several months. Congress passed the Civil Rights Act of 1991, which addressed victims of workplace sexual harassment. Many women were incensed at the all-male committee investigating and dismissing Hill and her claims, and in response they chose to run for political office themselves. The election year 1992 came to be seen as "the year of the woman," as twenty-four women won election to the House of Representatives and four women were elected to the Senate, bringing the total number to six. Most were Democrats. In 2018, Senator Dianne Feinstein of California was the minority leader of the Senate Judiciary Committee when the committee confronted another charge of sexual misconduct, this one made by Dr. Christine Blasey Ford against another Supreme Court nominee, Brett Kavanaugh. Yet the result was the same: despite the credibility of Ford's claims and a slightly more polite hearing, Kavanaugh was confirmed to the Supreme Court.

Explanation and Analysis of the Document

In this photograph, Anita Hill sits at the table on the right, alone. This was a fact not lost on the television audience tuned in to the Clarence Thomas hearings. In front of her in the Russell Caucus Room in the Capitol Building—to the left in the photo—sits the Senate Judiciary Committee, fourteen white men. Surrounding the participants are bright lights, hundreds of reporters and other audience members, and microphones. The effect was to make Anita Hill appear vulnerable and brave, tested and nervous, professional and yet forced to relive the most unprofessional moments of her life. Senate Judiciary Committee chair Joe Biden would eventually apologize to Hill for her treatment during the hearing, specifically for situations like that depicted in this photo. Biden's apology did not come until he decided to run for president, however, and Hill was dissatisfied with his apology because he did not seem to understand how the hearings could have been handled differently—perhaps with more counsel, more allowance for credible witnesses on her behalf, and a greater reining in of the furious and baseless accusations made by Biden's Republican colleagues. It is significant that this photograph was reproduced in 2018 when Dr. Christine Blasey Ford came forward to testify against the Supreme Court candidacy of Brett Kavanaugh under similar circumstances—as an image, it seemed the model as to how *not* to take a critical charge of sexual harassment seriously.

—David Simonelli

Questions for Further Study

1. What does it appear is happening in this photograph? Where does the power appear to lie among its component parts?

2. Greg Gibson was presumably not the only photographer who obtained a shot like this one. What does that say about the Senate Judiciary Committee's concern for the optics of their questioning of Professor Hill?

3. How might you have reorganized the setting in which this questioning took place to have Professor Hill's testimony appear more dignified and to make it clear the committee took her charges of sexual harassment seriously?

Further Reading

Books

Foskett, Ken. *Judging Thomas: The Life and Times of Clarence Thomas*. New York: Morrow, 2004.

Hill, Anita. *Believing: Our Thirty-Year Journey to End Gender Violence*. New York: Viking Press, 2021.

Hill, Anita Faye, and Emma Coleman Jordan, editors. *Race, Gender, and Power in America: The Legacy of the Hill-Thomas Hearings*. New York: Oxford University Press, 1995.

Thomas, Clarence. *My Grandfather's Son: A Memoir*. New York: Harper, 2007.

Films

Anita: Speaking Truth to Power (documentary). Freida Mock, director. Chanlim Films, 2014.

Confirmation. Rick Famuwiya, director. HBO, 2016. https://confirmationhbo.com/.

Steve Greenberg: "Bill Clinton's Foreign Policy Vehicle" Cartoon

Author/Creator Steve Greenberg	**Image Type** Cartoons
Date 1994	**Significance** Called attention to President Bill Clinton's indecisive foreign policy during his first year in office

Overview

This editorial cartoon is a critique of President Bill Clinton's foreign policy. Drawn by cartoonist Steve Greenberg, it first appeared in the *Seattle Post-Intelligencer* in 1994. Greenberg's cartoon is a critique on the indecisiveness and half-measures that had become a trademark of Clinton's foreign policy.

During the presidential campaign of 1992, Clinton's lack of foreign policy experience had been a constant target for his opponents. Once in office, the Clinton administration quickly learned that being the world's lone superpower in the post–Cold War era presented a new set of challenges, including collapsing regimes, regional conflicts, and genocide. Although critical of the foreign policy of his predecessor, George H.W. Bush, during the 1992 presidential campaign, Clinton resorted to many of Bush's policies once in office and largely dealt with issues as they presented themselves rather than developing a proactive strategy.

About the Artist

An editorial cartoonist and freelance artist, Steve Greenberg was born in Los Angeles, California, in 1954. He attended California State University, Long Beach, where he received a bachelor of fine arts degree. While he was in college, his editorial cartoons ran in two campus newspapers. From 1995 to 1998, Greenberg was a regular contributor of cartoons to *Editor and Publisher* magazine. From 2002 to 2008, Greenberg was on staff to the *San Francisco Examiner*, *San Francisco Chronicle*, *Seattle Post-Intelligencer*, *Marin Independent Journal*, the *Daily News of Los Angeles*, and the *Ventura County Star*. He currently contributes to Crooksandliars.com, *SF Weekly*, the *Ojai Valley News*, and the *Jewish Journal of Greater Los Angeles*.

Reprints of Greenberg's work have been published in newspapers such as the *New York Times*, the *Washington Post*, the *Los Angeles Times*, the *Chicago Tribune*, and *USA Today*. His work has also been displayed in numerous museum exhibits, including San Francisco's Cartoon Art Museum, the Billy Ireland Cartoon Museum at Ohio State University and Library, the Charles M. Schulz Museum, and the Newseum. Greenburg has also written for Disney comics and written and drawn for *MAD* magazine. In 2008 he self-published *Fine-Tooning the Planet*, which consists of environmental cartoons.

Document Image

"Bill Clinton's Foreign Policy Vehicle"
(Steve Greenberg, *Seattle Post-Intelligencer*)

Greenburg's work has won numerous awards. These include first place in the 2020 Homer Davenport Cartoon Contest, Citations for Excellence in the 2015, 2007, and 2006 United Nations Ranan Lurie Political Cartoon Awards, and multiple awards from the Society of News Design. He was the first American cartoonist to be invited to join the Cartoonist Movement out of the Netherlands.

Context

As the first post–Cold War president, Bill Clinton's task was to devise a foreign policy that was not defined by the threat of the Soviet Union or the continuation of containment. Containment of communism in general, and of the Soviet Union's influence in particular, had been the basis for U.S. policy since the ideology was first proposed by George Kennan in 1947. The collapse of the Soviet Union in 1991 brought an end to containment, and the United States had emerged as the world's only remaining superpower. The Clinton administration had the opportunity to establish what U.S. policy would look like in this emerging post-Soviet world.

This was easier said than done. During the presidential campaign of 1992, Clinton's lack of international experience was a common target. Prior to his election as president, Clinton had spent his entire career serving at the state level, lastly as the governor of Arkansas. With no foreign policy record to stand on, the Clinton campaign focused on broad statements to define his views. These included updating and restructuring the U.S. military, shifting economics as the focus of international policy, and promoting democracy worldwide. How these goals were to be achieved was never addressed. At the same time, many of Clinton's internationalist, free-market statements were similar to those of his opponent, George H.W. Bush, whom he was critical of.

Upon entering the White House, the Clinton administration inherited a number of international issues. At the start of his presidency, U.S. troops were deployed in more nations than at any time since Harry Truman assumed the presidency. The U.S. Navy and Coast Guard were conducting a blockade of Haiti. Marines were in Somalia, and the U.S. Air Force had recently bombed positions in Iraq and were preparing airlifts into Bosnia.

During Clinton's first term, the administration sought to develop a unified foreign policy, a "Clinton Doctrine," which could replace the Cold War policy of containment. What developed was known as democratic enlargement. Based on four points, democratic enlargement sought to strengthen capitalism worldwide, promote and foster new capitalist democracies, support the liberalization of hostile states, and defend human rights through multinational intervention. Economics and humanitarianism emerged as the two guideposts of foreign policy during the Clinton presidency. Critics argued that the administration's foreign policy was determined more by public opinion rather than by any unified policy.

The post–Cold War world challenged Clinton from the start. President George H.W. Bush's humanitarian mission to Somalia turned tragic with the Battle of Mogadishu. Photographs of Staff Sergeant William David Cleveland's body being dragged through the streets of Mogadishu quickly turned U.S. opinion against the operation. This shift in public opinion led Clinton to order troops out of Somalia in March 1994. Clinton again bowed to public opinion against intervention in Africa when a humanitarian crisis and genocide emerged in Rwanda.

Other crises challenged Clinton's policies during his time as president. These included the overthrow of the democratically elected government of Haiti by a military junta, the disintegration of the Soviet Union, ethnic and regional conflicts in the Balkans, and the threat of a North Korean nuclear program. Clinton's firmness in some events and waffling in others led to critics emphasizing his inconsistency and his devotion to public opinion.

Explanation and Analysis of the Document

In his editorial cartoon "Bill Clinton's Foreign Policy Vehicle," Steve Greenberg depicts the inside of a manual transmission automobile. At the center of the drawing is a large gearshift. To the left of the gearshift is the driver's seat and steering wheel, and to the right is the glovebox, which is open to reveal numerous maps.

The automobile is used as an analogy for Clinton's foreign policy. Without seeing him, the viewer assumes that Bill Clinton, as president, is in the driver's seat.

On the gearshift there are six speeds—a low speed, an "easy does it," a slow, and three positions of reverse. This is meant to show the slowness and reversals of Clinton's foreign policy in light of the promises he made while campaigning in 1992. The maps spilling out of the glovebox represent specific examples of policy reversals from Clinton's first year in office.

The first map is labeled Haiti. Under the previous president, George H.W. Bush, the democratically elected president of Haiti, Jean-Bertrand Aristide, was ousted by a military coup led by Raoul Cédras. The Bush administration, in its support for Aristide, suspended all trade save food with the island nation. The coup also set off a refugee crisis as Haitians attempted to flee to the United States by boat. Under Bush, refugees were fleeing economic, not political, conditions and were to be returned to Haiti. Those who were not immediately returned were detained at the U.S. military base at Guantanamo Bay, Cuba. Clinton had campaigned against forced repatriation, but once in office, he continued the Bush policy. In an effort to pressure Cédras to step down, Clinton dispatched the USS *Harlan County* to Port-au-Prince. Met with protesters on the docks and fearing casualties, Clinton reversed his order and had the ship return to the United States.

The second map visible is labeled Bosnia. With the disintegration of Yugoslavia by January 1992, the successor states descended into nationalistic and ethnic violence. Serbian president Slobodan Milosevic fanned the flames of nationalism to instigate violence in neighboring states and strengthen his position at home. By May 1992 Croatia, Slovenia, and Macedonia had declared their independence. Bosnia-Herzegovina had also declared its independence, but violence erupted after Serbia invaded claiming to liberate the Serbian population. During the Bush administration, the Yugoslavian situation took a backseat to other events, such as the fall of the Soviet Bloc and the Persian Gulf War. As violence erupted, George H.W. Bush maintained it was a civil war that stemmed from historical ethnic tensions. Bush supported a United Nations weapons embargo on all the former Yugoslavian states. During the 1992 campaign, Clinton accused Bush of coddling dictators and called for the arming of Bosnian Muslims and NATO-backed airstrikes on Serbian positions. This became the Clinton administration's position, referred to as Lift and Strike, during its opening months. None of these measures halted the growing violence against Muslim Bosnians, including the establishment of concentration camps and Serbian attacks on United Nations safe zones. Rather than develop an all-out strategy for Bosnia, Clinton and his administration dealt with each incident individually as they emerged.

The third map is labeled North Korea. In 1985, North Korea joined the Nuclear Nonproliferation Treaty (NPT), which sought to stop the spread of nuclear weapons. During the Bush administration, it became common to offer incentives to encourage North Korea to abide by the treaty. These concessions included the removal of American tactical nuclear weapons from South Korea. A key issue that remained was inspections of North Korean nuclear sites as required by the NPT. This issue ballooned once Bill Clinton assumed the presidency. North Korea refused inspections and by March 1993 announced it was withdrawing from the NPT. Months of escalation followed as Clinton increased America's military presence in South Korea and increased international sanctions. North Korea threatened that any further sanctions would be taken as an act of war. While presenting a strong stance on one hand, the Clinton administration continued the Bush policy of concessions, including persuading South Korea to suspend major military exercises. As Clinton was considering the viability of a preemptive air strike on North Korean nuclear sites, former President Jimmy Carter moved into the limelight. Carter began the process that brokered the first bilateral treaty between the United States and North Korea, in which North Korea agreed to stop the production of weapons-grade nuclear material in exchange for the United States providing aid in building electrical plants.

All three examples in the editorial cartoon show how Clinton's early foreign policy was reacting to crises as they emerged and then only slowly addressing or reverting back to the previous policies of the Bush administration or, in the case of North Korea, Jimmy Carter. The use of the gearshift in the cartoon demonstrates that Clinton's foreign policies only move slowly or, in many cases, backward to previous administrations.

—Robert W. Malick

Questions for Further Study

1. Is the automobile and gearshift an effective analogy for Clinton's foreign policy? Why or why not? How might the use of a gearshift be lost by today's generation?

2. Haiti, Bosnia, and North Korea are highlighted by the artist. What do these countries have in common? Compare and contrast how the Clinton administration sought to address the issues in each of these countries.

3. Based on the image, what do you think are the artist's political opinions? What in the piece leads you to this conclusion?

Further Reading

Books

Berman, William C. *From the Center to the Edge: The Politics and Policies of the Clinton Presidency*. Lanham: Rowman & Littlefield Publishers, 2001.

Dumbrell, John. *Clinton's Foreign Policy between the Bushes, 1992–2000*. London: Routledge, 2009.

Articles

Brinkley, Douglas. "Democratic Enlargement: The Clinton Doctrine." *Foreign Policy* 106 (1997): 110. https://doi.org/10.2307/1149177.

Naím, Moisés. "Clinton's Foreign Policy: A Victim of Globalization?" *Foreign Policy* 109 (1997): 34. https://doi.org/10.2307/1149454.

Sweeney, John. "Stuck in Haiti." *Foreign Policy* 102 (1996): 142. https://doi.org/10.2307/1149266.

Websites

Daalder, Ivo H. "Decision to Intervene: How the War in Bosnia Ended." Brookings, December 1, 1998. https://www.brookings.edu/articles/decision-to-intervene-how-the-war-in-bosnia-ended/.

Steve Greenberg: "Contract with America" Cartoon

Author/Creator Steve Greenberg	**Image Type** Cartoons
Date 1995	**Significance** Criticized the Republican Party's "Contract with America" legislative agenda for cutting the social safety net that was meant to help those in need

Overview

Editorial cartoons have been an important form of political commentary, often capturing the irony of political action in vivid, easily remembered imagery that creates a lasting impression. This cartoon, entitled "Betsy Ross Gingrich" by its creator, Steve Greenberg, appeared in the *Seattle Post-Intelligencer* on February 27, 1995. The cartoon is a clever attack on the Contract with America from the perspective of those who favor the social welfare policies of the New Deal and Great Society. The Contract with America was the culmination of a conservative backlash against the welfare state created by the New Deal and Great Society. Seizing on the momentum of Ronald Reagan's victory in 1980 and the new world of policy possibilities brought about by the end of the Cold War and collapse of the Soviet Union in 1991, conservative Republican firebrands lined up behind Representative Newt Gingrich of Georgia, a Republican, and his Contract with America pledge for the 1994 midterm election. The Contract was a right-of-center wish list of proposals to replace the American political status quo that many felt had ossified in the last decades of the Cold War. With the Cold War's end, foreign policy assumptions were being reexamined. To many, this seemed to be the time to do the same with domestic policy. Gingrich's Contract with America provided a blueprint for how to do that. In November of 1994, much of the voting public was willing to give the plan a chance. Republicans took control of Congress for the first time since 1952, picking up fifty-four seats in the House for a thirteen-seat majority, and nine seats in the Senate for a two-seat majority. This 104th Congress would try to enact the policies called for in Gingrich's Contract with America, prompting Greenberg's attack in this cartoon.

About the Artist

Steve Greenberg has been a graphic designer, editorial cartoonist, copy editor, and freelance artist for several West Coast newspapers, including the *Seattle Post-Intelligencer*, *San Francisco Chronicle*, and *San Francisco Examiner*. From his first work for campus newspapers while pursuing a bachelor of fine arts degree from California State University, Long Beach, he has produced countless works and won numerous awards, both national and international. His work has been on display in some of the most prestigious museums dedicated to cartooning and news, such as Ohio State's Billy Ireland Cartoon Museum and Library, the Charles M. Schulz Museum, and the Newseum.

Document Image

"Betsy Ross Gingrich"
(Steve Greenberg, *Seattle Post-Intelligencer*)

A quick scan of his work shows his left-of-center perspective. Naturally, this led him to view the Contract with America with great skepticism. With a clear majority of 223 Contract with America signatories elected to the House of Representatives in 1994 and Republican control of the Senate, Republican leaders introduced bills to implement the provisions of the Contract with America as the first order of business on opening day of the new 104th Congress. The bills were a mix of structural reforms of American political institutions and policy changes. By February 1995 when Greenberg drew this cartoon, debate on the bills was well underway. Greenberg's cartoon directly attacks the Contract's policy changes that sought to dismantle the social welfare safety net for the impoverished created by the New Deal and Great Society. The most dramatic of these assaults occurred to the New Deal program Aid to Families with Dependent Children, commonly called welfare. The Contract with America called for less money to be spent on the program and outright bans on minors receiving benefits and existing recipients receiving benefits for additional children, as well as requirements that recipients work or pursue education.

Context

While the pace of change would increase in the twenty-first century, to those living in the 1990s, it seemed like a time of enormous change and dislocation. The overarching, defining dynamic of the global system, the Cold War, had ended. As a result, economies and political systems around the world were being restructured, and new policies were being tried. Ideas that had threatened pursuit of a nuclear balance of terror between the United States and Soviet Union during the Cold War suddenly emerged as potential options instead of dangerous experiments that could cause division and weaken the country in its perilous international struggle. It was in this environment of newfound policy potential that Representatives Newt Gingrich (R-Ga.) and Dick Armey (R-Tex.) crafted a ten-plank platform called the Contract with America to turn America into a pre–New Deal Republican vision. Not only would the plan bring back Republican policies of limited government, isolationism, and laissez-faire economic and social policy, they believed it would allow the Republican Party to displace the Democrats as America's dominant party and make the emerging, more conservative sunbelt wing—the southern and western states—transcendent within the party. All but a handful of Republican House candidates signed the Contract with America in a dramatic ceremony on the steps of the Capitol in late September of 1994.

The welfare state had long been a target of conservatives. No program symbolized the welfare state to its opponents more than Aid to Families with Dependent Children (AFDC). First passed as part of the New Deal's Social Security Act of 1935, the program provided federal government funds for states to distribute to households with children who had incomes below certain thresholds, which were adjusted for family size. While a godsend to many households during the height of the Depression, when unemployment and homelessness sank to never-before-seen levels, the program drew increasing criticisms in times of overall prosperity. Not only did critics oppose the expenditure of taxpayer funds for what many saw as a moral failing of poor work ethic and laziness, conservatives in particular saw it as creating a moral hazard that encouraged the immoral behavior of promiscuity and single-parent households. They cited the lack of limits on household size or time one could be on the program as causing people to have more children and to have children with no concern for whether the household conformed to a "male breadwinner, female caretaker" model. Basically, conservatives believed AFDC incentivized those receiving assistance to continuing having children to increase both the amount of their benefit, since larger households received larger payments, and the length of time the parents would be able to receive benefits, since one received money until children were eighteen.

To fix these perceived problems, point three of the Contract with America called for a Personal Responsibility Act. Specifically, this plank of the Contract called for fundamental changes to AFDC. It prohibited those collecting AFDC to gain increased payments for additional children born while in the program. It also established time limits for participation in the program, ultimately settling on a five-year lifetime maximum and two-consecutive-year maximum. Minors with children, a situation particularly concerning to AFDC's critics, were required to live under adult supervision with a parent or guardian to be eligible; if they had no parent or guardian, they received no help from the program either. Work, education, or community service requirements were also put in place for recipients. These changes, which eventually passed toward the end of the 104th Congress in 1996, radically changed cash government assistance to poor households. Nothing sums up the spirit of these changes better than the name chosen for the new policy. No longer Aid to Families with Dependent Children, the Contract with America version of cash assistance to poor households was called Temporary Assistance to Needy Families.

Explanation and Analysis of the Document

The foreground of the cartoon depicts Newt Gingrich posed like seamstress Betsy Ross, sewing a flag that represents the Contract with America. Gingrich is sewing the flag with thread made of America's social safety net. The Contract with America is thereby literally unraveling the social safety net of the New Deal and Great Society, which was an overtly stated talking point of those who campaigned under it. A logical conclusion of the cartoon's message is that with a weakened or destroyed safety net, the citizens it was meant to protect will fall through it instead, to their peril.

The cartoon is criticizing the Contract with America's proposals on welfare reform for severely weakening America's social safety net. The Contract sought to gut the level of income security provided to poor households by the Aid to Families with Dependent Children program. Right-of-center critics of AFDC were convinced that the poor were essentially using the program as their primary income and that they were having more and more children to maintain this livelihood. These critics feared that the result of this dynamic would be an increasing number of poor people, dependent upon on AFDC, who would continue to have children they did not have the fiscal resources to take care of. The critics also believed that AFDC removed incentives for maintaining a traditional nuclear family structure, and that this financial support was why children gave birth to children and was the reason for so many single-parent, generally female, households. Helping these people, critics feared, would only encourage the poor to have more children, refrain from marrying, refrain from working, remain poor, and proliferate.

Using the momentum of the Contract with America, the 104th Congress sought to avoid this feared scenario by replacing AFDC with TANF, Temporary Assistance to Needy Families, which limited program recipients' ability to stay on the program and receive support for more children. At the same time, it proposed to end the cycle of poverty and government dependence by forcing people to work or obtain job training to participate. This, they reasoned, would give program participants the experience and skills to be self-supporting, ultimately reducing and, perhaps ideally, eliminating the need for this type of safety net.

The Personal Responsibility Act section of the Contract with America and Greenberg's critique of it suggest several assumptions about TANF. Supporters contended that TANF would reduce the number of children in poverty as the incentive to have more children to maintain or increase government assistance would be gone. It follows from this that the goal of "cut spending for welfare programs" stated in the Personal Responsibility Act section of the Contract with America would also be achieved. Greenberg's critique, on the other hand, suggests that without the safety net of AFDC, the number of children in poverty would rise. The Personal Responsibility Act section of the Contract also calls for the policies in TANF to "discourage illegitimacy and teen pregnancy," so one would expect out-of-wedlock and teenage births to fall as well. On the socio-cultural front, the implied preference for traditional nuclear families and gender roles in the rhetoric used to support AFDC's replacement with TANF can be seen as an attack on the LGBQT community as non-traditional families are presumed inferior. Similarly, it can also be seen as counter to the women's rights movement since the focus on the traditional family suggests that women should conform to traditional caregiver roles rather than have the option to choose the role they desire in society.

TANF has now been federal policy for over twenty years. Looking at the data, the claims of its supporters and critics can be evaluated. The implication from the cartoon that the weakening of the social safety net by the Contract with America would place a higher percentage of children in poverty has not been born out. The percentage of children living in poverty declined slightly in the years after TANF replaced AFDC. It averaged 20.3 percent per year for the twenty years prior to Personal Responsibility Act's implementation, compared to an average of 18.9 percent for the twenty years after, a 6.9 percent decline. There was a decrease in spending on TANF (0.13 percent of GDP) as a percentage of the overall U.S. economy compared with AFDC (0.19 percent of GDP), although both amounts, representing less than one-fifth of one percent, are a negligible share of all economic activity. Perhaps the greatest change was in teen pregnancy, which fell from around 30 per 1,000 fifteen- to seventeen-year-olds in 1997 to a little over seven by 2019, a drop of more than 75 percent. Births to unwed mothers, however, increased from around 32.5 percent of all births in 1997 to 40 percent in 2019, a 23 percent increase. These statistics might suggest that some aspects of the Contract with America worked as intended while others did not. Other factors, as well, such as increased awareness of and access to birth control, might also have contributed to the changes.

—G. David Price

Questions for Further Study

1. What does the cartoon criticize about the Contract with America? What effects does it suggest the Contract with America will have?

2. Was the cartoon's criticism justified? Did the Contract with America undertake the actions implied by the cartoon? Did the actions have the effects suggested by the cartoon?

3. Given the purposes behind the Personal Responsibility Act and changes in child poverty rates, teen pregnancy rates, and births to unwed mothers after twenty years, would you consider it a success?

Further Reading

Books

Garrett, Major. *The Enduring Revolution: How the Contract with America Continues to Shape the Nation.* New York: Crown Forum, 2005.

Gingrich, Newt, et al. *Contract with America: The Bold Plan by Rep. Newt Gingrich, Rep. Dick Armey and the House of Republicans to Change the Nation.* New York: Random House, 1994.

Schorr, Alvin Louis. *Welfare Reform: Failure and Remedies.* Westport, CT: Praeger, 2001.

Articles

Harvey, Philip. "Gingrich's Time Bomb: The Consequences of the Contract." *American Prospect*, December 19, 2001. https://prospect.org/economy/gingrich-s-time-bomb-consequences-contract/.

Jacobson, Gary C. "The 1994 House Elections in Perspective." *Political Science Quarterly* 111, no. 2 (Summer 1996): 203–23.

Perlstein, Rick. "How Wily Newt Pulled the 'Contract with America' Scam." *Rolling Stone*, January 26, 2012. https://www.rollingstone.com/politics/politics-news/how-wily-newt-pulled-the-contract-with-america-scam-200577/.

Weaver, R. Kent. "Deficits and Devolution in the 104th Congress." *Publius: The Journal of Federalism* 26, no. 3 (Summer 1996): 45–85.

Documentaries

Congressional Republicans and the Contract with America. United States BBC Worldwide Americas, Inc./BBC Worldwide Learning.

Oklahoma City Bombing Photograph

Author/Creator	Significance
Staff Sergeant Preston Chasteen	Captured the aftermath of the bombing of the Alfred P. Murrah Federal Building in Oklahoma City, the worst act of domestic terrorism in American history and the worst terror attack in American history to that point
Date	
1995	
Image Type	
Photographs	

Overview

At 9:02 a.m. on April 19, 1995, a blast erupted from in front of the Alfred P. Murrah Federal Building in Oklahoma City, shaking the heart of the city's downtown and causing mass chaos in and around the structure. The building itself sustained a substantial amount of damage in the blast, and 300 other buildings and dozens of cars were severely damaged from the explosion as well. When the dust settled, 168 people (including nineteen children who had been in the daycare program in the building) had been killed in the blast, and hundreds more had been injured.

The media had a significant impact almost immediately on the investigation, with many outlets speculating that the bombing was the work of Muslim terror groups since it had occurred about two years after a similar bombing in the World Trade Center parking garage in New York City. CNN and similar twenty-four-hour news networks ran live coverage from the blast site, streaming images of the blast into the homes of viewers, while newspapers and magazines published photographs of the destruction and carnage. One of the most iconic photos to come out of the incident, taken by Charles Porter IV, was of a fireman pulling a badly injured child from the wreckage of the building; Porter went on to win the Pulitzer Prize for the image. In the case of the image depicted here, dated April 21, the sheer force of the blast can be seen in the wreckage of the cars in the foreground and the skeletal remains of the federal building in the background.

After the initial reports by the media that the bombers were Muslim extremists, FBI investigators were able to locate the rear axle of the Ryder truck that had carried the explosives and tracked it down to a rental facility that helped create a sketch of a suspect who witnesses later identified as Timothy McVeigh. The investigation turned from one of foreign terrorism to one of domestic terrorism, ostensibly stemming from disillusionment over a raid by federal agents at Waco, Texas, two years earlier.

About the Artist

The photographer, Staff Sergeant Preston Chasteen, was a member of the Oklahoma Air National Guard when the photograph was taken. He has photographed various missions of the Oklahoma Air National Guard,

Document Image

Photograph showing the destruction from the bombing of the Murrah Federal Building
(Staff Sergeant Preston Chasteen)

including its participation in rescue and recovery efforts at the site of the bombing.

Context

During the latter part of the twentieth century, right-wing militia groups were growing in size and influence around the United States in direct response to the perceived heavy-handedness of the American government in dealing with these groups. In 1992 at Ruby Ridge in Boundary County, Idaho, agents from the Federal Bureau of Investigation (FBI) and the Bureau of Alcohol, Tobacco, Firearms and Explosives (ATF) laid siege to property owned by Randy Weaver, who was accused of federal firearms charges. The siege lasted eleven days before a fierce shootout ended it. A year later in Waco, Texas, the Branch Davidians, led by David Koresh, engaged the FBI and ATF again in a siege for fifty-one days, from February 28 to April 19, 1993, before the FBI assaulted the structure and the building ignited (a series of fires later determined to have been started by the Branch Davidians themselves), resulting in dozens of lives lost. Many right-wing groups viewed such actions as proof that the government (now led by a Democratic Congress and president) were trying to strip away American freedoms and bring down the Constitution.

It was against this setting that Timothy McVeigh plotted the attack against the Alfred P. Murrah Federal Building in Oklahoma City, along with Terry Nichols, who helped manufacture the bomb. As a member of a group called the Michigan Militia, McVeigh, like many militia members, viewed his role as protecting the United States from the tyranny that was the federal government, particularly the Department of Justice. These groups believed in the concept of "posse comitatus," or the summoning of militias to protect the United States from its oppressors and invaders. This growing movement had been a part of a growing trend in the 1980s within the so-called "new right," which aimed to restore America to a more conservative state. These groups also sometimes participated in attacks against abortion clinics, claiming it was part of their moral duty as American citizens to protect the sanctity of human life.

The attack on Oklahoma City signified two significant issues confronting American law enforcement in the 1990s. The first issue was symbolized by the media's quick response to blame the attack on a foreign terror group such as Hamas or Hezbollah, resulting in increasing apprehension by Americans against the Muslim community and helping fuel the drive for recruitment for the militia groups. Attacks such as the one seen in New York City's World Trade Center in 1993 made these concerns understandable, and McVeigh's attack had sought to play into those fears to help plant the seeds of discord. That leads to the second issue that the FBI faced: the growing force and influence of the right-wing militias in the United States and the difficulty in using traditional heavy-handed approaches to dismantle those operations. The attack against the Alfred P. Murrah Federal Building was partly responsible for the congressional power shift in 1996 to the Republicans even though President Clinton would remain in office, as many Americans now felt that the safety of the nation (typically seen as the purview of the Republicans) was a number-one concern over social inequities (typically seen as the purview of the Democrats).

Explanation and Analysis of the Document

This image captured the sheer brutal destruction and force of the blast in Oklahoma City. Even two days after the blast, the wrecked hulks of cars sit like silent memorials to the power of the blast, while the rubble of what had been the front of a ten-story structure that housed many federal agencies and organizations seems to weep from the loss of life and destruction. Of the 361 people inside the building on the day of the explosion, 319 sustained injuries of some sort, and 163 of those (including 19 children) were killed in the blast. Many of the dead were found days later as rescuers shifted through the rubble in the front part of the building.

As the picture shows, the size and force of the blast were incredibly powerful thanks to the 4,800 pounds of ammonium nitrate that had been packed into the truck that served as the bomb. Nearly half of the building's front façade had been destroyed in the blast, which left an impact crater thirty feet wide by eight feet deep. The concussive forces of the blast can be seen by the lack of hoods, doors, wheels, and trunks on the cars in the parking lot, and its impact was felt in a four-block radius around the structure. Seismic readers dozens of miles away from the blast site would register the explosion as a 3.0 magnitude earthquake. The building's main support column collapsed in the blast, explaining the collapse of the structure seen in the photograph.

This photograph would have been taken as FBI and ATF teams combed the bomb site looking for clues as to the bomber's identity. Each vehicle is marked with a number to help investigators as they identified pieces of evidence, often small bits of shrapnel and debris that investigators would then use to complete the backward redesign of the bomb used in the blast. With the blast being the equivalent of 5,000 pounds of TNT, however, many of these pieces were either obliterated or incinerated in the blast, or embedded into vehicles in the parking lot as they were expelled out from the truck. To completely piece together the source of the explosion and analyze the events of that morning's blast, investigators had to comb through the wreckage around the blast site seeking any piece that might have had a serial number or vehicle identification number (VIN) engraved on it so they could begin tracing the original source of the blast and then find a paper trail leading to the suspect.

The Oklahoma City bombing was a significant turning point in American history as it shifted American focus to the growing right-wing domestic terror and militant movement growing within America's borders in the 1990s. Initially thought to be a localized, rural issue in places like Idaho (Ruby Ridge) and Texas (Branch Davidians), the attack on the Alfred P. Murrah Building represented a sudden awareness that the problem of right-wing extremism was more widespread than originally thought. The FBI and other intelligence and security agencies shifted their energies from foreign terror groups to American organizations, resulting in the arrests of numerous individuals on weapons and conspiracy charges in the 1990s. While these investigative efforts helped mitigate the threat of the domestic terror groups, there were some who believed that the shift of focus from external to internal threats paved the way for the failures to prevent the September 11, 2001, attacks on the World Trade Center and Pentagon.

—Ryan Fontanella

Questions for Further Study

1. The events at Ruby Ridge, in Waco, and then at Oklahoma City all represented a growing discontentment among right-wing radical groups in the United States. What historical events had triggered their resentment of the government, and why did they come to fruition in the 1990s rather than sooner?

2. Many Americans found it hard to believe that an American, particularly a U.S. Army veteran, could have been responsible for such a deadly attack on U.S. soil. Why were many Americans so quick to jump to the conclusion that Arab extremists and not American extremists must have committed the attack? What impacts could that have had internationally had the FBI not been so quick to identify McVeigh as the bomber?

3. Some scholars believe that the focus on domestic terrorism by federal agencies such as the FBI in the 1990s resulted in the failure to identify the warning signs of 9/11 six years after the Oklahoma City attack. Do you agree that America's focus on domestic terrorists might have reduced its ability to target and identify foreign terrorists operating in the United States? Why or why not?

Further Reading

Books

Linenthal, Edward. *The Unfinished Bombing: Oklahoma City in American Memory*. New York: Oxford University Press, 2003.

Wright, Stuart A. *Patriots, Politics, and the Oklahoma City Bombing*. New York: Cambridge University Press, 2007.

Websites

"FBI Records: The Vault—Oklahoma City Bombing." FBI. https://vault.fbi.gov/OKBOMB/OKBOMB%20Part%2001%20of%2001/view.

"Oklahoma City Bombing." Clinton Digital Library. https://clinton.presidentiallibraries.us/okc-bombing.

"Oklahoma City Bombing." History: Famous Cases and Criminals, FBI. https://www.fbi.gov/history/famous-cases/oklahoma-city-bombing.

Bush v. Gore Election Photograph

Author/Creator
Peter Cosgrove/AP Photos

Date
2000

Image Type
Photographs

Significance
Shows the chaos caused by the closeness of the 2000 presidential election, in particular the vote count in Florida, which was subject to weeks of post-election litigation

Overview

This montage from the Associated Press, showing different headlines from the same newspaper, the *Orlando Sentinel*, running the same day, perfectly captures the spirit of confusion and chaos that occurred as the votes of Florida were being counted, and ultimately recounted, in the wake of the 2000 election. There were 5,963,110 votes cast for president in Florida that year, and the major party candidates were neck and neck. Exit polling had predicted a very narrow victory for Vice President Al Gore, the Democratic nominee, yet his opponent, Governor George Bush of Texas, maintained a steady but essentially microscopic lead as votes were counted. Even before the closeness of the election was known, charges of voting irregularities and confusing ballots in Palm Beach County were impugning the results. As election night wore on and returns came in from other states, it became clear that the electoral votes of Florida would determine the presidency, yet the vote there was too close to call. After 2 a.m. the morning after election day, Gore called Bush to concede, only to call back in less than two hours to retract the concession. Reflecting this, the second and third headlines read "It's Bush" and "Is It Bush?" respectively.

The ultimate margin was a mere 537 votes, nine-thousandths of a percent (0.009). Florida law required any election closer than half of a percentage point (0.500) to undergo a machine recount. The Gore campaign requested a hand recount in four largely Democratic counties, assuming that the country was not patient enough for a hand recount of the entire state and that those counties would most likely be where uncounted Democratic votes were in sufficient numbers to matter. Republicans objected and began legal action to stop the recount. Both sides assembled high-powered legal teams. Legal proceedings dragged on for weeks, ultimately reaching the Supreme Court. In a five-to-four decision on December 12, 2000, the Court ruled that the recount in progress was unconstitutional and that there was not sufficient time to complete a recount that might pass constitutional muster before the Electoral College votes were to be certified. George W. Bush was now the president-elect of the United States in what is arguably the closest presidential election in American history.

Document Image

Montage of headlines from the Orlando Sentinel on November 8, 2000
(AP Images)

About the Artist

Peter Cosgrove was a photographer for both United Press International (UPI) and the Associated Press (AP). He had a long and distinguished career in journalism, beginning in 1957 and ending with retirement in 2005. Based in Florida in his later years, his final position was in the AP office in Orlando, Florida, from 1997 to 2005, where he took this photo. Well liked and respected by his colleagues, he was at the center of coverage for many of the late-twentieth-century's major events associated with Florida. Perhaps most famously, he is credited with saving the Pulitzer-winning image a colleague took of young Elián González's horrified face as federal agents seized the child to return him to Cuba.

Cosgrove is perhaps best known for his coverage of stories related to the National Aeronautics and Space Administration (NASA), so much so that NASA lists him in its Roll of Honor for media representatives and public affairs officers. His coverage of the space program began early, starting with coverage of a hometown parade held for astronaut John Glenn and reaching an apex in the late 1960s and early 1970s when he was shipboard for the pickups of four Apollo crews, including the crew from the first moon landing. As a wire service photographer, his images from these and other events received wide circulation in newspapers across the country. Cosgrove was able to enjoy several years of retirement after his exciting career, and he died of a heart attack in 2019.

Context

As the twenty-first century dawned, Americans found themselves very divided politically. These divisions had been foreshadowed by new political energy that sprang up in the 1990s with the ascension of globalization as the primary dynamic of world politics in the wake of the Cold War's end. Both major political parties were still controlled by the traditional centrist establishments as the decade began. They were soon challenged by insurgent movements that helped to polarize and muddle traditional American politics. A movement of nationalistic economic populism reacting against more liberal trade and immigration found a champion in Ross Perot and his Reform Party. Perot received almost 20 percent of the vote in the 1992 election. The most conservative elements of the Republican Party were on the ascent at the expense of the establishment with the rise of Newt Gingrich and the Contract with America, the party's legislative agenda. Although slower to coalesce, left-of-center critics of the status quo were also gaining momentum by the decade's end. The anger and frustration of youth embodied in grunge and hip-hop music began to explode in outbursts of violent rioting, such as the 1992 Los Angeles riot in response to the acquittal of the police officers who had brutally beaten Rodney King in 1991 and the anarchist-led "Battle for Seattle" protesting the 1999 World Trade Organization ministerial conference. A fledgling Green Party tried to harness this energy into a social justice and anti-corporate political movement.

Against this backdrop, Vice President Al Gore Jr. and Governor George W. Bush sought the presidency in 2000. Representing the anti-establishment extremes in the election were Pat Buchanan, running under the Reform Party banner after losing the Republican nomination to Bush, and Ralph Nader, an activist and long-standing critic of corporate America, making a second run for the Green Party. In many ways, Bush and Gore were embodiments of the establishments of their parties. Gore, the sitting vice president, a former senator, and the son of a longtime senator, was the consummate Washington insider and had a moderate record on most issues. Even in what was becoming his signature reform issue of environmental policy, his sizable holdings of petroleum stock and charges of illegal waste dumping on his family's land cut into his credibility. Bush, the governor of Texas, son of a former president, and grandson of a senator known as an Eisenhower Republican and birth control advocate, was trying to stake out ground in the Republican Party with promises of "compassionate conservativism."

This four-way presidential contest would by some measures be the closest in American history. Ultimately, Bush prevailed by two electoral votes despite losing the popular vote to Gore by 537,079 votes. The story encapsulated by the photo montage is that the closest vote to determine which slate of electors would get to vote was from the state of Florida, which had twenty-five electoral votes that were determined by a mere 537 out of 5,963,110 votes cast in the state. The winner of Florida's electoral votes would be president, yet several problems arose in determining who won in Florida. Complaints about confusing ballots and other election irregularities had to be resolved. Given the closeness of the election, lawsuits and recounts were inevitable. To further cast uncertainty into the legitimacy of vote count, George W. Bush's brother Jeb was the governor of Florida. After several recounts and legal maneuvers, the Supreme Court stepped in and, in the case of *Bush v. Gore*, ordered the recounting to stop and Bush's 537-vote margin to stand as the official result on December 12, 2000.

Explanation and Analysis of the Document

The photo is a montage of pictures of the four headlines produced on election night for different editions of the *Orlando Sentinel*. The practicalities of printing and delivering newspapers to subscribers required different editions. The *Orlando Sentinel* is a morning newspaper, which subscribers expect to be available to them when they wake up to go to work. It took time to get a physical copy of a newspaper to delivery people many miles from Orlando. The edition going to farthest locations had to be printed first. Its headline, "Oh, so close," reflects the uncertainty of the result when it went press. By the time the Metro edition went to press, headed for the suburbs, Bush's lead in Florida appeared to be holding and possibly growing slightly. Major news networks were beginning to call Florida for him, so the headline in this edition read "It's Bush." The situation was different when it came time to print the edition distributed within the city of Orlando. Bush's lead had eroded a good bit, and Gore was expected to continue to gain on him, prompting yet another headline change to "Is It Bush?" Once that edition was printed and out to delivery people, it was clear that a mandatory recount would be required and that the result of that recount would determine the presidency. That situation warranted an "extra" edition, so a small "election extra" edition was published with a headline appropriate to the situation: "Contested."

The back and forth of the election-night headlines reflected what would be a confused process of how to determine what fair electoral processes were in terms of both casting and counting ballots. Trying to resolve the issues exposed flaws in how elections were conducted and made many people aware of the complexities, and to some unfairness, of the Electoral College method of selecting the president.

The first issue that had to be addressed was what constituted a fair recount. Florida law required that races with a margin of a half of a percentage point or less had to undergo a machine recount. Essentially, the ballots had to be fed through vote-tabulating machines again. Florida law also allowed a candidate in such a close race to request a manual recount, a much more time-consuming process in which humans tabulated the ballots. The Gore campaign requested hand recounts in only four of Florida's sixty-seven counties. These were highly populous counties, containing over 30 percent of the votes cast in the disputed election. Nevertheless, Bush's attorneys questioned whether a partial hand recount was fair. If there are ballots that will be counted if observed by humans that were not counted by machines, shouldn't all of the ballots be recounted by hand? The Supreme Court sided with Bush, ruling that a partial hand recount violated the rights of voters in areas not recounted. It needed to be a complete hand recount or no hand recount.

Furthermore, it was unclear how those doing the hand recount should deal with ballots that did not explicitly indicate a preference. This proved to be an issue with punch-card ballots—those in which voters punched a hole in a perforated card beside the name of their preferred candidate. Sometimes the punch only partially opened the hole, resulting in a "hanging chad." At what point is the chad pushed through enough to be a sign of the voter's intent: most of the way through, halfway through, only one corner separated? There was no statewide standard. Also, some voters pointed out that on Palm Beach County ballots, the font on the candidate's name had been enlarged so much to make the names more readable that it no longer directly lined up with the hole that needed to be punched to select that candidate. While most everyone agreed that that design probably did cause some people who intended to vote for Gore to inadvertently vote for Reform Party candidate Buchanan, it was too problematic to redo the election, either in the county with the flawed ballot or in the country as a whole.

Finally, the election caused many people to question the Electoral College as a method of presidential selection. Despite losing the Electoral College by two votes, Gore won the nationwide popular vote by 537,079. Many Americans had no idea that one could get fewer votes than another candidate across the country and still win the presidency, although it had happened three times in the nineteenth century. As is indicated by President Donald Trump's refusal to accept his defeat in 2020—despite losing both the Electoral College and popular votes—the 2000 election was only the beginning of a questioning of the processes and rules of voting and of the use of the Electoral College.

—G. David Price

Questions for Further Study

1. Why did it take so long for the results of the presidential election of 2000 to be known? What problems arose in arriving at a final result?

2. What principles did the Supreme Court use to rule in the case of *Bush v. Gore*? Does the ruling seem fair to you?

3. What do you think about the fact that a person can come in second in the popular vote but win the Electoral College? Is it fair that the person who received fewer votes across the country as a whole becomes president?

Further Reading

Books

Brinkley, Douglas. *36 Days: The Complete Chronicle of the 2000 Presidential Election Crisis.* New York: Henry Holt, 2001.

Ceaser, James W., and Andrew Busch. *The Perfect Tie: The True Story of the 2000 Presidential Election.* Lanham, MD: Rowman & Littlefield, 2001.

Tauber, Steven C., et al. "Florida: Too Close to Call." In *The 2000 Presidential Election in the South: Partisanship and Southern Party Systems in the 21st Century*, edited by Laurence W. Moreland and Robert P. Steed: 149–68. Westport, CT: Praeger, 2002.

Wilcox, Clyde, and Stephen Wayne. *The Election of the Century and What It Tells Us about the Future of American Politics.* Armonk, NY: M.E. Sharpe, 2002.

Articles

Ashbee, Edward. "The Also-Rans: Nader, Buchanan and the 2000 US Presidential Election."
Political Quarterly 72, vol. 2 (April 2001): 159–69.

Websites

"Bush v. Gore." Oyez. https://www.oyez.org/cases/2000/00-949.

PHOTOGRAPH OF WORLD TRADE CENTER TOWERS AFTER 9/11 TERRORIST ATTACK

AUTHOR/CREATOR
Robert Fisch

DATE
2001

IMAGE TYPE
PHOTOGRAPHS

SIGNIFICANCE
Captures the moment United Airlines Flight 175 crashed into the World Trade Center's South Tower, the second of two terrorist-controlled aircraft to strike the trade center complex

Overview

This photograph was one of many captured by photographers in New York City following the terrorist attacks on September 11, 2001, and it reflected the shock and horror that many Americans felt as the incident played out on live national television. Many Americans were at school, at work, or at home watching television when the news broke of the first trade center tower, the North Tower, being hit by an airplane, and viewers watched in disbelief at what was initially thought to be an accident. At 9:03 a.m., a second airplane, Flight 175, crashed into the South Tower on live television and with hundreds of photographers on the ground taking photos of the moment of impact. Akin to the explosion of the space shuttle *Challenger* in 1986, the siege at the Branch Davidian complex in Waco, Texas, in 1993, and the bombing of the Murrah Building in Oklahoma City in 1995, this incident reveals the powerful ability of modern live-feed media to bring horror and tragedy into the homes of Americans and shape public opinion.

About the Artist

Robert Fisch was a professional photographer who had documented New York City life since the 1980s—from the graffiti to the architecture to the rise of the LGBTQ community in New York during the late 1980s and early 1990s. When the events of 9/11 occurred, he used his camera to document the attacks from the streets of Greenwich Village, an area just north of Lower Manhattan. His photography was widely seen in publications and news media around the country, including another iconic image of Flight 175 just before impact with the South Tower. Though still an active photographer, 9/11 would be the last major event he would actively photograph.

Context

In the 1980s and 1990s, America had adopted a more assertive role in the events in the Middle East; from the deployment of Marines to Beirut, Lebanon, to maintain the peace between the Lebanese and the Israelis, to America's alliance with Saudi Arabia against Saddam Hussein's invasion of Kuwait in 1990, the United States increasingly inserted itself in the political and economic affairs of the oil-rich region. While this part-

Document Image

The World Trade Center towers following the plane attacks on September 11, 2001
(Wikimedia Commons)

nership would bring economic and marginal political stability to the region throughout the 1990s, some Muslim extremist organizations found the American presence to be threatening to their culture and a challenge to the caliphates they had hoped to establish.

One particular organization that resented America's presence in the region was al-Qaeda, led by Osama bin Laden. The organization was formed by former Mujahideen fighters in Afghanistan who had sought to prevent the Soviet occupation and who now turned their efforts to the United States and its increasing involvement in the Middle East. As the Saudi princes struck deals with American and European governments for military hardware in exchange for oil and influence, al-Qaeda began to unleash terror attacks against Saudi Arabian and foreign targets in the late 1980s and early 1990s. Expelled from Saudi Arabia following the Persian Gulf War, which increased American presence (that is, influence), al-Qaeda set up its training facilities in the Sudan and continued to launch attacks against international targets. In 1993, al-Qaeda used a van packed with explosives to destroy the parking garage of the World Trade Center in New York City, killing six and marking the first time terrorist attacks hit American soil. In 1996, another attack by al-Qaeda, this time against U.S. Air Force personnel at the Khobar Towers in Riyadh, signaled another major strike against the United States by the growing terror organization. President Bill Clinton responded by launching missile strikes at al-Qaeda camps in the Sudan and forced bin Laden once again to relocate his training facilities, this time to the mountains of Afghanistan, where he was offered protection and support from the Taliban government.

Political upheaval caused by the 2000 election and the subsequent recounts and court challenges left the United States distracted from the threat of al-Qaeda, who now began the process of preparing for a systematic strike against multiple hard and soft targets in the United States. Though numerous agencies had various pieces of intelligence showing that al-Qaeda was planning something, the lack of bureaucratic cohesion and competition between those appointed by Clinton and those who were incoming under President George W. Bush resulted in a failure of law enforcement and national intelligence forces to prevent the attacks.

Explanation and Analysis of the Document

This photograph, particularly when combined with another photograph by Frisch shortly before showing Flight 175 as it flew toward the tower, captures the moment when many Americans realized that the crashes had been intentional and that the country was under attack. Looking toward Lower Manhattan from uptown, Frisch had a clear vantage point of the World Trade Center towers and the chaos that would result that morning as a result of the terror attacks. Taken presumably from the rooftop of an apartment building in Greenwich Village, he had a unique vantage point, able to see and capture the sequence of events that the taller buildings downtown would have obscured for many photographers and others closer to the scene.

The crash of the plane into the middle section of the South Tower, the combustion of jet fuel, and the ensuing heat weakened the structural integrity of the tower's supports, eventually resulting in its collapse (and the same was true of the North Tower). This event marked a turning point in American social and foreign relations history, thus rendering this image iconic for its capture of a pivotal moment of the 9/11 attacks and for representing the explosive reaction of America in response. Approximately one month after the attack, U.S. troops began to arrive in Afghanistan along with an international coalition of forces to root out al-Qaeda and remove the Taliban regime that had sheltered bin Laden and his followers. Around the world, increased counterterrorism raids sought to arrest or eliminate terrorist cells operating in Europe, Africa, and the United States, marking a notable shift from America's more traditional police-like approach to a more militaristic response.

At home as well, America saw significant changes in response to these attacks. Despite the contentious election of 2000 that had politically split the nation, the attacks unified Americans and brought political stability to the country. President Bush's approval rating swelled to 86 percent as Americans supported his aggressive response to the attacks on the World Trade Center, even though some of this came at the loss of individual freedoms. In October 2001, the United States passed the PATRIOT (Providing Appropriate Tools Required to Intercept and Obstruct Terrorism) Act, which allowed for special courts to secretly issue warrants for searches, wire taps, and arrests for those suspected of terrorism. It also created a special facility at Guantanamo Bay, a U.S. Naval base in Cuba, to incarcerate those suspected of terrorism without allowing them access to lawyers or consulate protections. Similarly, those who were suspected of aiding or supporting terrorists or of committing acts of terrorism could be detained without habeas corpus (legal protection against unlawful detention, the right to a lawyer, and a speedy trial) while the case was adjudicated in the courts.

One of the most significant responses to the 9/11 attacks came in 2002 when the United States created the Department of Homeland Security (DHS), an executive agency that combined twenty-two different federal departments into a unified agency. After the attacks, Congress launched an investigative committee that determined that one of the key causes for failure to prevent 9/11 was that many law enforcement and intelligence agencies did not communicate with one another. The result was akin to trying to have twenty-two people put together a single puzzle with parts of the puzzle in separate rooms: while all of the pieces were there, nobody could see the whole picture. The creation of DHS brought together many of these organizations into a single agency that now could coordinate and collate the information and prevent such a disaster from occurring again. From the Immigration Customs Enforcement Agency to Secret Service and Coast Guard, the United States increased the security of its borders from future terrorist attacks and added a single agency tasked with responding to all disasters, including natural disasters.

—Ryan Fontanella

Questions for Further Study

1. As images such as this one were seen on television, in newspapers, and on the internet in the wake of the attacks, how did they fuel the patriotic desire of Americans to unify despite a time of political chaos?

2. Previous terrorist attacks against the United States included the bombing of the Marines barracks in Beirut in 1983, the bombing of Pan Am Flight 103 over Lockerbie, Scotland, in 1988, the original World Trade Center attack in 1993, and the Khobar Towers bombing in Saudi Arabia in 1996. Why did the attacks of September 11, 2001, elicit such a different response from Americans? What role did the development of 24-hour media access play in the political and social changes of the United States post-9/11?

3. The U.S. response to 9/11 in the Middle East included the invasion of Iraq in 2003 and the use of drone strikes to target specific military and terrorist leadership in countries like Afghanistan and Yemen. How did the terror attacks depicted in this picture pave the way for such an aggressive response?

Further Reading

Books

National Commission on Terrorist Attacks. *The 9/11 Commission Report*. New York: Norton, 2004.

Wright, Lawrence. *The Looming Tower: Al-Qaeda and the Road to 9/11*. New York: Knopf Doubleday, 2007.

Websites

"9/11 Investigation." FBI. https://www.fbi.gov/history/famous-cases/911-investigation.

"Preventing Terrorism Overview." U.S. Department of Homeland Security. https://www.dhs.gov/preventing-terrorism-overview.

"September 11, 2001: The Day That Changed the World." 9/11 Memorial and Museum. https://www.911memorial.org/learn/resources/digital-exhibitions/september-11-2001-day-changed-world.

J. Scott Applewhite: "Mission Accomplished" Photograph

Author/Creator J. Scott Applewhite	**Image Type** Photographs
Date 2003	**Significance** Highlighted the erroneous belief of the Bush administration that the conflicts associated with the War on Terror could be quickly and easily won

Overview

This photograph is a textbook example of a photo opportunity, or "photo op," a staged photograph designed to portray the viewpoint of the subject depicted in it. The message in this particular photo, summed up in the "Mission Accomplished" banner, was that the war in Iraq was over and the United States would soon be able to withdraw its forces. From that, Americans were to infer that the Bush administration's promises of quick victory over Iraqi dictator Saddam Hussein and the establishment of a peaceful and democratic Iraq were being fulfilled. At the time of President George W. Bush's photo op, Iraq's regime had been overthrown and its leadership killed or driven underground, all in less than six weeks at the cost of 140 American lives. The sad reality, however, was that the mission was far from accomplished; the United States was destined to occupy Iraq for another eight years, continue sporadic military operations for years after that, and lose at least 4,446 more soldiers.

Although the administration worked incredibly hard to convince Americans that invading Iraq was part of the War on Terror that began with al-Qaeda's terrorist attacks of September 11, 2001, scholars generally conclude that it was an extension of the conflict between the United States and Iraq that had begun with President Bush's father, President George H.W. Bush. He had overseen a U.S.-led, United Nations–authorized multinational military operation to restore Kuwait's sovereignty and drive invading Iraqi forces out in 1991. The effort honored the UN mission objectives by stopping short of overthrowing Iraq's dictator, Saddam Hussein. Using the climate of fear created by al-Qaeda's 9/11 attacks, the second President Bush misled Congress and the public into supporting an invasion of Iraq to finally overthrow Hussein. Administration officials assured Congress and the public that the Hussein's government would make nuclear weapons available to terrorist groups like al-Qaeda and that Iraq's population would "greet us as liberators." No evidence of nuclear weapons was found, and an anti-U.S. insurgency and civil war among Iraqis led to a protracted U.S. occupation and the deaths of thousands more American soldiers after the declaration of victory depicted in the photo. To many, the "Mission Accomplished" photo op came to symbolize the complexities of intervention in Middle Eastern politics and the failure of the U.S. policy to remake the Islamic world into secular, capitalist democracies.

Document Image

Photograph of George W. Bush on May 2, 2002
(AP Images)

About the Artist

J. Scott Applewhite has been a photographer for the Associated Press (AP) since the 1970s. Inspired by adventures he had as student journalist at Western Kentucky University, he worked for several newspapers, including the *Louisville Courier-Journal*, *Palm Beach Post*, and *Miami Herald*, before becoming the primary stringer for the AP in Florida. His work documenting the 1980 Liberty City riots in Miami caught the eye of AP's upper management, and he was given a position in AP's Washington Bureau in the waning days of the Carter administration. From there he has covered seven presidential administrations, countless significant events, and eventually shifted focus from the White House to the Capitol, where he took some of the most dramatic images of its January 6, 2021, storming by insurrectionists trying to prevent certification of Joe Biden's election as president. He was inside the House Gallery when the rioters stormed the Capitol and was the sole person allowed to remain in the balcony while Capitol Police held the mob at bay. His coverage of the insurrection led him to be a Freedom of the Press honoree in 2021.

Over the years, his work has earned several prestigious awards and honors and led to his selection by his peers as chair of the Senate Press Photographers Gallery. He was further recognized by his colleagues in the White House News Photographers Association with a Lifetime Achievement Award in 2017. His photos contributed to the AP's Pulitzer Prizes for Feature Photography in 1993 for the US. presidential campaign and in 1999 for coverage of President Bill Clinton's impeachment. He was nominated for an individual Pulitzer for his images of the United Nations relief effort in Somalia in 1992–93 and received an Honored Finalist Award. As the AP's primary White House photographer, Applewhite was part of the press corps that followed President George W. Bush on his trip to San Diego for this photo op on the USS *Abraham Lincoln*. For a man who has had the long and exciting career that Applewhite has had, that assignment was all in a day's work.

Context

The 9/11 attacks radically altered the trajectory of U.S. and global politics. One way they did this was to give the Bush administration the opportunity to push for an invasion of Iraq, a goal George W. Bush and his key foreign policy advisors had sought from the beginning of his presidency. Iraq had been largely defanged after the U.S.-led United Nations (UN) force liberated Kuwait from Iraqi occupation in 1991. In addition to thoroughly defeating Iraq's military, the United States and its allies enforced no-fly zones in northern and southern Iraq, effectively precluding Iraqi military operations outside the center of the country. There was a personal dimension to the U.S.-Iraq conflict as well. Saddam Hussein's intelligence agency had tried to assassinate former President George H.W. Bush when he visited Kuwait in the spring of 1993. Although using the rhetoric of protecting American national security, many observers believe revenge for the Hussein's failed assassination attempt on his father was the reason for the second President Bush's insistence that the Iraqi regime had to be overthrown as part of the War on Terror.

One reason people look for a motivation beyond the War on Terror as rationale for the Bush administration's zealous drive to invade Iraq is that there was absolutely no connection between Saddam Hussein and al-Qaeda, the terrorist group responsible for 9/11. Relations between the two groups were hostile. Al-Qaeda sought the establishment of an Islamic Fundamentalist regime for the Islamic world. Saddam Hussein's regime was secular and based on the Pan-Arab Socialism of the Ba'ath Party, which was at odds with Islamic Fundamentalism. The al-Qaeda presence in Iraq consisted of small cells based in the Kurdish areas of northern Iraq, which were ironically protected from destruction by Saddam's forces by the U.S. no-fly zone. While the Bush administration did everything in its power to conflate Saddam's past aggressions with the violent Islamic Fundamentalism of al-Qaeda and confuse the American public, the administration knew it needed different rationale for foreign policy experts in Congress and its overseas allies.

The Bush administration seized on Iraq's previous possession of weapons of mass destruction (WMD) and its designation as a State Sponsor of Terrorism to promote the idea that Iraq would give WMD to terrorists. Labeling Iraq as part of a dangerous "Axis of Evil," Bush repeatedly told Americans that Iraq was building WMD and would soon give them to terrorists. To prevent this, Bush insisted that the United States had to act unilaterally and with force if necessary. Again, however, just as there were no connections between Iraq and al-Qaeda for the Bush administration to justify attacking Iraq, there was also no firm evidence that Iraq had or was currently developing WMD.

Despite 700 inspections in Iraq from November 2002 to March 2003, UN teams found no evidence that Iraq had built new WMD. The United States and some allies rejected the UN's findings, demanding Iraq give up the WMD the UN concluded it did not have. The Bush administration flooded the public with flimsy evidence to support its claims and tried to discredit UN inspections that concluded otherwise. Officials such as National Security Advisor Condoleezza Rice dismissed objections to their evidence as dangerously nitpicky, most famously warning Americans that "we don't want the smoking gun to be a mushroom cloud." With the American public still shellshocked by the horror of the 9/11 attacks, the administration succeeded. By the time of the invasion, more than 70 percent of Americans supported overthrowing Saddam Hussein. With overwhelming military superiority, U.S. forces easily defeated Iraq's military, most of whom surrendered or deserted, and Iraq's leaders went into hiding. President Bush thought these circumstances sufficient to declare America's mission in Iraq "accomplished."

Explanation and Analysis of the Document

The "Mission Accomplished" photo op took place May 2, 2003, on the deck of the aircraft carrier USS *Abraham Lincoln*. It was returning home from several months at sea, its last action having been supporting the Iraq invasion. The speech President George W. Bush gave at the event reiterated the administration's false claims that Iraq was "an ally of al-Qaeda" and furthered its efforts to conflate Saddam Hussein with the 9/11 attacks by saying the defeat of "Iraq is one victory in a war on terror that began on September the 11th, 2001." The administration was clearly trying to make the public think its efforts at avenging and preventing future 9/11 style attacks were being fulfilled by overthrowing Saddam Hussein.

While Bush's claims of the destruction of Saddam Hussein's regime were accurate, his boast that "major combat operations in Iraq have ended" was not. Seventy-two days had elapsed from the initial invasion to Bush's "Mission Accomplished" photo op. In those seventy-two days, 140 Americans in Iraq were killed, roughly two per day. The death rate of U.S. soldiers declined to about 1.5 per day for the next nine months or so, but it began to spike upward in the spring of 2004. From March 10, 2004, through September 16, 2007, a total of 1,285 days, 3,220 Americans died serving in Iraq, a rate of over 2.5 people per day. Looking at the most intense period, June 26, 2006, to June 26, 2007, the rate was almost three per day. If a death rate of two U.S. soldiers per day occurred during a time of major combat operations, it would seem hard to argue that the intensity of fighting was diminished for the more than three years that the rate was a sustained 25 percent higher.

The number of troops involved also indicates the intensity of involvement. When President Bush gave his "Mission Accomplished" speech, there were a little over 147,000 U.S. troops in Iraq. The number dwindled to an average of around 121,000 in the nine succeeding months when casualties fell as noted above. For the three and a half years after that, through mid-September 2007, troop levels, like casualties, were again substantially higher, averaging 142,970. Combat operations, four and a half years after Bush proclaimed their end, were as intense as they were before and had been for most of that period.

While Bush acknowledged that other aspects of the Iraq War mission, such as neutralizing Iraq's WMD and establishing a free and democratic Iraq, were yet to be completed, his rhetoric and tone suggested they would be successfully accomplished in short order. Caches of old chemical weapons from the Iran-Iraq War of the 1980s were discovered in Iraq. About half of these were widely known about and had been sealed in bunkers by UN inspectors during the 1990s and subject to constant surveillance by U.S. Air units as part of the enforcement of the no-fly zones. These posed virtually no threat as any attempt by the Iraqis to retrieve them would have resulted in U.S. airstrikes to deny access to them. The remainder were scattered along abandoned frontline positions from the Iran-Iraq War, potentially accessible and usable, although Saddam's forces neither moved them nor used them against Americans, calling into question the degree to which they were even aware of their existence. No evidence of the much-discussed biological and nuclear weapons the administration claimed existed was found, consistent with the UN's conclusion that they did not exist.

"Free" and "democratic" are ultimately in the eye of the beholder, although scholars have made numerous attempts to quantify the concepts so that comparisons can be made. The most comprehensive effort to do this, considering both defined concepts and length of time for which data is analyzed, comes from the V-Dem Institute in Gothenburg, Sweden. By its measures, Iraq made noticeable gains in the degree to which the population was "free" (in the sense of the population's civil liberties being protected) and the degree to which the country was democratic (in the population's ability to participate politically and hold the government accountable) since Hussein's regime was overthrown. Nevertheless, when compared against all countries, Iraq remained decidedly in the range of unfree countries, scoring well below the countries of the European Union and North America and more akin to other members of the Arab world such as Kuwait, Lebanon, and Morocco. Other indices, such as Freedom House's annual "Freedom in the World" report, come to the same conclusion.

All in all, the mission to neutralize Iraq as a threat and to make it a free, democratic society was certainly not fully accomplished by May 2, 2003. Thousands more Americans would die in pursuit of the mission. Few, if any, WMD that could realistically be given to terrorists to attack the United States were found. While the Iraqi people have more freedoms and political rights now than under Saddam Hussein, they are still not considered free in the senses understood by the American public, and their government is not considered a functioning democracy.

—G. David Price

Questions for Further Study

1. What motivated the U.S. invasion of Iraq in 2003? Consider both the stated reasons and other motives that scholars have advanced.

2. What resulted from the U.S. invasion both for the United States and Iraq?

3. Given the motives and results of the invasion, to what degree was the mission the United States set out for Iraq accomplished by the time the photograph was taken? To what degree has it been accomplished today?

Further Reading

Books

Harvey, Frank P. *Explaining the Iraq War: Counterfactual Theory, Logic and Evidence.* New York: Cambridge University Press, 2011.

Keegan, John. *The Iraq War.* New York: Knopf, 2004.

Phillips, David L. *Losing Iraq: Inside the Postwar Reconstruction Fiasco.* New York: Westview Press, 2005.

Steed, Brian, editor. *Iraq War: The Essential Reference Guide.* Santa Barbara, CA: ABC-CLIO, 2019.

Websites

Bryan, Wright, with Douglas Hopper. "Iraq WMD Timeline: How the Mystery Unraveled." NPR, November 15, 2005. https://www.npr.org/2005/11/15/4996218/iraq-wmd-timeline-how-the-mystery-unraveled.

"Fatalities." Iraq Coalition Casualty Count. http://icasualties.org/App/Fatalities.

"WE THE PEOPLE ARE GREATER THAN FEAR" FLYER

AUTHOR/CREATOR
Shepard Fairey; Ridwan Adhami

DATE
2017

IMAGE TYPE
FLYERS

SIGNIFICANCE
Conveys a message to a politically divided American public about increasing dialogue and cooperation and making sure to represent a largely unheard voice in the American politic

Overview

This political image is an example of American iconography that was intended to convey a specific political message and is comparable to the iconic image of the "Hope" poster created by Shepard Fairey for Barack Obama's 2008 presidential election campaign. This image was a part of a larger collection of images aimed at promoting unity following a very divisive election campaign in 2016. The posters were displayed throughout Washington, D.C., on inauguration day and published as advertisements in the *Washington Post* and other newspapers.

This poster was particularly powerful thanks to its imagery of a Muslim woman wearing an American flag, a conceptual reimagination by Shepard Fairey of a photograph taken for the five-year anniversary of 9/11 by Ridwan Adhami. During the election campaign, the rise of the extreme right not just in the United States but also in France, Germany, and other countries resulted in white people attacking Muslims, in particular Muslim women, who often could be identified by the visible identifiers of their faith like the hijab.

About the Artist

Shepard Fairey is a contemporary American street artist whose most notable work was the 2008 Barack Obama "Hope" poster from his 2008 election campaign. In 2014, Fairey painted a mural nine stories tall in Johannesburg, South Africa, dedicated to Nelson Mandela as well as a mural in Germany that focused on ending the war in Afghanistan in 2014. Though he is an artist, he is more broadly classified as a humanitarian through the sales of his artwork and the donation of profits to various charities and organizations he supports.

Ridwan Adhami is a photographer and filmmaker. For the fifth anniversary of 9/11, he photographed a woman wearing an American flag as a hijab near Ground Zero, an image he titled "I Am America." Fairey adapted Adhami's image ten years later as a conceptual poster for the Amplifier organization's "We the People" media campaign.

Context

During the 2016 presidential election, President Donald Trump held numerous rallies that amplified and

Document Image

"We the People Are Greater Than Fear"
(Shepard Fairey, Ridwan Adhami)

emboldened the growing alt-right movement. Many pundits classified the presidential race between Trump and Hillary Clinton, the Democratic candidate, as divisive and even abusive at points, with a proliferation of hostility in the debates and in campaign speeches that focused more on negative language than on the political issues at hand. Clinton referred to "half of Trump supporters" as a "basket of deplorables," adding, "They're racist, sexist, homophobic, xenophobic, Islamophobic—you name it." Though Clinton would walk back her comments after backlash from the Trump campaign, Trump had indeed declared that "I think Islam hates us" and voiced his desire to disallow all Muslims from entering the United States and to investigate mosques as potential sites for training and recruiting domestic terrorists. Despite condemnation from both sides of the political aisle, Trump continued to push a strong anti-Muslim rhetoric to appeal to the more radicalized voters of the Republican Party.

Though Trump would win the election in November, he failed to secure a plurality of the vote, earning only 46 percent of the popular vote, compared to Clinton's 48 percent. Trump nonetheless carried the electoral college vote by 304 to 227, resulting in a large number of voters who felt disenfranchised by Clinton's loss. As the nation made plans for the inauguration in January 2017, large groups of left-wing protesters organized protests to show their dissatisfaction with the election results and protest Trump's presidency, which prompted the creation of this poster campaign.

Much like Obama's "Hope" poster, which used a similar color scheme and aesthetic, the idea behind "We the People" was to symbolize unity rather than division for the public in a way that was easy to disseminate and communicate. Due to the restrictions in place at the time of the inauguration, these posters had to be distributed rather than posted around the city. As such, they were run as full-page, colored advertisements in local newspapers, which would be large enough for people to display to send a message of unity in the crowd of inauguration attendees as well as in the countless protest marches that occurred in the afternoon. Some of these posters were also distributed as stickers that people could affix to their clothing, their electronic devices, or anywhere else they desired to show their support for the unity of the nation and an understanding that America was a collection of cultures, not just a singular ethnic or racial identity.

While the posters may have sought to unify America, the events of the inauguration on January 20, 2017, showed a nation that was anything but united. Three thousand law enforcement officers and National Guard soldiers were deployed to secure the streets of Washington, D.C., as protestors numbered in the tens of thousands, with some historians estimating upward of 200,000 protestors for the Women's March the day after Trump's inauguration. The protests were mostly peaceful, but in a few incidents such as Franklin Square, officers and civilians were injured when objects from the crowd were thrown at officers and multiple buildings were vandalized. Just as Trump's campaign had mobilized the extreme right-wing voters during the election, it had also resulted in left-wing anarchist groups seeing an opportunity to cash in on the discord and use violence to create chaos and convey their message. Growing calls for resistance echoed not just in Washington, D.C., but across the country as America's political gaps were expanded into ever-growing crevices and divides. This was seen in the 2020 election when President Donald Trump refused to recognize the election results and prompted a mob to break into the Capitol Building as the election results were being certified on January 6, 2021.

Explanation and Analysis of the Document

Below the image of a woman wearing the U.S. flag as a hijab appear the words "We the People" in large letters, and "Are Greater Than Fear" below that in smaller letters. The color palette is red, blue, and off-white or yellow. This poster was created when a greater divide was apparent in America politically than had been seen in previous elections, including the contentious 2000 and 2008 elections. The imagery was meant to remind Americans that despite the election of Donald Trump in 2016, the United States still represented a very diverse population. In the days immediately following the election, numerous protests by women's rights groups and organizations such as Black Lives Matter sought to increase awareness of the misogynistic and racist attitudes conveyed by the newly elected president during several speeches as well as on-camera events prior to his candidacy.

The political divide was not lessened but, if anything, exacerbated during the Trump's administration. Tensions led to events such as the "Unite the Right" white nationalist rally in Charlottesville, Virginia, in August

2017 that resulted in the death of a thirty-two-year-old woman; professional athletes' refusal to stand for the national anthem; and, in May 2020, Minneapolis police officer Derek Chauvin's murder of George Floyd, whom he was detaining on the suspicion of passing a counterfeit twenty-dollar bill. In various tweets and social media posts, President Trump continued to press the divide by refusing to admonish the actions of white supremacists and even trying to shift the blame for these incidents onto groups like Black Lives Matter and Antifa. In a 2019 Pew Research poll, 56 percent of Americans surveyed said that Trump's presidency made race relations in the United States worse. These tensions continued to remain a prominent issue into the 2020 election campaign as President Trump repeatedly voiced allegations of election fraud, particularly in battleground states such as Pennsylvania, Arizona, and Nevada, furthering a divide between conservatives and liberals in the United States.

In light of such tension, the "We the People" poster recalled the concept of hope that had driven the Democrats' push for the election of Barack Obama in 2008, and the use of the same color palette and similar iconography helped convey a similar message of American unification behind change and progress. While the political divide remained, the notion that America could still be great and celebrate its ethnic and cultural diversity was a pivotal point throughout the midterm elections in 2018 and then the election of 2020, which saw a shift in power (albeit slight) back to the Democrats.

—Ryan Fontanella

Questions for Further Study

1. What is the significance of the imagery in the poster—the color palette as well as the iconography of the image? Do you see this as a message of unity, a call for resistance, or something else? Please explain.

2. Political campaign and message posters have a long history in the United States. Imagery is often more powerful than written or spoken word, and images in the twenty-first century can spread especially rapidly thanks in part to social media. How might this image be seen as reflective of the power of social media in connecting Americans to a common voice and thought?

3. One of the key takeaways from the presidential election of 2016 was that America was politically divided to a point where extremist views became loud and noticeable on both sides of the political spectrum. What political issues and events divided America going into the election?

Further Reading

Websites

Avins, Jenni. "The Story behind Shepard Fairey's Powerful Posters for Donald Trump's Inauguration." *Quartz*, January 18, 2017. https://qz.com/887358/the-story-behind-shepard-faireys-powerful-posters-for-donald-trumps-inauguration/.

"An Examination of the 2016 Electorate, Based on Validated Voters." Pew Research Center, August 9, 2018. https://www.pewresearch.org/politics/2018/08/09/an-examination-of-the-2016-electorate-based-on-validated-voters/.

"Shepard Fairey's Plan for Trump's Inauguration." *Phaidon*. https://www.phaidon.com/agenda/art/articles/2017/january/17/shepard-fairey-s-plan-for-trump-s-inauguration/.

Solis, Steph. "Shepard Fairey's Inauguration Poster: The Meaning behind the 'We the People' Art." *USA Today*, January 16, 2017. https://www.usatoday.com/story/news/politics/onpolitics/2017/01/16/we-the-people-activists-make-art-inauguration/96627614/.

MIHOKO OWADA: PHOTOGRAPH OF RIOTERS BREACHING THE U.S. CAPITOL

AUTHOR/CREATOR Mihoko Owada	**IMAGE TYPE** PHOTOGRAPHS
DATE 2021	**SIGNIFICANCE** Documents the seditious assault on the U.S. Capitol for the purpose of preventing the lawful tally of electoral votes by Congress

Overview

This photograph taken January 6, 2021, depicts a mob of supporters of outgoing President Donald Trump attacking the Capitol Building in Washington, D.C.

After losing the presidential election, Donald Trump dishonestly propagated the idea that he actually won the election, making multiple unsupported accusations of voter fraud, all of which were disproved. Despite the reality of the situation, Trump clung to the fantasy that he could hold onto power by preventing Congress from counting the electoral votes on January 6. To that end, he and a circle of advisors called for and organized a rally on that date with the express purpose of stopping Congress from certifying the victory of Joe Biden. Trump and a number of his allies gave increasingly inflammatory speeches to the assembled crowd at the perniciously titled "stop the steal" rally. After the speeches, which called for violence and indicated that the only way Trump could hold onto power would be to interrupt Congress from counting the votes, the mob marched on the Capitol.

Over the course of several hours, the mob overwhelmed the Capitol police and broke into the building, killing one officer and injuring several others in the pursuit of Vice President Mike Pence and the member of Congress, forcing them to flee the floor of Congress and to hide in protected areas throughout the building. The mob proceeded to ransack the Capitol, looting offices and threatening violence against Pence and congresspeople. After more than three hours, Trump ordered his followers to go home, which they did. After the Capitol was secured and the House floor was cleaned up, Congress proceeded to certify Biden's election, formally completing the process at 3:32 a.m. on January 7.

About the Artist

Mihoko Owada is a professional freelance photographer from Japan who is currently living in Washington, D.C. Her work has appeared in the *Catholic Standard*, a variety of websites, and newspapers in both the United States and Japan.

Context

In 2016, Donald Trump was elected president of the United States, winning in the Electoral College but receiving fewer actual votes than Democratic candidate

Document Image

Photograph showing rioters breaching the Capitol on January 6, 2021
(AP Images)

Hillary Clinton. Trump immediately claimed that he had also won the popular vote, the first of a series of false claims he made about the elections of 2016 and 2020.

As the campaign began in 2020, Trump was asked a number of times if he would accept the outcome of the election if he were defeated, a question heretofore never asked of an incumbent president because it was completely unnecessary. Trump initially answered these queries by confidently predicting victory. As the race wore on, he began to imply, then outright state, that any outcome besides his victory would automatically be fraudulent and that he would try to overturn it.

On election day, despite the fact that the votes had not been completely counted, Trump declared victory. In fact, he had lost both the popular vote and in the Electoral College decisively. Trump and his advisors immediately began claiming that the only possible explanation for this outcome was fraud, and a series of investigations and legal challenges began. Over the next two months, all of the legal challenges failed, and a thorough investigation by the Department of Homeland Security and several state election boards determined that there was no reason to doubt the outcome. The Department of Homeland Security declared the election the safest in American history, and the handful of fraudulent votes discovered were almost all cast on behalf of Trump.

Despite all of the evidence, Trump and some of his advisors, along with a number of Republican politicians and conservative talking heads on Fox News and other outlets, continued to make dishonest claims about the election. Trump's false claims of fraud and victory became known as the Big Lie. As the last of the increasingly spurious legal challenges failed, all of the states certified the outcome of the election.

The final step in the process was the official counting and certification of the electoral votes by Congress as required by the Constitution and codified by the Electoral Count Act of 1887. The act established January 6 as the date for this final administrative process, whereby Congress meets jointly to open, count, and certify the electoral votes sent in by the states. The vice president presides over the counting and announces the result. If electors are challenged, the House and the Senate have to meet separately to resolve the challenge, then resume the joint session to complete the counting. Trump initially hoped that he could convince some of the states that Biden won to send phony slates of electors to disrupt the count and perhaps swing the election. When that gambit failed, he called on Republicans in Congress to challenge the electors in a few states, which did happen, but this only delayed the count as there was no evidence that supported a challenge. Trump also called on Vice President Pence to simply reject some of Biden's electoral votes and then either call for yet another investigation or a revote, or just declare that Trump actually won. Pence refused to commit this blatantly illegal act.

Trump's final hope was to organize a rally by supporters on January 6 to physically disrupt Congress and prevent the certification of Biden's victory. The beginning of the mob's attempt to carry out Trump's plan is seen in the photograph.

Explanation and Analysis of the Document

The picture shows the mob of Trump supporters that had marched from the site of the initial rally and speeches to the Capitol Building. They are in the process of breaching the initial police barricades that surrounded the Capitol. In the background, part of the mob has already occupied the balcony on which the inauguration would take place two weeks later, with the mob on the right and left of the photo occupying the grandstands set up for the inauguration. The mob in the background of the picture is on the verge of completely overwhelming the Capitol police and entering the building. The photographer appears to be in the midst of the rear of the mob, shooting up toward the Capitol.

The mob is decked out in Trump-branded paraphernalia, carrying Trump or American flags. The defeated president had spent the preceding sixty days lying to his supporters, feeding them a daily deluge of dishonest claims, echoed by commentators and interviewees on Fox News, Newsmax, and One America News as well as by some of Trump's aides, advisors, and attorneys supported by some Republican senators and congresspeople. Again, all of the evidence and facts supported the actual truth: Joe Biden defeated Donald Trump in the 2020 election. Republican officials in Georgia and Arizona certified that fact. State and federal judges throughout the country, including a number appointed by Trump, dismissed all of the legal challenges to the election due either to a lack of evidence or to overwhelming evidence that the claims put forward by Trump's attorneys were false. The Department of Homeland Security investigated numerous claims of fraud on behalf of Biden and found none of them to be true.

Nonetheless, the steady, daily propagation of the Big Lie had the desired effect. A majority of Republicans polled believed the Big Lie and refused to accept the truth that Trump had been soundly defeated. Thus, Trump was able to have his team organize a rally for January 6, confident that several thousand supporters would show up convinced that the Big Lie was true and willing to do whatever Trump wanted them to do to support it.

With the assistance of domestic terrorist groups like the Proud Boys and the Oath Keepers, the rally was planned for January 6. At the rally, a series of Republican speakers, including Missouri senator Josh Hawley, Alabama congressman Mo Brooks, and attorney Rudy Giuliani, spoke to the crowd, encouraging them to fight to keep Trump in the White House and to "do what they had to do" to make that happen. Trump also spoke at the rally, calling on Vice President Pence to illegally throw out Biden electors and declare Trump the victor, and stating that Pence would no longer be his friend if he did not do so.

After the speeches, the mob marched to the Capitol Building, first surrounding it and occupying the grandstands set up for the inauguration. They then began assaulting the heavily outnumbered police, spraying them with mace, hitting them with flags, pipes, fists, and pieces of the torn-down barricades, and finally overwhelming them entirely and breaching the Capitol, the moment captured by the photograph from the rear of the mob.

Shortly after this picture was taken, the mob entered the Capitol, threatening violence against Pence and House Speaker Nancy Pelosi. They did not find the vice president or any members of Congress; they did break into the floor of Congress and into several offices and stole computers, flags, and the like. While this was happening, Trump refused to call off the mob despite entreaties from several congressional Republicans, aides, family members, and conservative pundits. For three hours the mob ransacked the Capitol before Trump finally issued a statement that they disperse. It took another three hours for the FBI, National Guard, and D.C. and Capitol police to fully secure the building.

Congress then reassembled, and after a handful of frivolous challenges to electors by a few Republicans, Vice President Pence announced after midnight on January 7 that Joe Biden would be the next president of the United States.

—Richard M. Filipink

Questions for Further Study

1. After losing the election of 2020, what was the purpose of the rally Donald Trump called for on January 6?

2. What message does this picture convey about who was responsible for the attack on the Capitol?

3. How does the action compare with previous insurrections against the government?

Further Reading

Books

Karl, Jonathan. *Betrayal: The Final Act of the Trump Show.* New York: Dutton, 2021.

Raskin, Jamie. *Unthinkable: Trauma, Truth, and the Trials of American Democracy.* New York: Harper, 2022.

Woodward, Bob, and Robert Costa. *Peril.* New York: Simon & Schuster, 2021.

Websites

"The January 6 Insurrection" (collection of articles). *Washington Post.* https://www.washingtonpost.com/january-6-capitol-riot/.

Select Committee to Investigate the January 6th Attack on the U.S. Capitol, U.S. Congress. https://january6th.house.gov/.

Steve Helber: Photograph Of Robert E. Lee Statue Removal

Author/Creator Steve Helber/AP Photo **Date** 2021 **Image Type** Photographs	**Significance** Documents the removal of one of the largest remaining Confederate monuments in the United States from its pedestal in Richmond, Virginia, the former Confederate capital

Overview

This document is an example of a mass media photograph, commonly used in the twentieth and twenty-first centuries. The first photographs in the United States were used to report on important events during the American Civil War, with images from the battlefield making their way to living rooms across the nation for the first time in the nation's history. By the twentieth century, the medium was commonplace, and photography helped influence public opinion in the nation (and world) on numerous occasions, such as during the modern civil rights movement and the Vietnam War, when images shocked Americans by bringing the reality of those events to the forefront of people's daily lives.

This particular photograph documents the removal of the statue of Confederate general Robert E. Lee from its pedestal in Richmond, Virginia, former capital of the Confederate States of America, in the summer of 2021—an important event in the ever-changing and multifaceted landscape of American civil rights and politics.

After the deadly shooting and murders of nine African Americans in a church in Charleston, South Carolina, in 2015 by a white supremacist, the nation began to have a discussion about Confederate flags, symbols, and monuments, many of which were still prominently displayed. It was a heated debate, with arguments from both sides, but gradually flags and monuments began to come down, viewed by many as symbols of slavery and hatred rather than heritage.

This debate took center stage once again after the murder of George Floyd by police officer Derek Chauvin in 2020, which sparked mass protests across the country, the Black Lives Matter movement, and further debate about Confederate imagery in the public domain. The statue of Confederate general Robert E. Lee, which stood atop a monument in Richmond, the former capital of the Confederacy, was one of those targeted by protesters and a focal point of the debate about the place of such memorials in twenty-first-century America.

About the Artist

Associated Press photographer Steve Helber is an American photographer whose work has appeared in

Document Image

A statue of Robert E. Lee being removed from its pedestal in Richmond, Virginia
(AP Images)

over fifty different periodicals and news outlets, including *Bloomberg News, El País, Fox News, HuffPost, MSN, Washington Post, Time, USA Today, Yahoo News, ABC News, CBS News, New York Post, The Atlantic, US News & World Report, Chicago Tribune, People, Toronto Star, Globe and Mail, Christian Science Monitor, Cleveland Advocate, Global News, Houston Chronicle, Seattle Times, Sports Illustrated, Star Tribune, Boston Globe, Mercury News, Times of Israel, Vanity Fair, Epoch Times, Irish Independent*, and *Miami Herald*.

Helber and his colleague Sarah Rankin were the first journalists covering the white supremacist rally in Charlottesville, Virginia, in 2017 to receive an alert about a car plowing into protesters. They were the first to have a named official saying the suspected driver was arrested, and they were also the first with a named source saying that one person, Heather Heyer, had been killed. Helber continued taking photographs, shooting award-winning pictures, while being hit with pepper spray and other items from the crowd.

Context

During the early part of the twenty-first century, the United States was engaged in an intense debate over how to study its past, including how to memorialize those who fought against the Union and for the Confederacy during the Civil War (1861–65).

Monuments to supporters of the Confederacy can be traced to the post–Civil War ideology of the Lost Cause. The Lost Cause is a mythology that claims the cause of the Confederacy was just, heroic, and not centered on slavery. Since 1866, it has continued to influence racism, gender roles, and religious attitudes in the South. Lost Cause proponents typically praise the traditional culture of honor and chivalry of the antebellum South. They argue that enslaved people were treated well and deny that their enslavement was the central cause of the war. The first major period of Lost Cause activity was around the turn of the twentieth century, when efforts were made to preserve the memories of dying Confederate veterans. This was done predominantly through actions such as building Confederate monuments and creating Lost Cause organizations, which often constructed the memorials.

One such Lost Cause memorial was the statue of Robert E. Lee, commanding general of the Army of Northern Virginia, erected in 1890 in the former Confederate capital, Richmond, Virginia, Lee's home state. The statue was sculpted by Antonin Mercié, a French sculptor in France with funds from the Lee Monument Commission led by Lee's nephew and the governor of Virginia, Fitzhugh Lee. The monument was unveiled before a crowd of more than 10,000, which included Lee's daughters, on May 29, 1890. A time capsule was placed beneath the monument.

After the white supremacist "Unite the Right" rally in Charlottesville in 2017, calls began for the removal of Confederate monuments, including a statue of Lee in Charlottesville. Following the murder of George Floyd and subsequent protests in 2020, Governor Ralph Northam of Virginia announced plans to remove the statue in Richmond. In response, a judge issued a temporary injunction against the monument's removal. Several more legal battles kept the statue standing into 2021, when the state Supreme Court ruled that the governor had the legal authority to remove it.

Following Black Lives Matter protests in the summer of 2020, the traffic circle in Richmond where the statue stood was updated with a sign saying "Welcome to Beautiful Marcus-David Peters Circle, Liberated by the People MMXX." This honored Marcus-David Peters, a Black man from Richmond who was shot and killed by the police in 2018. The monument itself was covered with images, slogans, and other graffiti after the protests. The *New York Times* deemed it to be among the most influential American protest artworks since World War II.

Following the ruling from the Virginia Supreme Court, the monument was removed on September 8, 2021, and taken to a storage facility. It was later announced that the statue and other monuments would be transferred to the Black History Museum and Cultural Center of Virginia. The pedestal was removed in 2022, and it is now a traffic circle with a patch of grass.

Explanation and Analysis of the Document

One of the first aspects of this photograph that likely strikes the viewer is that the photographer, Steve Helber, captured the removal in action. The statue, General Robert E. Lee on a horse, has been removed from the base or pedestal of the monument and hangs from a crane. The viewer is also likely drawn to the pedestal itself in the background, covered in graffiti. This graffiti is new and came from the protests that centered on the removal of the statue, which arose mostly during the summer of 2020 and into 2021, after the murder of George Floyd on May 25, 2020. The words "Black & Brown Unity" are easily readable, prominently displayed on the base of the memorial in yellow. These bright words seem to contrast with the statue of Lee, which is being hoisted away.

The imagery and message are clear: it is the dawn of a new era, one of increased racial equality. The statue, which to many symbolized the hatred and racism of the past, is being removed. This is shown in real time, and for many it is part of a healing process that has been a long time coming.

That this monument was one of the largest remaining Confederate monuments in the United States to be removed is significant, as is the fact that it stood in the middle of the former capital of the Confederate states and honored a man whom many still hold in high regard.

—Seth A. Weitz

Questions for Further Study

1. Is removing a monument from a park the same as erasing history? Explain your reasoning.

2. What should communities do with monuments that are removed from public squares?

3. What does this photograph show us about the power of protest?

Further Reading

Books

Allison, David, ed. *Controversial Monuments and Memorials: A Guide for Community Leaders.* Lanham, MD: Rowman & Littlefield, 2018.

Levinson, Sanford. *Written in Stone: Public Monuments in Changing Societies.* Durham: Duke University Press, 2018.

Websites

"Confederate Monument Interpretation Guide." Atlanta History Center. https://www.atlantahistorycenter.com/learning-and-research/projects-initiatives/confederate-monument-interpretation-guide/.

"Whose Heritage?" Southern Poverty Law Center. https://www.splcenter.org/whose-heritage.

Documentaries

POV: The Neutral Ground. C. J. Hunt, director. PBS, 2021.

List of Documents by Category

Artifacts
"Remember Wounded Knee" Patch

Cartoons
Benjamin Franklin: "Join, or Die" Cartoon
Cartoon Mocking Women's Rights Conventions
Currier & Ives: "Congressional Scales" Cartoon
Elkanah Tisdale: "The Gerry-mander" Cartoon
Herbert Block: "I Got One of 'em" Cartoon about Selma, Alabama
Herbert Block: "National Security Blanket" Cartoon
Herbert Block: "Strange How Some Choose to Live Like That" Cartoon
John H. Goater: "Irish Whiskey and Lager Bier" Cartoon
John L. Magee: "Forcing Slavery Down the Throat of a Freesoiler" Cartoon
John T. McCutcheon: "A Wise Economist Asks a Question" Cartoon
Joseph Keppler: "The Modern Colossus of (Rail) Roads" Cartoon
"King Andrew the First" Cartoon
Louis Dalrymple: "School Begins" Cartoon
Louis Maurer: "Progressive Democracy—Prospect of a Smash Up" Cartoon
Nathaniel Currier: "The Drunkard's Progress" Cartoon
Nathaniel Currier "The Way They Go to California" Cartoon
"The Only Way to Handle It" Cartoon
Pat Oliphant: "There He Goes Again" Cartoon
Philip Dawe: *Edenton Tea Party* Satirical Print
"Reconstruction" Cartoon
Richard Doyle: "The Land of Liberty" Cartoon
Rube Goldberg: "Peace Today" Cartoon
Steve Greenberg: "Bill Clinton's Foreign Policy Vehicle" Cartoon
Steve Greenberg: "Contract with America" Cartoon
Thomas Nast: "The American River Ganges: The Priests and the Children" Cartoon
Thomas Nast: "This Is a White Man's Government" Cartoon
"The Times, a Political Portrait" Cartoon

Flyers
Buffalo Bill's Wild West Flyer
Cherokee Delegation to England Portrait
Civilian Conservation Corps Poster
Dockside at Virginia Tobacco Warehouse Illustration
Fazil Movie Poster
"Gee! I Wish I Were a Man": Navy Recruiting Poster
Haymarket Mass Meeting Flyer
"Indian Land for Sale" Poster
John Gast: *American Progress* Painting
"Kultur-terror" Pro-German, Anti-American Propaganda Poster
McCormick's Patent Virginia Reaper Flyer
Nova Britannia Recruiting to the Colonies Flyer
Paul Revere: *The Bloody Massacre* Flyer
Philip Dawe: *Edenton Tea Party* Satirical Print
Philip Dawe: "Tarring & Feathering" Satirical Print
"Silence = Death" Flyer
Slaves for Sale Advertisement

"We Can Do It!" Rosie the Riveter Poster
"We the People Are Greater Than Fear" Flyer
William McKinley Campaign Poster

Illustrations
Alfred Rudolph Waud: "The First Vote" Illustration
"Camp-Meeting" Lithograph
Colonial Cloth Makers Illustration
Dockside at Virginia Tobacco Warehouse Illustration
James E. Taylor: "Selling a Freedman to Pay His Fine" Engraving
John White: Village of Secotan Illustration
Judge Magazine Cover: The Roaring Twenties
Lowell Offering Masthead
Painting of a Newly Cleared Small Farm Site
Picking Cotton, Georgia, 1858 Illustration
"Reconstruction" Cartoon
Robert Cruikshank: "President's Levee" Illustration
Smallpox Epidemic among the Aztec Illustration
William Henry Bartlett: Erie Canal, Lockport Illustration
Woman's Party Campaign Billboard

Maps
Brockett's Map of New Haven
Castello Plan: New Amsterdam Map
Dockside at Virginia Tobacco Warehouse Illustration
John White: Village of Secotan Illustration
Nova totius Map of the World
"A View of Savannah" Map

Newspapers
Thomas Jefferson: Advertisement for a Runaway Slave
William Bradford: "Expiring: In Hopes of a Resurrection to Life Again" Newspaper Protest

Paintings
Carl Rakeman: "The Iron Horse Wins—1830" Painting
Cherokee Delegation to England Portrait
Edward Hopper: *Automat* Painting
George Caleb Bingham: *The County Election* Painting
Jacob Lawrence: *The Great Migration* Painting
John Gast: *American Progress* Painting
The Old Plantation Painting
Painting of a Newly Cleared Small Farm Site
The Plantation Painting
Robert Feke: Portrait of Isaac Royall and Family

Photographs
Alfred T. Palmer: "Detroit Arsenal Tank Plant (Chrysler)" Photograph
American Indians Occupy Alcatraz Photograph
Andrew J. Russell: Ruins of Richmond Photograph
Ansel Adams: "Manzanar Relocation Center" Photograph
Assembly Line Photograph
Bush v. Gore Election Photograph
"Dreamland at Night" Photograph of Coney Island
Edgar Thomson Steel Works Photograph

"Emerson School for Girls" Photograph
Fred Blackwell: Woolworths Lunch Counter Sit-In Photograph
Greg Gibson: Photograph of Anita Hill Testifying before the Senate Judiciary Committee
Hélène Roger-Viollet: Drive-in Restaurant Photograph
Jacob Riis: "Bayard Street Tenement" Photograph
J. Scott Applewhite: "Mission Accomplished" Photograph
Louis Wickes Hines: Photograph of Boys Working in Arcade Bowling Alley
Marty Lederhandler: Photograph of Gasoline Rationing
Mihoko Owada: Photograph of Rioters Breaching the U.S. Capitol
NAACP: "A Man Was Lynched Yesterday" Photograph
Oklahoma City Bombing Photograph
Photograph after Raid on IWW Headquarters
Photograph of Anti-Busing Rally in Boston
Photograph of Berlin Wall Teardown
Photograph of Black Panther Party Demonstration
Photograph of Bread Line, New York City
Photograph of B-17 Formation over Schweinfurt, Germany
Photograph of Cab Calloway and Dancing Couples
Photograph of Carlisle Indian School Students
Photograph of Congested Chicago Intersection
Photograph of Freed Slaves at a County Almshouse
Photograph of Garment Workers Strike
Photograph of Harlem Hellfighters Regiment
Photograph of Health Inspection of New Immigrants, Ellis Island
Photograph of Interstate 10 under Construction in California
Photograph of Joseph McCarthy
Photograph of Levittown, Pennsylvania
Photograph of Navajo Code Talkers
Photograph of Nicodemus, Kansas
Photograph of Powder Monkey on USS *New Hampshire*
Photograph of the 107th U.S. Colored Infantry
Photograph of the 101st Airborne Division outside Little Rock Central High School
Photograph of Vietnam War Destruction
Photograph of World Trade Center Towers after 9/11 Terrorist Attack
Steve Helber: Photograph of Robert E. Lee Statue Removal
Thomas J. O'Halloran: "Kitchen" Debate Photograph of Richard Nixon and Nikita Khrushchev
Tom Olin: "Wheels of Justice" March Photograph
United Farm Workers Strike Photograph
Warren K. Leffler: Photograph of Phyllis Schlafly at White House Demonstration

Sculptures
John Foster's Gravestone

INDEX

Volume numbers are indicated in bold before each page number.

A

ADA. *See* Americans with Disabilities Act
Adams, Abigail, **1:**120
Adams, John, **1:**116–17, **1:**169
Adams, John Quincy, **1:**168, **1:**186
Adams, Samuel, **1:**135
Addams, Jane, **2:**377
Adhami, Ridwan, **3:**696–97
AFDC (Aid to Families with Dependent Children), **3:**668–69
African Americans, **1:**110–11, **1:**232–36, **2:**264, **2:**267, **2:**270–71, **2:**277, **2:**282–83, **2:**286–90, **2:**364–65, **2:**462–64, **2:**468–69, **2:**474–76, **3:**480, **3:**516, **3:**546–47
   civil rights of, **2:**268, **2:**276, **2:**280, **2:**286, **2:**288–89, **2:**306, **2:**342, **3:**544, **3:**588, **3:**650, **3:**708
   conservative, **3:**654
   education of, **2:**337
   emancipation of, **2:**264, **2:**282, **2:**288
   Great Migration of, **2:**306, **2:**450, **2:**472–76
   images and depictions of, **3:**511
   lynching of, **1:**184, **1:**186, **1:**229, **2:**283, **2:**346, **2:**412–13, **2:**460, **2:**460–64, **2:**474, **3:**511
   military units, **2:**262, **2:**264, **2:**289, **2:**410–14
   in public office, **2:**276, **2:**342
   voting rights, **2:**265, **2:**286, **2:**288–89, **3:**534, **3:**570
Agricultural Workers Organizing Committee (AWOC), **3:**588
AIDS (HIV/AIDS), **3:**486, **3:**638, **3:**640–43, **3:**663, **3:**668–69
AIDS pandemic, **3:**638, **3:**640–43
Albany Plan of Union, **1:**66–69
Alcatraz Island, **3:**580, **3:**583–84, **3:**602
Alcott, Louisa May, **1:**210
Alfred Rudolph Waud: "The First Vote" Illustration, **2:**274–78
Alfred T. Palmer: "Detroit Arsenal Tank Plant (Chrysler)" Photograph, **3:**514–19
Algonquin people, **1:**10–12
American colonies
   colonial assemblies, **1:**54, **1:**57, **1:**63, **1:**66, **1:**68, **1:**92
   Colonial Williamsburg, **1:**82, **1:**112
   militias, **1:**68
   New England, **1:**54
   protests, **1:**81, **1:**96
   southern, **1:**56
   trade, **1:**63, **1:**92
   Virginia, **1:**63–64
   women in, **1:**8, **1:**10, **1:**22–24, **1:**26, **1:**28–30, **1:**32–33, **1:**50–52, **1:**56–58, **1:**62–63, **1:**68–70, **1:**74–75, **1:**80–82, **1:**92–94, **1:**98–99, **1:**104–6
American Indian Movement, **3:**602, **3:**604–5, **3:**607
American Indians Occupy Alcatraz Photograph, **3:**580–84
Americans with Disabilities Act (ADA), **3:**648, **3:**651
American West, **1:**151, **1:**192, **1:**216, **1:**220, **1:**222
Andrew J. Russell: Ruins of Richmond Photograph, **2:**256–60
Ansel Adams: "Manzanar Relocation Center" Photograph, **3:**496–501
Anthony, Susan B., **2:**240, **2:**242
Antietam, Battle of, **2:**256
Appleby, George, **1:**72, **1:**74
Applewhite, J. Scott, **3:**690, **3:**690–95
Armey, Dick, **3:**668, **3:**671
Armstrong, Louis, **2:**434, **2:**468
Army-McCarthy hearings, **3:**528–30
Assembly Line Photograph, **2:**426–31
Astaire, Fred, **3:**635
Atlas, Charles, **2:**434
Auberger, Mike, **3:**651
Austin, George, **1:**72, **1:**74
AWOC (Agricultural Workers Organizing Committee), **3:**588
Aztec Empire, **1:**2, **1:**4–6

B

Bache, Benjamin Franklin, **1:**117
Bagley, Sarah, **1:**175
Baillie, James, **1:**226
Bain, George Grantham, **2:**380
Bake, Henry, **3:**502
Baker, Josephine, **2:**469
Banks, Dennis, **3:**602, **3:**607
Barker, Penelope, **1:**105
Barker, Thomas, **1:**105
Bartlett, William Henry, **1:**160–61, **1:**163
Bartlett, Willian Henry, **1:**160
Basire, Isaac, **1:**42, **1:**44
Bates, Daisy, **3:**532
Baum, L. Frank, **3:**605
Beattie, William, **1:**160
Beecher, Lyman, **1:**210, **1:**216
Bell, John, **2:**244
Bellecourt, Clyde, **3:**602
Belmont, August, **2:**289
Bender, Albert, **3:**498
Benjamin Franklin: "Join, or Die" Cartoon, **1:**66–70
Bennett, John, **1:**96, **1:**98
Berlin, Irving, **2:**468
Bernstein, Carl, **3:**599
Bevel, James Luther, **3:**568, **3:**570

Biddle, Nicholas, **1**:157
Biden, Joe, **3**:605, **3**:654, **3**:656–57, **3**:702, **3**:704–5
Bingham, George Caleb, **1**:220–21, **1**:223, **1**:225
Black Panther Party, **3**:574–78
Blackwell, Antoinette Brown, **2**:238
Blackwell, Fred, **3**:556–57, **3**:559
Blaeu, Willem, **1**:16–17
Blanche, Bruce Kelso, **2**:276
Bleeding Kansas, **1**:228, **1**:230, **2**:246, **2**:306
Block, Herbert, **3**:568–72, **3**:596–99, **3**:626–29
Bloody Massacre Flyer, **1**:90–95
"Bloody Sunday" incident in Selma, Alabama, **3**:568
Boston Massacre, **1**:90, **1**:92–95, **1**:98
Boston Port Act, **1**:99
Boston Tea Party, **1**:69, **1**:92, **1**:98, **1**:104
Bowman, Bryan, **2**:344
Braddock, Edward, **2**:364
Bradford, William, **1**:78–81
Bradley, Tom, **2**:474
Brady, Matthew, **2**:262
Brahe, Tycho, **1**:14
Brando, Marlon, **3**:582, **3**:604
Brandt, Willy, **3**:646
Brantner, Theodore, **2**:272
Bratt, Benjamin, **3**:582
Breckinridge, John C., **2**:244, **2**:246–47
Brewster, Francis, **1**:28
Brice, Fanny, **2**:468
Bridport, Hugh, **1**:148, **1**:150–52
British colonies, **1**:8, **1**:20, **1**:22, **1**:56, **1**:66, **1**:69, **1**:78, **1**:86, **1**:126
Britton, John, **1**:160
Brock, Sallie, **2**:260
Brockett, John R., **1**:26, **1**:28
Brockett's Map of New Haven, **1**:26–29
Brougham, John, **2**:274
Brown, Dee, **3**:605
Brown, Elaine, **3**:577
Brown, John, **2**:306, **2**:472
Bryan, William Jennings, **2**:354, **2**:356
Bryant, Anita, **3**:640
Bryant, William Cullen, **2**:276
Buchanan, James, **2**:246
Buchanan, Pat, **3**:680
Budd, James, **3**:552
Buena Vista, Battle of, **2**:336
Buffalo Bill Cody. *See* Cody, William F.
Buffalo Bill's Wild West Flyer, **2**:346–50
Bull, John, **2**:337
Bull Run, Battle of, **2**:274
Burn, Harry, **2**:401
Burnham, Daniel H., **2**:374, **2**:379
Burns, Lucy, **2**:400
Burr, Raymond, **3**:480

Bush, George H.W, **3**:635, **3**:648, **3**:651, **3**:654, **3**:656, **3**:660, **3**:662–63, **3**:690, **3**:692
Bush, George W., 3:678, 3:680, 3:686, 3:690–93
Bush, Jeb, 3:681
Bush v. Gore Election Photograph, **3**:678–82

C

Cage, Nicholas, **3**:505
Calamity Jane, **2**:434
Caldwell, James, **1**:93
Calhoun, John, **2**:283
Calhoun, John C., **1**:199
California gold rush, **1**:190, **1**:192–94
Calley, William, **3**:593
"Camp-Meeting" Lithograph, **1**:148–52
Cantor, Eddie, **2**:434, **2**:468
Carlisle Indian School. *See* Photograph of Carlisle Indian School Students
Carl Rakeman: "The Iron Horse Wins—1830" Painting, **1**:142–46
Carnegie, Andrew, **2**:310, **2**:362, **2**:364–65, **2**:367
Carr, Patrick, **1**:93
Cartelyou, Jacques, **1**:32–33
Carter, Jimmy, **3**:498, **3**:610, **3**:623, **3**:628, **3**:634–35, **3**:663
Carter, Rosalynn, **3**:623
Cartoon Mocking Women's Rights Conventions, **2**:238–42
Cass, Lewis, **1**:229
Castello Plan: New Amsterdam Map, **1**:30–34
Catholic immigrants, **1**:178, **1**:216
Catlin, George, **1**:192
Catt, Carrie Chapman, **2**:401–2
CCC (Civilian Conservation Corps), **3**:478–82
Centers for Disease Control (CDC), **3**:638, **3**:641
Chaplin, Charlie, **2**:431
Charlottesville, Virginia, white supremacist rally, **3**:698, **3**:710
Chávez, César, **3**:586, **3**:588–89
Cherokee Delegation to England Portrait, **1**:42–46
child labor, **2**:368, **2**:370–72
Christy, Howard Chandler, **2**:404
Civilian Conservation Corps Poster, **3**:478–82
Civil Rights Act, **3**:534, **3**:564, **3**:570, **3**:576, **3**:622, **3**:657
civil rights movement, **3**:534, **3**:538, **3**:558–60, **3**:580, **3**:588, **3**:616–17, **3**:620, **3**:650
Civil War, **1**:150, **1**:152, **1**:186–87, **1**:192–93, **1**:222–23, **1**:234–35, **2**:240–41, **2**:247–48, **2**:252–54, **2**:258–72, **2**:276–78, **2**:285–86, **2**:288–89, **2**:300–301, **2**:342–44
Clark, Mark, **3**:577
Clay, Cassius Marcellus, **1**:210
Clay, Henry, **1**:168–69, **1**:199–200
Cleaver, Eldridge, **3**:577

Cleveland, Grover, **2:**324, **2:**336–37, **2:**352
Cleveland, William David, **3:**662
Clinton, Bill, **2:**337, **2:**468, **3:**570, **3:**610, **3:**635, **3:**656, **3:**660, **3:**662–64, **3:**674, **3:**686, **3:**692, **3:**698
Clinton, Hillary, **3:**698, **3:**704
Cloud, John, **3:**570
Cody, William F., **2:**346, **2:**348–50
Cohan, George M., **2:**406
Cohn, Roy, **3:**526, **3:**528–29
Cold War, **3:**520, **3:**523–24, **3:**530, **3:**538, **3:**540–42, **3:**608, **3:**610–11, **3:**644, **3:**646, **3:**660, **3:**662, **3:**666, **3:**668
Colonial Cloth Makers Illustration, **1:**120–24
Colson, Charles, **3:**598
Columbus, Christopher, **1:**4
Concord and Lexington, Battles of, **1:**92
Continental Congress, **1:**74, **1:**82, **1:**128
Coolidge, Calvin, **2:**406, **2:**420
Cooper, Peter, **1:**142, **1:**144
Cortelyou, Jacques, **1:**30, **1:**32, **1:**34
Cosgrove, Peter, **3:**680
Costigan, Edward P., **2:**463
Cotton Club, **2:**434, **2:**466–70
cotton gin, **1:**122, **1:**222–23, **1:**232
Cozzens, Eleanor, **1:**56
Creek nation, **1:**168
Creel, George, **2:**406
Crofutt, George A., **2:**298, **2:**301
Cruikshank, George, **1:**166
Cruikshank, Robert, **1:**166–69
Cuming, Alexander, **1:**42, **1:**44
Currier, Nathaniel, **1:**178–79, **1:**181, **1:**190–91, **1:**193–94, **1:**196, **1:**226, **2:**246
Currier & Ives, **1:**190, **1:**192, **1:**194, **1:**196–99
Currier & Ives: "Congressional Scales" Cartoon, **1:**196–200
Curtis, Harriot F., **1:**174
Curtis Act, **2:**389
Czolgosz, Leon, **2:**354

D

Daguerre, Louis, **1:**208, **3:**644
Dall, Caroline, **2:**238
Dalrymple, Louis, **2:**334–35, **2:**337, **2:**339
Damsleth, Harald, **3:**508, **3:**510–11
Dana, Richard Henry, Jr., **1:**210
DATP. *See* Detroit Arsenal Tank Plant
Davenport, John, **1:**26, **1:**28
Davis, Jefferson, **2:**283
Dawe, George, **1:**104
Dawe, Philip, **1:**96–99, **1:**102–5
Dawes, Henry, **2:**324, **2:**388
Dean, John, **3:**598
Dean, John W., **1:**132

Deans, Fiona, **2:**290, **2:**296
Declaration of Independence, **1:**68, **1:**84, **1:**86–87, **1:**135
Democratic Party, **1:**158, **1:**170, **1:**222–24, **1:**228–29, **2:**244, **2:**246–47, **2:**278, **2:**283, **2:**286, **2:**288–90, **2:**292, **2:**294, **2:**342–43, **2:**398, **2:**400, **3:**534–35, **3:**570–71, **3:**598–99, **3:**635, **3:**637, **3:**657, **3:**668, **3:**674, **3:**699
Democratic-Republican Party, **1:**114, **1:**116–18
Department of Homeland Security (DHS), **3:**687–88, **3:**704–5
Detroit Arsenal Tank Plant (DATP), **3:**514–15, **3:**517–19
Detroit Photographic Company, **2:**362, **2:**428–29
Dewey, George, **2:**336
Dickens, Charles, **2:**240
Dillingham, William Paul, **2:**422
Dix, Dorothea, **2:**343
Dixon, Aaron, **3:**577
Dixon, Elmer, **3:**577
Dixon, Elmer James, III, **3:**577
Dockside at Virginia Tobacco Warehouse Illustration, **1:**60–64
Dorsey, Tommy, **2:**468
Douglas, Aaron, **2:**469
Douglas, Stephen A., **1:**199, **1:**228–29, **2:**244, **2:**247–48, **2:**286
Douglass, Frederick, **1:**235, **2:**240, **2:**264, **2:**472
Doyle, Arthur Conan, **1:**184
Doyle, Richard, **1:**184–85, **1:**187–88
"Dreamland at Night" Photograph of Coney Island, **2:**358–61
Dred Scott v. Sandford, **1:**223
Dreiser, Theodore, **2:**451
du Bois, W.E.B., **2:**277, **2:**460
Durante, Jimmy, **2:**468
Dutch colonies, **1:**17, **1:**57
Dutch East India Company, **1:**14, **1:**16
Dutch West India Company, **1:**16, **1:**30, **1:**32–34
Dyer, Leonidas, **2:**463

E

Earhart, Amelia, **2:**406
Earle, Daniel, **1:**104
East India Company, **1:**22
Eckford, Elizabeth, **3:**532
Edenton Tea Party Satirical Print, **1:**102–6
Edgar Thomson Steel Works Photograph, **2:**362–67
Edward Hopper: *Automat* Painting, **2:**438–42
Edwards, Sarah, **2:**288
Ehrlichman, John, **3:**598
Eisenhower, Dwight D., **2:**324, **3:**532, **3:**540–41, **3:**547, **3:**552
Elizabeth I (Queen of England), **1:**10

Elkanah Tisdale: "The Gerry-mander" Cartoon, **1**:132–36
Ellis Island, **2**:392–96, **2**:422
Ellison, Ralph, **2**:474
Emancipation Proclamation, **2**:264, **2**:270, **2**:280, **2**:342
Emergency Immigration Act, **2**:420, **2**:422
Emerson, George, **1**:210
Emerson, John, **1**:223
Emerson, Ralph Waldo, **1**:210
"Emerson School for Girls" Photograph, **1**:208–11
Equal Rights Amendment. *See* ERA
ERA (Equal Rights Amendment), **3**:544, **3**:620, **3**:622–24, **3**:629, **3**:634
Erie Canal, **1**:142, **1**:144, **1**:160–64
Everett, Edward, **1**:210
"Expiring: In Hopes of a Resurrection to Life Again" Newspaper Protest, **1**:78–82

F

Fairey, Shepard, **3**:696–97
Faubus, Orval, **3**:532
Fauci, Anthony, **3**:640
Fauset, Jessie Redmon, **2**:469
Fazil Movie Poster, **2**:444–47
FBI (Federal Bureau of Investigation), **3**:529, **3**:577, **3**:602, **3**:604, **3**:607, **3**:656, **3**:674–76, **3**:688, **3**:705
FDIC (Federal Deposit Insurance Corporation). *See* Federal Deposit Insurance Corporation (FDIC)
Federal Art Project (FAP), **3**:478, **3**:482
Federal Bureau of Investigation. *See* FBI
Federal Deposit Insurance Corporation (FDIC), **2**:457–58
Federalist Party, **1**:114, **1**:116–18, **1**:132, **1**:134–36
Feinstein, Dianne, **3**:657
Feke, Robert, **1**:54–57
Female Labor Reform Association, **1**:175
Field, Cyrus West, **2**:310, **2**:313
Fifteenth Amendment, **3**:620
Fifteenth Amendments, **2**:282, **2**:342
Finkelstein, Avram, **3**:638
First Continental Congress, **1**:80
Fisch, Robert, **3**:684
Fischer, Adolph, **2**:316, **2**:318
Fischer, Jean, **3**:562
Fisher, Walter Lowrie, **2**:388
Fitzgerald, F. Scott, **2**:432
Flagg, James Montgomery, **2**:407
Fleischmann, Maximilian, **2**:450
Fletcher, Zack T., **2**:306–7
Floyd, George, **3**:699, **3**:708, **3**:710–11
Fonda, Jane, **3**:582
Ford, Christine Blasey, **3**:657
Ford, Gerald, **3**:634–35

Ford, Henry, **2**:310, **2**:426, **2**:429, **2**:431
Forrest, Nathan Bedford, **2**:289
Forsyth, James W., **3**:605
Foster, Abby Kelley, **2**:240
Foster, John, **1**:36–40
Fourdrinier, Paul, **1**:48, **1**:50
Fourteenth Amendment, **2**:276, **2**:282, **3**:498
Fraitor, Leon, **2**:412
Fraley, Naomi Parker, **3**:484
Franklin, Benjamin, **1**:56, **1**:66–70, **1**:80, **1**:82, **1**:117, **1**:214, **2**:339
Fred Blackwell: Woolworths Lunch Counter Sit-In Photograph, **3**:556–60
Freedmen's Bureau, **2**:270, **2**:272, **2**:282, **2**:342, **2**:344
freed slaves, **2**:262, **2**:264, **2**:268, **2**:270, **2**:280, **2**:282, **2**:304, **2**:306, **2**:341–43
Free Soil Party, **1**:204, **1**:228
Frémont, John C., **2**:264
French and Indian War, **1**:66, **1**:68, **1**:70, **1**:78, **1**:90, **1**:92, **1**:102
French colonists, **1**:66, **1**:68
French Revolution, **1**:114, **1**:116–17, **1**:166, **1**:169
Frey, John, **3**:577
Frick, Henry Clay, **2**:365
Friedan, Betty, **3**:622
Fry, Joshua, **1**:60, **1**:62–63
Fuchs, Karl, **3**:523
Fugitive Slave Act, **1**:84–88, **1**:199
fugitive slaves, **2**:241, **2**:246
Funk, Isaac Kaufmann, **2**:420

G

Gadsden, Christopher, **1**:69
Garbo, Greta, **2**:446
Gardner, Alexander, **2**:262
Garfield, James, **2**:312
Garment Workers Strike, **2**:380–81, **2**:383, **2**:385
Garrity, Wendell Arthur, Jr., **3**:614
Gast, John, **2**:298–99, **2**:301, **2**:303
gay rights movement. *See* LGBTQA+ rights movement
"Gee! I Wish I Were a Man": Navy Recruiting Poster, **2**:404–8
George Caleb Bingham: *The County Election* Painting, **1**:220–25
George II (King of England), **1**:42, **1**:44–45, **1**:48
George III (King of England), **1**:82, **1**:99
George IV (King of England), **1**:168
Gerry, Elbridge, **1**:134
"Gerry-mander" Cartoon, **1**:132–36
Gershwin, George, **2**:468
Gettysburg, Battle of, **2**:256
Ghost Dance, **3**:604–5. *See also* Native Americans
Gibson, Althea, **2**:474
Gibson, Charles Dana, **2**:406

Gibson, Greg, **3:**654–55, **3:**657
Giles, John Lawrence ("J.L."), **2:**280
Gill, De Lancey Walker, **2:**386, **2:**388
Giuliani, Rudy, **3:**705
Glenn, John, **3:**635, **3:**680
Goater, John H., **1:**214–15, **1:**217
Godman, John D., **1:**150
Gold, Harry, **3:**523
Goldberg, Rube, **3:**520, **3:**522–24
Goldman, Emma, **2:**418
Goldwater, Barry, **3:**634
Gompers, Samuel, **2:**318, **2:**380
Goodman, Benny, **2:**468
Goodrich, Charles, **1:**134
Goodyear, Stephen, **1:**28
Gordon, Peter, **1:**48, **1:**50
Gould, Jay, **2:**310, **2:**313
Grant, Spencer, **3:**614–16
Grant, Ulysses S., **2:**258, **2:**283, **2:**286, **2:**288, **2:**294
Great Awakening, **1:**86
Great Depression, **2:**304, **2:**307, **2:**428, **2:**435, **2:**438, **2:**444, **2:**448, **2:**450–52, **2:**454, **2:**456–58, **2:**463, **3:**478, **3:**480, **3:**486, **3:**547
Greeley, Horace, **2:**240
Green, Ernest, **3:**532, **3:**535
Green, Jesse, **1:**222
Greenberg, Steve, **3:**660–63, **3:**666–67, **3:**669, **3:**671
Greg Gibson: Photograph of Anita Hill Testifying before the Senate Judiciary Committee, **3:**654–58
Gregory, Dick, **3:**582
Griffiths, Martha, **3:**622
Grignion, Charles, **1:**60, **1:**62
Gumpertz, Samuel, **2:**361

H

Haakon VII (King of Norway), **3:**510
Hall, Theodore, **3:**523
Hamilton, Alexander, **1:**117–18
Hammond, James Henry, **1:**234
Hampton Roads, Battle of, **2:**250
Hancock, John, **1:**92
Hanley, Alfred, **2:**412
Hansberry, Lorraine, **2:**474
Hardart, Frank, **2:**440, **2:**442
Harding, Warren G., **2:**420
Harlem Hellfighters, **2:**410, **2:**413–14
Harlem Renaissance, **2:**344, **2:**413, **2:**434, **2:**466, **2:**468–70, **2:**474
Harper, Fletcher, **2:**240
Harriot, Thomas, **1:**8, **1:**10
Hart, Gary, **3:**635
Hawes, Johnson, **1:**208
Hawes, Josiah Johnson, **1:**208

Hawkins, Ralph, **2:**412
Hawkins, William, **1:**28
Hay, John, **2:**336
Hayman, Francis, **1:**60, **1:**62
Haymarket Mass Meeting Flyer, **2:**316–21
Hearst, William Randolph, **2:**336, **2:**406, **3:**552
Helber, Steve, **3:**708–11
Held, John Jr., **2:**432
Hélène Roger-Viollet: Drive-in Restaurant Photograph, **3:**562–66
Hemings, Sally, **1:**86, **1:**88
Hennigan, James, **3:**616
Henry, Patrick, **1:**80, **1:**135
Herbert Block:
    "I Got One of 'em" Cartoon about Selma, Alabama, **3:**568–72
    "National Security Blanket" Cartoon, **3:**596–600
    "Strange How Some Choose to Live Like That" Cartoon, **3:**626–30
Herblock. *See* Block, Herbert
Hernández, Francisco, **1:**2
Heyer, Heather, **3:**710
Hill, Anita, **3:**654–57
Hill, William R., **2:**306
Hilliard, Benjamin, **2:**401
Hine, Lewis, **2:**372
Hines, Louis Wickes, **2:**368–69, **2:**371
Hispanics, **2:**450
Hitchcock, Alfred, **2:**440
HIV/AIDS. *See* AIDS movement
Ho, Ahn Chang, **3:**550
Holley, Alexander, **2:**364
Holliday, Billie, **2:**468
Hollings, Ernest, **3:**635
Homer, Winslow, **2:**240
Honey, Frederick R., **1:**26
Hoover, Herbert, **2:**406, **2:**456, **3:**480, **3:**610
Hoover, J. Edgar, **3:**529, **3:**577
Hopkins, Harry, **3:**481
Hopper, Edward, **2:**438–39, **2:**441–42
Horn, Joseph, **2:**440
Horne, Lena, **2:**468
Howard, Brian, **3:**638
Hudson, Henry, **1:**32
Huerta, Dolores, **3:**586, **3:**588
Hughes, Charles Evans, **2:**401
Hughes, John, **2:**294
Hunt, E. Howard, **3:**598
Hunter, David, **2:**264
Husher, Edwin H., **2:**362, **2:**428
Hussein, Saddam, **3:**684, **3:**690, **3:**692–94
Hutchinson, Thomas, **1:**93
Hutton, Robert, **3:**577

I

immigration, **1**:178, **1**:180, **1**:216–17, **2**:288, **2**:290, **2**:292, **2**:316, **2**:318–20, **2**:328, **2**:330, **2**:368, **2**:370, **2**:377, **2**:394–96, **2**:422–24, **3**:680, **3**:687
Immigration Act of 1882, **2**:395
Immigration Restriction Act, **2**:420, **2**:422
indentured servants, **1**:62, **1**:140
"Indian Land for Sale" Poster, **2**:386–90
Indigenous American populations, **1**:4–5, **1**:44, **1**:140, **1**:232. *See also* Native Americans
Industrial Workers of the World. *See* IWW
International Ladies Garment Workers Union (ILGWU), **2**:380, **2**:382–83
International Working People's Association, **2**:318
Interstate Commerce Commission, **2**:313
Iraq War, **3**:632, **3**:695
"The Iron Horse Wins—1830" Illustration, **1**:142–46
Iroquois Confederacy, **1**:68
Ives, James, **1**:180
Ives, James Merritt, **1**:198
IWW (Industrial Workers of the World), **2**:416, **2**:418–19

J

Jackson, Andrew, **1**:154, **1**:156, **1**:158, **1**:166, **1**:168, **1**:170, **1**:193, **1**:214, **1**:222, **2**:324, **2**:386
Jackson, Janet, **2**:468
Jackson, Jimmie Lee, **3**:570
Jackson, Michael, **2**:474
Jacob Lawrence: *The Great Migration* Painting, **2**:472–76
Jacob Riis: "Bayard Street Tenement" Photograph, **2**:328–33
James E. Taylor: "Selling a Freedman to Pay His Fine" Engraving, **2**:268–72
James I (King of England), **1**:22
Jamestown Virginia, **1**:20, **1**:22–24, **1**:62, **1**:232, **1**:234
January 6 riots, **3**:702–6
Japanese Americans, **3**:496, **3**:498–501
Jazz Age, **2**:432, **2**:466
Jefferson, Peter, **1**:60, **1**:62–63, **1**:84, **1**:86
Jefferson, Thomas, **1**:60, **1**:62, **1**:84–88, **1**:116–17, **1**:123, **1**:134, **1**:162, **1**:169, **1**:172, **2**:256, **2**:300, **2**:386
Jeffersonian Republicans, **1**:132, **1**:134–35
Jefferys, Thomas, **1**:60, **1**:62–63
Jessop, George H., **2**:432
Jewell, Mary, **2**:274
Jim Crow, **2**:265, **2**:280, **2**:283, **2**:462–63, **2**:475
Jim Crow era, **3**:556, **3**:558–59
John Foster's Gravestone, **1**:36–40
John Gast: *American Progress* Painting, **2**:298–303
John H. Goater: "Irish Whiskey and Lager Bier" Cartoon, **1**:214–18
John L. Magee: "Forcing Slavery Down the Throat of a Freesoiler" Cartoon, **1**:226–30
Johnson, Andrew, **2**:282, **2**:288
Johnson, Eastman, **1**:192
Johnson, Frank, Jr., **3**:571
Johnson, Henry, **2**:413
Johnson, Herschel V., **2**:244, **2**:246–47
Johnson, Jack, **2**:468
Johnson, James Weldon, **2**:469
Johnson, Lyndon B., **3**:570–71, **3**:576, **3**:588
Johnson, Otis, **2**:413
Johnson, Robert, **1**:20, **1**:22, **1**:24
Johnston, Joseph E., **2**:258
Johnston, Oliver, **3**:638
Johnston, Philip, **3**:502, **3**:504–5, **3**:507
John T. McCutcheon: "A Wise Economist Asks a Question" Cartoon, **2**:454–58
John White: Village of Secotan Illustration, **1**:8–12
"Join, or Die" Cartoon, **1**:66–70
Jones, Bobby, **2**:434
Jones, George, **1**:48, **1**:50
Jones, James Earl, **2**:474
Jones, Lois Mailou, **2**:469
Jones, Mary Harris, **2**:319
Jones, Noble, **1**:48, **1**:50
Jones, William R., **2**:364
Jordan, I. King, **3**:651
Joseph Keppler: "The Modern Colossus of (Rail) Roads" Cartoon, **2**:310–14
J. Scott Applewhite: "Mission Accomplished" Photograph, **3**:690–95
Judge Magazine Cover: The Roaring Twenties, **2**:432–36

K

Kahn, Albert, **2**:429
Kansas-Nebraska Act, **1**:226, **1**:228–30, **2**:244, **2**:246
Käsebier, Gertrude, **2**:348
Kavanaugh, Brett, **3**:657
Keane, Tom, **3**:640
Keating, Edward, **2**:401
Keller, Helen, **2**:340
Kelley, Clarence M., **3**:577
Kennan, George F., **3**:523–24, **3**:540, **3**:542, **3**:662
Kennedy, David, **1**:148
Kennedy, John F., **3**:558, **3**:596, **3**:599
Keppler, Joseph Ferdinand, **2**:310, **2**:312, **2**:334
Khrushchev, Nikita, **3**:538–42
King, Elizabeth, **1**:105
King, Martin Luther, Jr., **3**:558–59, **3**:568, **3**:570, **3**:576, **3**:616
King, Rodney, **3**:680
"King Andrew the First" Cartoon, **1**:154–58
Kirk, George H., **3**:502–3, **3**:505

Klann, William, **2:**428
Knights of Labor, **2:**318–19
Know-Nothing Party, **1:**214, **1:**216
Knudsen, William, **3:**516–18
Koch, Robert, **2:**395
Koresh, David, **3:**674
Kramer, Larry, **3:**638
Krelff, Charles, **3:**638
Ku Klux Klan, **2:**276, **2:**283, **2:**289, **2:**422, **2:**463
Kultur-terror" Pro-German, Anti-American Propaganda Poster, **3:**508–12

L

LaFeber, Walter, **3:**540, **3:**542
Lane, Joseph, **2:**244, **2:**246–47
Laurens, Henry, **1:**72, **1:**74–75
Lawrence, Eugene, **2:**292
Lawrence, Jacob, **2:**469, **2:**472–76
Lederhandler, Marty, **3:**608–9, **3:**611–12
Lee, Fitzhugh, **3:**710–11
Lee, Robert E., **2:**258, **2:**264, **2:**280, **2:**283, **3:**708–11
Leffler, Melvin P., **3:**540, **3:**542, **3:**620
Leffler, Warren K., **3:**620–21, **3:**623
Lemlich, Clara, **2:**380, **2:**383, **2:**385
Leslie, Frank, **2:**240, **2:**286, **2:**312
Leupp, Francis E., **2:**388
Levitt, Abraham, **3:**544, **3:**546
Levitt, William, **3:**544, **3:**546
Lewinsky, Monica, **3:**656
Lewis, Arnold, **2:**376
Lewis, Charles, **1:**86–87
Lewis, John, **3:**568
LGBTQA+ rights movement, **3:**640–42, **3:**669, **3:**684
Liddy, G. Gordon, **3:**598
Liliuokalani (Queen of Hawaii), **2:**337
Lincoln, Abraham, **1:**214, **1:**228, **2:**244, **2:**247–48, **2:**258–59, **2:**264–65, **2:**270, **2:**277, **2:**280, **2:**286, **2:**288, **2:**294, **2:**342
Lindbergh, Charles, **2:**434
Lione, Chris, **3:**638
Lister, Joseph, **2:**395
Little Bighorn, Battle of, **2:**388
Little Rock school integration. *See* Photograph of the 101st Airborne Division outside Little Rock Central High School
Livingstone, William A. Jr., **2:**362, **2:**428–29
Loewen, James, **2:**412
Logan, Rayford, **2:**412
Lord Dunmore, **1:**87
Louis, Joe, **3:**511
Louis Dalrymple: "School Begins" Cartoon, **2:**334–39
Louis Maurer: "Progressive Democracy—Prospect of a Smash Up" Cartoon," **2:**244–48, **2:**348
Louis Wickes Hines: Photograph of Boys Working in Arcade Bowling Alley, **2:**368–72
Lowell Offering Masthead, **1:**172–76
Lucas, William, **1:**148
Lynch, Charles, **2:**462
lynching. *See* African Americans, lynching of

M

MacArthur, Douglas, **2:**406
Macham, Samuel, **1:**22
Madden, Owen, **2:**468
Madison, James, **1:**116–18, **1:**135, **2:**256, **3:**552
Magee, John L., **1:**226–29
Malcolm X, **3:**576
Malcom, John, **1:**96, **1:**98–100
Mandela, Nelson, **3:**696
manifest destiny, **2:**298, **2:**300–303, **2:**334, **2:**336, **2:**339
Manzanar Relocation Center. *See* Ansel Adams: "Manzanar Relocation Center" Photograph
Marshall, Thurgood, **3:**654
Martha (Crown Princess of Norway), **3:**510
Marty Lederhandler: Photograph of Gasoline Rationing, **3:**608–12
Mason, George, **2:**256
Mason-Dixon Line, **1:**186
Mather, Richard, **1:**36
Maurer, Louis, **2:**244–45, **2:**348
Mayo, Joseph C., **2:**259
McCabe, Edward P., **2:**307
McCallum, Daniel C., **2:**258
McCarthy, Joseph R., **3:**526–30, **3:**570, **3:**628
McClellan, George B., **2:**258, **2:**264
McCormick, Cyrus H., **1:**202, **1:**204–6
McCormick, Robert, **1:**204
McCormick's Patent Virginia Reaper Flyer, **1:**202–6
McCutcheon, John T., **2:**454–55, **2:**457
McGready, James, **1:**151
McIntosh, Elizabeth, **1:**57
McIntosh, Henry, **1:**57
McKay, Claude, **2:**469
McKinley, William, **2:**336, **2:**352, **2:**356
McLane, Louis, **1:**157
McVeigh, Timothy, **3:**672, **3:**674–75
Means, Russell, **3:**604
Medill, William, **2:**324
Meese, Edwin, **3:**629
Mellon, Andrew W., **2:**310
Merritt, Ralph, **3:**498–500
Mexican Americans, **3:**588–89
Mexican-American War, **1:**184, **1:**186–87, **1:**192–93, **1:**196, **1:**198, **1:**204, **1:**228, **2:**256, **2:**301, **2:**334, **2:**336
Mihaly, David H., **2:**407
Mihoko Owada: Photograph of Rioters Breaching the U.S. Capitol, **3:**702–6

Miller, Glenn, **2**:468
Miller, J. Howard, **3**:484
Milton, John, **2**:283
Minuit, Peter, **1**:32
Missouri Compromise, **1**:186, **1**:198, **1**:223, **1**:228
Mitchell, Billy, **3**:492
Mitchell, George, **3**:602
Mondale, Walter, **3**:635
Monroe, James, **2**:300
Monroe Doctrine, **2**:300, **2**:336
Moody, Anne, **3**:556
Moore, Walter J., **2**:444
Morgan, Tallulah, **3**:616
Morland, Henry, **1**:96
Morrison, Toni, **2**:474
Morse, Samuel, **1**:193
Mothershed, Thelma, **3**:532
Mulford, Don, **3**:574
Murray, Pauli, **3**:564
Muskie, Edmund, **3**:599
Mussolini, Benito, **2**:406

N

NAACP (National Association for the Advancement of Colored People), **2**:460–64, **3**:558, **3**:616
NAACP: "A Man Was Lynched Yesterday" Photograph, **2**:460–64
Nader, Ralph, **3**:680, **3**:682
NASA (National Aeronautics and Space Administration), **3**:680
Nast, Sarah, **2**:288
Nast, Thomas, **2**:240, **2**:286–90, **2**:292–93, **2**:295–96
Nathaniel Currier:
    "The Drunkard's Progress" Cartoon, **1**:178–82
    "The Way They Go to California" Cartoon, **1**:190–94
National American Woman Suffrage Association. *See* NAWSA
National Association for the Advancement of Colored People (NAACP). *See* NAACP (National Association for the Advancement of Colored People)
National Child Labor Committee (NCLC). *See* NCLC (National Child Labor Committee)
National Farm Workers Association (NFWA), **3**:588
National Institutes of Health (NIH), **3**:638, **3**:640–41
National Park Service, **3**:480, **3**:501, **3**:583
National Woman's Party (NWP), **2**:398, **2**:400–402
National Women's Rights Conventions, **2**:240, **2**:242
Native American, education of, **2**:322, **2**:388
Native Americans, **1**:8–12, **1**:32–33, **1**:66, **1**:68, **1**:87, **1**:99, **1**:126, **1**:128, **1**:222, **2**:282, **2**:326, **2**:349–50, **2**:388–90, **2**:410, **2**:450
    assimilation, **3**:582
    assimilation of, **2**:386

enslaving, **1**:5
forced removal of, **2**:300, **2**:324, **2**:348
land rights, **1**:92
property rights of, **2**:325
sale of lands to settlers, **2**:386–90
trade with Dutch settlers, **1**:16
Trail of Tears, **1**:156
NAWSA (National American Woman Suffrage Association), **2**:398, **2**:400
NCLC (National Child Labor Committee), **2**:370
NDAC (National Defense Advisory Commission), **3**:516, **3**:518
Newman, Pauline, **2**:382
Newton, Huey P., **3**:574, **3**:577–78
Nicholas Brothers, **2**:468
Nichols, Terry, **3**:607, **3**:674
Nicodemus. *See* Photograph of Nicodemus, Kansas
Nixon, Richard, **3**:539, **3**:541, **3**:583, **3**:588, **3**:596, **3**:598–99, **3**:610, **3**:628, **3**:632, **3**:635
Nordwall, Adam, **3**:580, **3**:582
Northam, Ralph, **3**:710
Nova Britannia Recruiting to the Colonies Flyer, **1**:20–24
Nova totius Map of the World, **1**:14–18
Nute, Alfred, **2**:394
NWP. *See* National Woman's Party

O

Oakes, Richard, **3**:580, **3**:583–84
Oakes, Yvonne, **3**:582
Oakley, Annie, **2**:346, **2**:348
Obama, Barack, **3**:696, **3**:699
Oglethorpe, James Edward, **1**:48, **1**:50–53
O'Halloran, Thomas J., **3**:528, **3**:538
Oklahoma City Bombing Photograph, **3**:672–73, **3**:675–76
Old Plantation, The, Painting, **1**:108–12
Olin, Tom, **3**:648–49, **3**:651
Oliphant, Pat, **3**:632–33, **3**:635
"The Only Way to Handle It" Cartoon, **2**:420–24
Oukanaehah, **1**:45–46

P

Painting of a Newly Cleared Small Farm Site, **1**:126–30
Palmer, Alfred T., **3**:514–15, **3**:517, **3**:519
Palmer, A. Mitchell, **2**:418, **2**:422
Palmer, Fanny, **1**:192
Palmer, Mary McIntosh, **1**:57
Parsons, Albert, **2**:319
Parsons, Lucy, **2**:319
Pasteur, Louis, **2**:395
Paterson, Paul, **1**:166
Patillo, Melba, **3**:532, **3**:535
Pat Oliphant: "There He Goes Again" Cartoon, **3**:632–36

Paul, Alice, **2**:400, **2**:402
Paul Revere: *The Bloody Massacre* Flyer, **1**:90–95
Pelham, Henry, **1**:93–94
Peltier, Leonard, **3**:604, **3**:607
Pendleton, John, **1**:178, **1**:180, **1**:190, **1**:192
Perkins, Granville, **2**:240
Perot, Ross, **3**:680
Philip Dawe:
Edenton Tea Party Satirical Print, **1**:102–6
"Tarring & Feathering" Satirical Print, **1**:96–99
Phillips, Wendell, **2**:238, **2**:242
Photograph after Raid on IWW Headquarters, **2**:416–19
Photograph of Anti-Busing Rally in Boston, **3**:614–18
Photograph of B-17 Formation over Schweinfurt, Germany, **3**:490–94
Photograph of Berlin Wall Teardown, **3**:644–47
Photograph of Black Panther Party Demonstration, **3**:574–78
Photograph of Bread Line, New York City, **2**:448–52
Photograph of Cab Calloway and Dancing Couples, **2**:466–70
Photograph of Carlisle Indian School Students, **2**:322–26
Photograph of Congested Chicago Intersection, **2**:374–79
Photograph of Freed Slaves at a County Almshouse, **2**:340–44
Photograph of Garment Workers Strike, **2**:380–85
Photograph of Harlem Hellfighters Regiment, **2**:410–14
Photograph of Health Inspection of New Immigrants, Ellis Island, **2**:392–96
Photograph of Interstate 10 under Construction in California, **3**:550–54
Photograph of Joseph McCarthy, **3**:526–30
Photograph of Levittown, Pennsylvania, **3**:544–49
Photograph of Navajo Code Talkers, **3**:502–7
Photograph of Nicodemus, Kansas, **2**:304, **2**:304–8
Photograph of Powder Monkey on USS *New Hampshire*, **2**:250–54
Photograph of the 101st Airborne Division outside Little Rock Central High School, **3**:532–36
Photograph of the 107th U.S. Colored Infantry, **2**:262–67
Photograph of Vietnam War Destruction, **3**:590–94
Photograph of World Trade Center Towers after 9/11 Terrorist Attack, **3**:684–88
"Picking Cotton, Georgia, 1858" Illustration, **1**:232–35
Pierce, Franklin, **1**:229, **2**:246, **2**:340
Pike, Johnathan, **2**:276
Pinkerton, Allan, **2**:264
Pizarro, Francisco, **1**:4
Plantation, The, Painting, **1**:138–41
Playfair, Hugo, **1**:166
Polk, James K., **1**:184, **1**:186, **1**:193
Ponce de Leon, Juan, **1**:4
Pop Warner, **2**:324
Porter, Charles, IV, **3**:672
Porter, Rufus, **1**:193
Pratt, Richard Henry, **2**:322, **2**:388
Preston, Thomas, **1**:93
Proclamation of 1763, **1**:68

Q
al-Qaeda, **3**:686, **3**:688, **3**:690, **3**:692
Quarles, Francis, **1**:38
Quinn, Anthony, **3**:582
Quisling, Vidkun, **3**:508

R
Racial Imbalance Act, **3**:614, **3**:616
railroads, **1**:142, **1**:144, **1**:163
Rainey, Joseph H., **2**:282
Rakeman, Carl, **1**:142–43, **1**:145
Rakeman, Eva, **1**:142
Raleigh, Walter, **1**:8, **1**:10
Rankin, Sarah, **3**:710
Ray, Gloria, **3**:532, **3**:535
Reagan, Ronald, **3**:576, **3**:610, **3**:626, **3**:628–30, **3**:632, **3**:634–36, **3**:640, **3**:666
Reconstruction, **2**:272, **2**:276–78, **2**:280, **2**:282–86, **2**:288–90, **2**:303–4, **2**:306, **2**:308, **2**:342–44
Reconstruction Acts, **2**:274, **2**:277, **2**:282, **2**:288–89
Reconstruction Amendments, **2**:342–43
"Reconstruction" Cartoon, **2**:280–85
"Remember Wounded Knee" Patch, **3**:602–7
Remington, Frederic, **2**:348
Republican Party, **2**:247, **2**:276, **2**:278, **2**:282–83, **2**:286, **2**:288, **2**:290, **2**:292, **2**:294, **2**:352, **2**:354–55, **3**:666, **3**:668, **3**:680, **3**:698
Revels, Hiram, **2**:282
Revere, Paul, **1**:90–93, **1**:95
Revolutionary War, **1**:69, **1**:106, **1**:138, **1**:150, **1**:187
Reynolds, Joshua, **1**:44
Reynolds, William H., **2**:358
Rich, Buddie, **2**:468
Richard Doyle: "The Land of Liberty" Cartoon, **1**:184–88
Rider, Alexander, **1**:148, **1**:150–51
Riis, Jacob, **2**:328–33
Roaring Twenties, **2**:432–36, **2**:448, **2**:450, **2**:454, **2**:466
Robert Cruikshank: "President's Levee" Illustration, **1**:166–70
Robert Feke: Portrait of Isaac Royall and Family, **1**:54–58

Roberts, Charles Luckyth, **2**:413
Roberts, Terrence, **3**:532
Robeson, Paul, **2**:468
Robinson, Jackie, **2**:474
Rockefeller, John D., **2**:310, **2**:312
Rockwell, Norman, **3**:484
Rodgers, Richard, **2**:468
Roger-Viollet, Hélène, **3**:562–63, **3**:565
Romney, George, **1**:44
Roosevelt, Franklin D., **2**:389, **2**:406, **2**:457, **2**:463, **3**:478, **3**:480, **3**:486, **3**:496, **3**:498, **3**:510, **3**:516–17, **3**:552, **3**:570, **3**:628, **3**:650
Roosevelt, Theodore, **2**:288, **2**:294, **2**:330–31, **2**:336, **2**:349, **2**:352, **2**:355, **2**:412
Rose, Ernestine, **2**:238, **2**:240
Rose, John, **1**:108, **1**:110
Rosie the Riveter. *See* "We Can Do It!" Rosie the Riveter Poster
Ross, Diana, **2**:474
Ross, Harold, **2**:432
"Rough Riders," **2**:336, **2**:349
Roundtree, Simon P., **2**:306
Royall, Isaac, Jr., **1**:54–57
Rube Goldberg: "Peace Today" Cartoon, **3**:520–24
Ruby Ridge incident, **3**:674–75
Russell, Andrew J., **2**:256–57, **2**:259
Russell, Andrew Joseph, **2**:258
Russell, Bill, **2**:474
Ruth, Babe, **2**:434

S
Sacco, Nicola, **2**:422
Saint Francis of Assisi, **1**:4
Salter, John, **3**:556, **3**:559–60
Sandburg, Carl, **2**:376
Sanger, Margaret, **2**:434
Savage, Augusta, **2**:469
Sayer, Robert, **1**:96, **1**:98
Schine, David, **3**:526, **3**:528–29
Schlafly, Phyllis, **3**:620–24
Schmid, Hans Jakob, **2**:362
Schreyvogel, Charles, **2**:348
Schwarzmann, Adolph, **2**:312
SCLC (Southern Christian Leadership Conference), **3**:558, **3**:568
Scott, Dred, **1**:223
Seale, Bobby, **3**:574, **3**:577–78
Searle, Ronald, **3**:632
Selden, George, **2**:429
Seminole nation, **1**:168
Senate Judiciary Committee, **3**:654–57
Seneca Falls Convention, **2**:240–41, **2**:398
Seward, William H., **2**:336

Seymour, Horatio, **2**:286
Sharp, Granville, **1**:86
Shaw, Robert, **2**:262
"Silence = Death" Flyer, **3**:638–43
Sirica, John, **3**:598
Sissle, Noble, **2**:413
Sitting Bull, **3**:605
slavery, **2**:244, **2**:246–47, **2**:264–65, **2**:268, **2**:270–72, **2**:276–77, **2**:280, **2**:282, **2**:289, **2**:292, **2**:294, **2**:342, **2**:344, **2**:462, **2**:464
  abolition of, **1**:56, **1**:68, **1**:184, **1**:186, **1**:196, **1**:198–99, **1**:226, **1**:228, **2**:282, **2**:294, **2**:342–43
  among American settlers, **1**:192
  and the Declaration of Independence, **1**:87
  in England, **1**:184
  expansion of, **1**:86, **1**:193, **1**:226, **1**:228, **1**:236, **2**:244, **2**:247
  fugitive slaves, **1**:84, **1**:87, **1**:186, **1**:199
  importation of slaves, **1**:74–75
  opposition to, **1**:50, **1**:74
  runaway slaves, **1**:76, **1**:84–85, **1**:87
  slave rebellions, **1**:74, **1**:86–87
  and tobacco, **1**:62, **1**:64
Slaves for Sale Advertisement, **1**:72–76
Slosson, Preston W., **2**:435–36
smallpox, **1**:2–3, **1**:5–6, **1**:58, **1**:72, **1**:75, **1**:87
Smallpox Epidemic among the Aztec Illustration, **1**:2–6
Smith, Bessie, **2**:469
Smith, Jenny, **2**:306
Smith, John, **1**:22
Smith, Kathleen, **3**:577
Smith, Margaret Bayard, **1**:169
Smith, Thomas, **1**:22
Smith, William Morris, **2**:262
SNCC (Student Nonviolent Coordinating Committee), **3**:558–59, **3**:568, **3**:576
Soccarás, Jorge, **3**:638
Somerset, James, **1**:86
Somerset Decision, **1**:86
Southworth, Albert Sands, **1**:208
Spanish-American War, **2**:339, **2**:352, **2**:354, **2**:404
Stamp Act, **1**:68, **1**:78, **1**:80–82, **1**:92, **1**:98–99
Stamp Act Congress, **1**:68, **1**:80
Stanford, Leland, **2**:310
Stanton, Elizabeth Cady, **2**:238, **2**:240, **2**:242
Stephens, Alexander Hamilton, **2**:282
Stephenson, George, **1**:145
Steve Greenberg:
  "Bill Clinton's Foreign Policy Vehicle" Cartoon, **3**:660–64
  "Contract with America" Cartoon, **3**:666–71
Steve Helber: Photograph of Robert E. Lee Statue Removal, **3**:708–11

Stevens, Robert, **3**:529
St. John, John, **2**:306
Stone, Lucy, **2**:240
Stono Rebellion, **1**:74–76
Stowe, Harriet Beecher, **1**:210, **1**:216
Strong, Caleb, **1**:135
Strong, Thomas W., **1**:214
Student Nonviolent Coordinating Committee. *See* SNCC
Stuyvesant, Peter, **1**:32–33
Sullivan, Anne, **2**:340

T

Taft, William Howard, **2**:388
Tait, Arthur Fitzwilliam, **2**:246
Tammany Hall, **2**:247, **2**:288, **2**:292, **2**:294–96, **2**:310, **2**:332
Tapping, Joseph, **1**:38
"Tarring & Feathering" Satirical Print, **1**:96–99
Taylor, Edward T., **2**:401
Taylor, Frederick Winslow, **2**:426
Taylor, Herbert, **2**:412
Taylor, James E., **2**:268
Taylor, Zachary, **1**:196, **1**:199–200
Tea Act, **1**:98, **1**:104
Thackeray, William Makepeace, **2**:240
Thirteenth Amendment, **2**:270–71, **2**:282, **2**:342
Thomas, Clarence, **3**:654, **3**:656–58
Thomas, Jefferson, **3**:532
Thomas Jefferson: Advertisement for a Runaway Slave, **1**:84–88
Thomas J. O'Halloran: "Kitchen" Debate Photograph of Richard Nixon and Nikita Khrushchev, **3**:538–42
Thomas Nast:
   "The American River Ganges" Cartoon, **2**:292–96
   "This Is a White Man's Government" Cartoon, **2**:286–90
Thomson, Edgar, **2**:364–65, **2**:367
Thomson, John Edgar, **2**:362
Thorpe, Grace, **3**:582
Thorpe, Jim, **2**:324
Tilden, Samuel, **2**:283
Till, Emmett, **3**:534
Tillman, Benjamin, **2**:336
"Times, The, a Political Portrait" Cartoon, **1**:114–18
Tisdale, Elkanah, **1**:132–33, **1**:135
Tom Olin: "Wheels of Justice" March Photograph, **3**:648–52
Toomer, Jean, **2**:469
Tousey, Frank, **2**:432
Town, Charles, **1**:44
Townshend, Charles, **1**:104
Treaty of Guadalupe Hidalgo, **1**:186, **1**:192, **1**:196, **1**:228, **2**:301, **2**:336

Trenchard, Hugh, **3**:492
Trevithick, Richard, **1**:145
Trist, Nicolas, **1**:192
Trudell, John, **3**:582
Truman, Harry S., **3**:493, **3**:499, **3**:522, **3**:528, **3**:540, **3**:662
Trumbauer, Joan, **3**:558
Trump, Donald, **3**:629, **3**:632, **3**:634, **3**:681, **3**:696, **3**:698, **3**:702, **3**:704–6
Trumpauer, Joan, **3**:556
Tubman, Harriet, **2**:265, **2**:472
Tucker, Sophie, **2**:468
Tumball, John, **1**:134
Tutankhamen (King of Egypt), **2**:434
Twain, Mark, **2**:277

U

Umberto (Crown Prince of Italy), **2**:406
United Farm Workers Strike Photograph, **3**:586–89
U.S. war with Mexico. *See* Mexican-American War

V

Valentine, Robert Grosvenor, **2**:388
Valentino, Rudolph, **2**:434, **2**:446
Van Buren, Martin, **1**:156, **1**:222
Vanderbilt, Cornelius, **2**:310
Vanderbilt, William Henry, **2**:310, **2**:313
Van Der Zee, James, **2**:469
Velásquez, Diego, **1**:2
Vermeer, Johannes, **1**:14
Victoria (Queen of England), **2**:348
Vietnam War, **3**:570, **3**:588, **3**:590, **3**:592–94, **3**:610–11, **3**:628, **3**:632, **3**:648, **3**:708
"View of Savannah" Map, **1**:48–53
Vingboons, Johannes, **1**:30, **1**:32–33
Virginia Company of London, **1**:20
Virginia Reaper, **1**:202, **1**:204–5
Vogel, Clayton B., **3**:502, **3**:504
Voting Rights Act, **3**:568, **3**:571–72, **3**:576

W

Wagner, Robert F., **2**:463
Wales, James Albert, **2**:432
Walker, Edwin, **3**:532
Wallace, George C., **3**:570–71
Wallace, Henry, **3**:528
war on terror, **3**:690, **3**:692–93
Warren K. Leffler: Photograph of Phyllis Schlafly at White House Demonstration, **3**:620–24
Washington, George, **1**:87, **1**:116–18, **1**:169, **1**:187, **1**:222, **2**:256, **3**:552
Washington, Jesse, **2**:460
Waters, Ethel, **2**:468–69
Waud, Alfred Rudolph, **2**:274–75, **2**:277

Weaver, Randy, **3**:671, **3**:674
Webster, Daniel, **2**:283
"We Can Do It!" Rosie the Riveter Poster, **3**:484–88
Weitenkampf, Frank, **1**:154
Welch, James, **3**:529
West, Mae, **2**:468
Westmoreland, William, **3**:592
"We the People Are Greater Than Fear" Flyer, **3**:696–700
Whig Party, **1**:200, **1**:216, **1**:222–24, **1**:228–29
White, Hugh, **1**:90
White, John, **1**:8–11
Whitehouse, Jane, **1**:94
Whitney, Eli, **1**:122, **1**:222
Whittier, John Greenleaf, **1**:210
Wilhelmina (Queen of the Netherlands), **3**:510
Wilkes, John, **1**:99
William Bradford: "Expiring: In Hopes of a Resurrection to Life Again" Newspaper Protest," **1**:78–82
William Henry Bartlett: Erie Canal, Lockport Illustration, **1**:160–64
William McKinley Campaign Poster, **2**:352–56
Williams, Charles, **2**:307
Williams, Hosea, **3**:568
Williams, Joe, **2**:412
Williams, Serena, **2**:474
Willis, Nathaniel Parker, **1**:160, **1**:162
Wilmot Proviso, **1**:198–99
Wilson, Alexander, **1**:150
Wilson, August, **2**:474
Wilson, Richard, **3**:604
Wilson, Woodrow, **2**:276, **2**:398, **2**:401–2, **2**:404, **2**:413
Winters, Jonathan, **3**:582
Winthrop, John, **1**:38
Woman's Party Campaign Billboard, **2**:398–402
women, **2**:238, **2**:240–41, **2**:319, **2**:340, **2**:343, **2**:382–83, **2**:400–401, **2**:434–36, **2**:440–41, **3**:480–81, **3**:484, **3**:486–88, **3**:541, **3**:583, **3**:622–23
   in the Black Panther Party, **3**:577
   during World War II, **3**:484, **3**:486–87, **3**:502, **3**:544, **3**:547
   education of, **1**:208, **1**:210, **1**:212
   and the Equal Rights Amendment, **3**:620–24
   in the military, **3**:623
   Muslim, **3**:696
   rights of, **1**:120, **1**:175, **2**:238, **2**:240–42, **3**:484, **3**:486, **3**:516, **3**:620, **3**:622, **3**:624, **3**:669
   voting rights, **2**:240, **2**:242, **2**:398, **2**:400–402, **2**:412, **2**:434
   in the workplace, **2**:380, **2**:383, **3**:486, **3**:516, **3**:654
Women Airforce Service Pilots (WASP), **3**:484
Women's Health Action and Mobilization (WHAM), **3**:640
Women's March of 2017, **3**:698
Women's Trade Union League (WTUL). *See* WTUL (Women's Trade Union League)
Woodward, Bob, **3**:599
Works Progress Administration. *See* WPA
World Anti-Slavery Convention, **2**:240
World War I, **2**:400, **2**:404, **2**:406–8, **2**:410, **2**:412, **2**:414, **2**:416, **2**:420, **2**:422–23, **2**:432, **2**:434–35, **2**:454, **2**:456
World War II, **2**:272, **2**:344, **2**:413, **2**:440, **3**:484, **3**:487–88, **3**:492–94, **3**:501–2, **3**:504, **3**:506–8, **3**:510, **3**:512, **3**:514, **3**:516–20, **3**:522–23
Wounded Knee massacre, **2**:324, **2**:388, **3**:583–84, **3**:602, **3**:604–7
WPA (Works Progress Administration), **3**:478, **3**:481–82
Wright, Richard, **2**:469, **2**:474
WTUL (Women's Trade Union League), **2**:380, **2**:382–83

Y
Young, Charles, **2**:410

Z
Ziegfeld, Florence, **2**:434
Ziegfield, Hugo, **2**:444